HOW CONVERSATION
WORKS

THE LANGUAGE LIBRARY

EDITED BY DAVID CRYSTAL

HOW CONVERSATION WORKS

Ronald Wardhaugh

Basil Blackwell
in association with
André Deutsch

601.542
W21h
14 51 56
Sept. 1988

Basil Blackwell Publisher Ltd
108 Cowley Road, Oxford OX4 1JF, UK

Basil Blackwell Inc.
432 Park Avenue South, Suite 1503,
New York, NY 10016, USA

in association with André Deutsch Limited,
105 Great Russell Street, London WC1B 3LJ, England

British Library Cataloguing in Publication Data

Wardhaugh, Ronald
    How conversation works. – (The Language Library)
    1. Conversation
    I. Title   II. Series
    808.56   P95.45

    ISBN 0–631–13921–4
    ISBN 0–631–13939–7 Pbk

Library of Congress Cataloging in Publication Data

Wardhaugh, Ronald
    How conversation works.

    (Language library)
    Bibliography: p. 227
    Includes index.
    1. Conversation.   I. Title.   II. Series.
    P95.45.W37 1985   001.54'2   84–14524
    ISBN 0–631–13921–4
    ISBN 0–631–13939–7 (pbk.)

Typeset by Oxford Publishing Services, Oxford
Printed in U.S.A.

Contents

Preface

This is a book about conversation, specifically about what happens when people talk to one another. It is not a technical treatise on that subject. Many such treatments already exist, but they are neither very accessible nor, once found, easy to read. Instead, this book tries to avoid technicalities and jargon in favour of 'plain speaking'. But obviously what follows could not have been written without the kinds of scholarly effort that have been applied in recent years to the study of conversation. In particular, knowledgeable readers will see in the following pages the influence of scholars such as J. L. Austin, Malcom Coulthard, Harold Garfinkel, Erving Goffman, H. P. Grice, Gail Jefferson, William Labov, Harvey Sacks, Emanuel Schegloff, and J. R. Searle, to name only the most prominent.

I have tried to explain simply why people say the kinds of things they say in a wide variety of circumstances. In one sense the answers are easy, but in another sense that very simplicity is a delusion. Those of us who spend our lives working with languages quickly learn that there is really very little that is simple in the languages we use or in the ways in which we use them. Hence the fascination of our work. It is my hope that this book will illustrate some of the attractions that the study of one aspect of language, conversation, can have for others than card-carrying linguistic scholars. It should also be useful to those who seek an introduction to recent observations that have been made about conversation but who might be put off by their first reading of some of the literature.

Each chapter concludes with a suggested list of further reading. These items should be found in any good library. Full bibliographical information is given at the end of the book.

I

The Social Basis of Talk

Our concern is with talk and the types of language used in talk. The major emphasis will be on conversation, the most generalized form of talk. We will also be concerned with both speakers and listeners, since talk is, as we shall see, essentially a cooperative undertaking. We will not be concerned with how language is used for private thought nor with speculations and theories about the nature of language itself. These topics we can safely leave to the appropriate experts who, we can be sure, have lots of ideas to challenge many of the beliefs we are likely to hold on such matters. The focus of our concern will be what happens when two or more people exchange words for some reason. Why does one person say one thing and the other reply as he or she does?

We will also ignore talking to yourself because of the very special characteristics of such talk. Talking to yourself is permissible only in a very narrow set of circumstances. It must be done privately, and with great care so as not to be overheard, or it must be deliberately intended to be overheard and in that respect viewed as a 'performance' of sorts. No one can prevent you from thinking aloud, reprimanding yourself, rehearsing a story, or recapitulating some event that you have been involved in. But it is risky for you to do any of these things so openly as to be caught in the act. You must not 'go public'. Those who persist in doing so – on crowded city streets, for example – are considered to be 'strange' at least and possibly even 'crazy'. If you do talk aloud to yourself – and most of us do on some occasion or other – you must be quite conscious of what you are doing and recognize that your private performance may become a public one at any moment. Indeed, you certainly can utter a prayer, mumble, mutter, exclaim, or swear to yourself, and you can even talk to your dog, but you must not forget where you are and what you are doing. You can pray aloud, but only in appropriate circumstances; you can exclaim, but only when an exclamation seems clearly called for; and you should talk to your dog about suitable topics for dog talk – not, for example, about nuclear physics, except perhaps jokingly. Private talk to yourself nearly always runs the risk of becoming public performance. Caught talking to yourself, you may be quite embarrassed and you will also embarrass those who catch you at it. However, if you talk to yourself with the deliberate intention that others should overhear what you are saying, then we can argue that what you are really doing is indulging in talk as a social, not private, activity. And that *is* our concern.

We can see some of the differences between private and public talk in a play like *Hamlet*. The play itself is a series of conversations performed for the benefit of a special public, the audience. They are meant to be overheard or there would be no play. But within the play there are various kinds of overhearings: soliloquies or musings aloud; deliberate self-revelations to overhear; and observations of others' speaking to either self or third parties, real or imagined. The result is a considerable complexity in the kinds of talk we find in the play and one of the play's fascinations to audiences and critics alike.

Talk is usually a social activity and therefore a public activity. It involves you with others, and each time you are involved with another person you must consider him or her. You must be aware of that person's feelings about what is happening, and you have some right to require him or her to do the same for you, to be aware of you and your feelings. In this sense talk is a reciprocal undertaking. Involvement in conversation therefore requires the two (or various) parties to be conscious of each other's needs, particularly the need not to be offended. Public life is possible only when the opportunities for being seriously offended are reduced to near zero. If the risks in an activity are great, you may be wise to refrain from that activity unless the potential gains are correspondingly great or you have no alternative. As we shall see, conversation is an activity which makes use of many devices in order to reduce the risks to participants. Consequently, skilled conversationalists rarely get 'hurt'.

There remains for most of us, however, a certain element of risk in any conversation. You may be hurt or you may inflict hurt in that one of the participants can emerge from the conversation diminished in some way. While it is unlikely that you insulted someone or you yourself were insulted, many lesser hurts are possible. You may have criticized another or have been criticized yourself; you may have incurred an obligation that you did not seek or made a suggestion that another could not refuse; someone may have complimented you, thereby requiring you not only to acknowledge acceptance of that compliment but to live up to it; you may have skirted a topic which others expected you to confront, you may have offered an excuse or an apology but be left with the feeling that it was not necessarily accepted completely – someone's sincerity may therefore be suspect. During a conversation some subtle change in relationships between the parties is likely to have occurred; many conversations result in the participants having definite, residual feelings about them: of pleasure, displeasure, ease, frustration, anger, alarm, satisfaction, and so on. We are not loath to judge conversations in such terms. When we do so, we are in an important sense evaluating the risks we took, counting our gains and losses as a result of taking them, and adding everything up on our mental score cards. That we do such things is apparent from the comments we sometimes make following conversations or reporting on them to others, comments such as *He was pretty short with her, You should have heard her go on about it, Why didn't you speak up?, She shouldn't have spoken to me like that, He just grunted, never said a word*, or that sure sign that a relationship is in trouble: *You're not listening; you never listen!*

Indeed, if all participants in a conversation are to feel happy with it, each must feel that he or she got out of it what was sought. If you wish to appear as a 'sensitive' participant in a conversation, you will therefore try to make sure that all the participants get to share in the various aspects of the conversation that will make it 'successful': in selecting the topics that will be talked about; in having adequate and timely opportunities to speak; in feeling at ease in saying what needs to be said; in achieving a sense of orderliness and adequacy about what is going on and doing this as one of a group of two or more; and so on. None of these characteristics can be prescribed in advance – unless the conversation is a very formal one, for example, a meeting of some kind – so it is necessary for you at all times to be aware of just what exactly is happening in any conversation in which you participate. You must be aware of both what has gone before and what may come next, as well as where you seem to be at the moment. You must be aware that a complicated array of possibilities exists and that each choice must necessarily preclude others. You must exhibit a certain sensitivity if you are to avoid some choices so that no one may feel arbitrarily cut off either from the topic or from other participants. Your goal must be to see that everyone leaves the conversation satisfied.

What we can infer from all this is that if you want to be a successful conversationalist you must command a wide variety of skills. You must have a well developed feeling about what you can (or cannot) say and when you can (or cannot) speak. You must know how to use words to do things and also exactly what words you can use in certain circumstances. And you must be able to supplement and reinforce what you choose to say with other appropriate behaviours: your movements, gestures, posture, gaze, and so on. You must also attune yourself to how others employ these same skills. This is a considerable task for anyone – or *everyone*, as it turns out – to perform, so it is not surprising that individuals vary widely in their ability to be successful in conversation. You can bungle your way through or you can be witty, urbane, and always sure to say the right thing. And some can even exploit the ability they have for ends that are entirely selfish.

The actual requirements will vary from group to group

and culture to culture. Some situations may require considerable amounts of silence and others considerable amounts of talk. Others may be partly defined by who gets to talk and in what order, for not everyone necessarily has a right to speak: contrast a state ceremonial with a Quaker meeting. And once speaking has begun, it has to stay within the bounds of the occasion: you do not deliver a lecture at a cocktail party; you do not tell a dirty joke while conveying bad news; and you do not (any longer in many places now) make sexist or racist remarks in public and hope to win or keep public office. In this broad sense linguistic behaviour may be described as appropriate or not, and it is this sense of appropriateness that is the subject of studies by those who work in a discipline known as the ethnography of speaking: the study of who speaks to whom, when, how, and to what ends.

Certain basic conditions seem to prevail in all conversation, and many of the details of individual conversations are best understood as attempts that speakers (and listeners) make to meet these conditions. Above all, conversation is a social activity and, as such, it shares characteristics of all social activities. These characteristics we usually take for granted so that it is only their absence we notice. When there is some kind of breakdown in society, we notice the absence of principles, conventions, laws, rules, and so on, which guided or controlled behaviour in better times. Or, alternatively, we become aware of these same principles only when we have too readily accepted certain things as 'normal' and then find out that we have been deceived, as when someone has tricked or 'conned' us by pretending to do one thing (apparently quite normal) but actually doing another. We may not feel quite as bewildered as Rosencrantz and Guildenstern in Tom Stoppard's play of the same name, but we will recognize their predicament.

Conversation, like daily living, requires you to exhibit a considerable trust in others. Life would be extremely difficult, perhaps even impossible, without such trust. It is this trust that allows you to put money in a bank in the expectation that you will get it back on demand, to cross the street

at a busy intersection controlled by either lights or a policeman, to eat food prepared by others, to plan for the future,
and so on. But there is also the more general trust we have in
the evidence of our senses, in the recurrence of both natural
and other events, and in the essential unchanging and possibly unchangeable nature of the world and of the majority of
its inhabitants. Trust in other people is the cornerstone of
social living: to survive we must believe that people do not
change much, if at all, from day to day and from encounter
to encounter, and also that the vast majority do not set out
deliberately to deceive or harm us. Indeed, we must believe
them to be benevolent rather than malevolent. Without such
trust in others and in what they do and say we could not get
very far in coping with the world in which we find ourselves.
So far as conversation is concerned, we would have little or
no shared ground on which to build, and communication
would become next to impossible. States of enmity and war
or 'not speaking' are good examples of the kinds of conditions that exist when trust is broken. However, it is important to realize that even in such cases there is almost never a
complete breakdown, since the antagonists usually continue
to observe certain rules and decencies. Not everything
becomes 'fair', which in such a case could mean only that
absolutely anything might be possible, a situation therefore
in which no rules of any kind would apply, an example of
'savagery' in its mythical, pathological form.

We cannot survive without putting trust in others, but it
must be a trust tempered with a certain amount of caution.
We cannot insist on viewing the world with wide-eyed inno-
cence and hope we will never be disappointed. If you want to
survive and minimize the hurts you will experience, you
must employ a little bit of common sense too. You must
exercise certain powers of judgement and you must make
sound decisions constantly. For example, in any encounter
with another person, you must try to work out exactly what
is going on. That requires you to exhibit characteristics for
which terms like 'intelligence' and 'sensitivity' are often used:
you must judge the actual words you hear in relation to the

possible intentions of the speaker, in order to come up with a decision as to what the speaker really means. In abstract, theoretical terms, the possible permutations of meaning are immense. Fortunately, in reality, most of those possibilities are extremely unlikely. You can rule them out, and you must do so – otherwise you could never decide anything at all: you could never be in any way sure about anything anyone said to you. But that ruling-out is not done haphazardly. Certain basic principles that prevail in most conversations help you to narrow down the possibilities to a manageable set: mutual trust, the sincerity of participants, the validity of everyday appearances, and 'common sense'. A certain scepticism may obtain in our views of life and of human motivation, but it must have 'healthy' limits. We cannot question and doubt everything or suspect every motive and still insist that we be regarded as normal people. We must seriously restrict such questioning, doubt, and suspicion; they are indicators, or markers, of very special kinds of conversation – interviews, psychiatric consultations, seminars, investigations – and such special activities must be clearly 'framed' in some way to indicate their special character. In order to participate in a conversation, you must be a willing party to a certain world-view. In that respect conversation is a collusive activity. You may have reservations about certain matters, but unless you are prepared to meet others on common ground and ignore differences which can only be divisive there is little hope that any kind of meaningful communication will occur.

Ethnomethodologists – those who study common-sense knowledge and reasoning as they pertain to social organisation – tell us that we are all parties to an agreement to inhabit a world in which things are what they appear to be and people do not in general go scratching beneath the surface of appearances. Scientists may do that, but that is the hallmark of the *scientific* enterprise. Living is largely a collusive activity, one in which you find yourself united with me because we both use our common sense and our goodwill to blind ourselves to things that do not seem to be important: we do not ask tough questions of each other; we do not seek rigid proofs; we do accept contradictions and uncertainty; and we do prefer to go along with others in most circumstances. That is how ordinary life is lived and must be lived.

Because conversation necessarily has a social basis, we must try to meet each other on common ground. For example, there is a general unspoken agreement among people that what we actually inhabit is a consistent, even mundane, world. It is essentially a world of the common-place and the things in it do not change much, if at all. These 'things' are also what they appear to be; they are not some-thing else. Consequently, we tend to be amused when a 'petrol station' really turns out to be a fast-food restaurant or one of James Bond's cars turns into a submarine·and another into an aeroplane. Magicians exploit this kind of amusement. But if such situations and such trickery happened continually we would undoubtedly find them stressful, or, alternatively, we would be forced to recast our image of fast-food outlets, automobiles, and trickery. That world too is one of simple causation: it is a recurrent world in which day follows night and night follows day, and so on. We see ourselves and others as consistent objects within that world; we believe we behave consistently and we tend to grant the same con-sistency to others.

We also tend to accept what we are told, taking any words spoken to us at close to face value unless we appear to have some very good reason for doing otherwise. For example, we seek only occasional clarification of remarks made to us. We are prepared to tolerate a remarkable amount of unclarity and imprecision in what we are told. We hold our peace and trust that everything will eventually work itself out to our satisfaction. So when we listen to interchanges that do involve considerable questioning and commenting, we know we are observing conversations of a special kind: for example, interrogations, psychiatric interviews, exchanges between teachers and students, and so on. If you suddenly let flow a stream of questions during what is otherwise just an ordinary conversation, you may effectively stop, or at least change, what is happening. You may well be perceived to be trying to turn something commonplace into an investigation and to be violating the basic condition of trust between participants. If I do not believe what you are telling me, I can challenge your truthfulness or I can start probing your account with questions. In either case you are likely to react in much the same way. You will become 'defensive', for your trust in what we were doing *together* will be weakened as you find yourself under attack. I will have violated the normal unspoken agreement that I will believe what you say because in return you will believe what I say. For, after all, are not both of us reasonable, sincere, and honest individuals? Some people regard defensive behaviour as 'bad' behaviour or evidence of some kind of guilt; it need be neither, being just a normal reaction to unwarranted offensive behaviour from others.

Each party in a social encounter has a certain amount of 'face' to maintain; many of the things that happen are concerned with maintaining appearances. I do not want to attack you in any way nor do I want you to attack me. We are, in a sense, parties to an agreement each to accept the other as the other wishes to appear. We may even go further and try to support a particular appearance the other proposes for himself or herself. If you want to act in a manner which I find somewhat peculiar, I may have very great difficulty in 'calling' you on what you are doing. It is much more likely that I will go along with your performance and keep my doubts to myself. After all, you may have a good motive unknown to me for your behaviour, so my initial reaction is likely to be to go along with what you are doing, to help you maintain the 'face' you are presenting, rather than to propose some kind of change in your behaviour. Those individuals who go around trying to 'un-face' others, as it were, may find themselves unwelcome, even to each other, being constantly in violation of this norm that 'good' social behaviour is based on mutual trust in appearances.

It is not surprising, therefore, that people rather infrequently resort to such expressions as *Who do you think you are?*, *Why do you speak to me like that?*, and *What gives you the*

right to tell me what to do? Such remarks are quite definitely
confrontational, but they do not confront the other person's
right to speak. Rather, what they confront is the precise role
the other has chosen to adopt, therefore the 'face' he has
chosen for himself. In similar vein, one of the difficulties we
might experience in saying *No* to a request made of us may
well arise from the feeling that to do so is to offer an affront
to the other's face. The extreme of request-type face is, of
course, that adopted by the beggar who sits head bowed and
silent before a container of some kind or with hand out-
stretched and eyes averted so as not to affront the faces of
passers-by or further diminish his or her own when refused.

Conversation proceeds on the basis that the participants are
reasonable people who can be expected to deal decently with
one another. There must be a kind of reasonableness, a sort
of 'commonsenseness', in the actual choice of the words and
expressions we employ. There must also be a certain rightness in the quantity as well as the quality of those words. You
have to say enough to do the job that must be done: not too
little must be said nor, on the other hand, too much. Too
little and someone will feel deprived of information; too
much and someone will feel either imposed upon or the
unwilling beneficiary of a performance rather than of a
genuine instance of communication. Unreasonable language
may also produce obscurity or even rouse someone to challenge what has been said. It may create problems which the
participants can solve only when they have re-established the
basic preconditions of trust that are necessary if anything
positive is to be accomplished.

You must assume, too, that most others with whom you
come into contact can deal adequately with the world, just as
adequately as you believe you yourself deal with it. You do
not readily question another's ability to state simple facts, or
to ask and give directions, or to add new information to old.
When you ask another person for directions, you expect that
he or she will employ a scheme for giving the directions that
will be adequate for the occasion. For example, if you have
asked for a description of the interior of a house, you expect

to get that description according to an acceptable pattern of spatial organization. You also expect certain kinds of information and not other kinds and to get information that is adequate for the purpose you have in mind, if you have made that purpose clear in some way. And that expectation is generally fulfilled. 'Basic' information is fairly easily accessible, but we should notice how difficult it is quite often to gain certain further kinds of information – or to supply that information if we are asked for it. A lot of 'information' that we actually have access to never becomes part of that body of information we rely on for ordinary living and routine communication with others. Police officers, for example, have to be specially trained to observe certain kinds of details that are, indeed, accessible to the general public. But what they observe and report is very different from what we, commonplace actors in a commonplace world, observe and are therefore able to report. We actually see the same things but we do not observe and record them in the same way; there is really no need to do so, for we know that everyday life does not usually require that intensity of observation. The events in our everyday world are necessarily mundane: life would quickly become unbearable if it were not so ordered and predictable and consequently so unworthy of close and continuing attention.

Even those who are scientifically trained do not usually carry over the scientific attitude into every aspect of life. Adequate functioning requires some disjunctions between the world of science and the world of everyday existence. One parent was reminded of this fact when one winter morning she said to her six-year-old son *Ah, the sun's finally rising!* only to have him offer her the sharp rebuke *But, mummy, the sun doesn't rise: the earth goes round the sun!* Whereas she had separated the two, the scientific and the ordinary, he had learned his basic facts about the solar system from his parents, and had not. It was not surprising that his teacher in school found him both precocious *and* disruptive!

Our sense of adequacy can show itself in many other ways. We all have some sense of what adequate and appropriate behaviour is in particular circumstances. We may actually refuse to do certain things because we know that we lack the requisite skills and we do not want to make fools of ourselves. What is in a way surprising is how adequate we feel in general, not how inadequate. We also know the bounds of our adequacy. If you consider the kinds of things you know that allow you not only to survive in society but sometimes even to flourish, they quickly add up to a formidable list. For example, you know how to behave in a doctor's or dentist's waiting room, in a queue, on a crowded bus or tube train, with a bank teller, in the company of a close friend of either the same or opposite sex, and possibly with a traffic policeman. You know in conversation in such circumstances what topics are suitable, how much you can or must reveal or, alternatively, hide, and what is likely to be quite inappropriate or even taboo. You also know when it is appropriate to speak and when it would be wise to be silent. These skills you must have if you are not to appear ill mannered, out of place, or social deficient in some way. And most of us have them. Actually, many of the skills you must display will have become highly ritualized, so that you no longer have to think about what you are doing. To use one limited domain as an example, you know how to occupy space among strangers and deal with them, and you are aware of the need to avoid potentially offensive remarks, of the importance of 'safe' topics, and of the care you must take to accept and treat others as you want them to accept and treat you. The ability to appear adequate and normal is one of your most precious possessions, but one which you must also grant to others. Inadequacy and abnormality are inherently judgements about social behaviour and clearly indicate some kind of failure in that behaviour.

'Adequacy' and 'normality' are, of course, culture-laden concepts. What is adequate and normal among one group of people may be entirely inappropriate among certain other groups. Those who have travelled in different parts of the world can readily attest to this fact. But many such differences are these days often readily observable on one's own doorstep. Many cities and towns now draw their populations from a variety of cultural and linguistic groups with rather different views of what is 'proper'. Consequently, it is not surprising that linguistic and behavioural differences have become a concern of many who live in such communities, and that the schools have on numerous occasions become the battlegrounds for the disputants.

Most of us have a very good idea of what 'normal' behaviour is and just how much variation is possible without drawing attention to itself. It is not the same idea that everyone else has because the norm does vary from one group to the next, but even widely divergent groups within the same society are likely to share certain values. It is those shared values which make it possible to speak of the *same* society. We readily recognize abnormal social behaviour: 'antisocial' or 'bad' conduct in public; 'inappropriate' manners in a restaurant; 'rudeness' in a shop; 'crazy' behaviour on the street; and so on. We even have a very good idea of the 'normal' bounds for many activities. We have an idea of 'how far' we can go: how far it is possible to ignore the various rules and regulations having to do with driving and parking; how much we can stretch the truth in certain circumstances; and even possibly how to 'fudge' one's tax return in some small way. However, when we witness a gross violation of the norm, we may be seriously offended, as when 'unspeakable' crimes are committed or certain conduct leaves us 'speechless' with rage. Such deliberate, even violent, breaking of norms threatens us all, striking as it does at those very principles of cooperative endeavour on which all social life depends. Punishment of such violations may be over-severe, since there is a tendency to over-react when norms are deliberately flouted. Instances are numerous: we need only to think back to widespread reactions in the 1960s and 1970s to 'long' hair, to 'bad' courtroom behaviour, to 'free speech', and to large-scale but essentially peaceful public protests, and so on.

When you violate a norm, you are indulging in a type of communicative behaviour. You are definitely 'saying' something. You may be demonstrating either ignorance of the norm or a complete disregard for it. While we may find it easier to excuse ignorance than deliberate flouting, the same principle seems to apply here as in legal matters: ignorance of the law is not viewed as an acceptable defence. You should know the law and you should be aware of the norm. In other words normative behaviour is *expected* behaviour; indeed, it is the *required* behaviour. Anything else is likely to be treated as behaviour critical of the norm itself. Aberrant behaviour, by definition, immediately brings to consciousness one's beliefs about what 'normal' means, and once instilled, such beliefs are quickly defended: something is 'not right', or is 'unacceptable', 'deviant', or 'inappropriate', or should not have been said or done. Sanctions are likely to follow quite quickly, particularly when the relationships are unequal, as between governors and the governed, mothers and children, and teachers and pupils.

The kind of world in which we see ourselves and others existing is also one in which personal behaviour is consistent – or should be. When we meet another person repeatedly, we assume that that person's behaviour is consistent. The other is the 'same' person from encounter to encounter and there is little, if any, fluctuation in behaviour. When a person is consistently inconsistent, which is therefore a consistent fact in itself, we assume that he will continue to be inconsistent. Indeed, if you notice a change in consistency when you meet someone, you are likely to make a comment to that effect or express some concern, possibly to others rather than to the person himself. You may quietly ask yourself *What is up with him?* or *What have I done to make Sally say that?* Or, having noticed John's 'peculiar' behaviour, you may ask Bill *Why is John behaving the way he is these days?* The relative infrequency of such expressions of concern indicates how 'normal' most continuing encounters are; the everyday sameness of behaviour and routine does not require notice or comment, except perhaps about that very sameness: *What's new? Nothing!*

Just as we expect the behaviour of others to be consistent,

so we also view the world consistently; our beliefs about it and about how its various bits and pieces relate to one another change slowly, if at all. We tend to have rather fixed ideas about our place within that world, of who we are and how we relate to others, and this observation is true even of those whose world is partly a world of fantasy. Only schizophrenics inhabit more than one world, thereby appearing to inhabit one world inconsistently. Each of us has a picture or self-image of himself or herself and of the various others in our environment, and we seek to keep these pictures consistent. A particular picture may also have more than a single dimension to it: for example, we may have both a public image and a very different private one. If we do, we must try to keep the two apart. The private lives of public figures are of interest to us not only because they show us quite different aspects of character, but also because we can try to judge how successful the individuals are in separating the two existences. We may also be tempted to evaluate one existence, particularly the public one, against what we come to know of the other. Much of the appeal of biographies lies in attempts to reconcile the various images of the subjects.

In looking at the world, we see it one way rather than another. In a real sense, however, we see what we want to see. We even ignore certain aspects of our surroundings. Sometimes that ignoring is part of a general agreement that prevails in society: we agree that only certain kinds of things should be noticed and others must be ignored. Not everything around us is equally accessible either to view or to comment. Sometimes certain things cannot even be acknowledged either to be happening or to have happened. Some people, objects, and events are therefore public in the picture; others are deliberately disregarded, for example, reporters and cameras at public events. Some bits of an individual and of his or her behaviour are publicly in the same sense, and others are usually treated as private. Candid photography reminds us of this fact: it makes public what are essentially private moments. We should not be at all surprised, then, that there is so much controversy in the modern world about 'rights to privacy' and the 'public's right to know', and that considerable disagreement exists concerning where the first set of rights ends and the second begins.

The same distinction can be carried over into the private domestic world. Some parts of that world are accessible to others and some are not. As a guest, you do not go into certain parts of your host's house unless invited. Children in a household may have their 'own' rooms. You do not go through your spouse's pockets or purse. You do not read another's diary. Conventions like these are observed by a great many people and violations are found to be offensive and to require explanation. Part of 'normal' living, then, requires us to observe the convention that not everything available to our senses must be examined and some things must be ignored.

We function in a world of normal appearances and usually do not probe beneath the surface of events, and in general, we believe that everybody else behaves in that respect much as we do, sharing with us a similar approach to daily existence. Those who probe are people like scientists and psychiatrists, but even their probing is restricted to a very narrow range of activities. Indeed, we go further and assume that those with whom we deal share much specific information about the world. One simple way of convincing yourself that this is so, that there is considerable shared background knowledge in any conversation, is to insist that each party make everything quite explicit in the very next conversation you have. That conversation will quickly degenerate: you may find yourself accused of being crazy, pedantic, or disruptive, or you may be assigned some other clearly antisocial label. Tempers are also likely to become frayed. Another way is to attempt to find out from newspapers, magazines, or radio and TV reports what is happening on some issue by using only the actual words you read or hear on a single specific occasion, completely disregarding any previous knowledge you might have of the topic. You will probably not be able to make much sense of what you either read or hear. One of the great difficulties you encounter in reading a local newspaper in a place you happen to be visiting is your lack of the background knowledge necessary to interpret what you are reading. This lack makes many items of local news either obscure or elusive: you lack knowledge of the people, the events, and the issues and have little or nothing on which to hang any details you are presented with. But the locals do not experience this difficulty.

Common knowledge, then – that is, 'what everyone knows' – is necessarily something that is culture-loaded and varies from group to group. Much of what everyone knows is also either scientifically unwarranted or very superficial. For example, there are numerous stereotypes in this kind of knowledge – ideas we have about the 'typical' behaviour and characteristics of people or objects. But that should not surprise us, because, after all, that is essentially what norms themselves are in one sense – abstractions based on certain kinds of experiences which apparently typify some kind of general behaviour. Many people go through life holding the view that common knowledge and stereotypes characterize a sort of truth about the world; others are somewhat more critical and conscious of the complexities that lie behind such a simple belief. What we must not assume, however, is that common knowledge is always false and stereotyping is always bad; social harmony is possible only if there are things we can agree on, and there are measures of agreement. What may be important is how fixed are the measures any society uses, not the existence of the measures themselves.

In periods of rapid social change old norms and stereotypes come under attack at a time when new ones are not available, so it is not surprising that confusion results. Linguistic behaviour at such times tends to reflect the disorder. Some strive to preserve the old ways, as conservative factions in Greece did in the 1960s to reimpose a 'high' variety of Greek. Others want to create a new set of conditions, for example, to rid a language of a *tu–vous* distinction in address forms, as did both the French and Russian revolutionaries (but eliminating the *vous* form in one case and the *tu* form in the other). Eventually new norms emerge, new appearances, new conventions, and new ways of using language to express these new norms with all the advantages, and disadvantages, of the old, offering as they do a way of constructing a certain kind of reality as well as providing blinkers which make other realities somewhat inaccessible to view.

One consequence of all this is that we must set limits on the amount of trust we place in others and in our view of the world. Similarly, in conversation we should not trust absolutely: that is too severe a demand to make both of ourselves and of others. Those who give their absolute trust to others are almost certain at one time or another to be disappointed. But we must also be aware that distrust cannot be the norm either, for a climate in which everyone distrusts everyone else would prohibit entirely all hope of mutually beneficial social contact. Therefore, we must err at all times on the side of trust. Unfortunately, those who would deceive us know that too, and, having confidence in their ability to exploit this basic social need, proceed to do so, often with impunity.

For any particular conversation it is also possible to show that there are differences between the parties in the specific things that they know in contrast to the kinds of background knowledge that they share. No two people have identical backgrounds, so in any conversation the participants will have different kinds of knowledge about almost any topic that is likely to be mentioned. If only two people, Fred and Sally, are involved, there will be certain matters known to both, some because 'everybody knows such things' and others because both Fred and Sally happen to know them. Then there will be matters known to only one of the speakers, so that Fred will know something that Sally does not know, or Sally something that Fred does not know. In addition, there will be partly known information: Fred or Sally, or both, may partly know something or know parts of something, but not necessarily the same parts. And Fred or Sally, or both again, may believe that the other knows something that the other actually does not know. As we can see, there are numerous possible permutations in who knows what, who believes who knows what, and so on. Again, there are predictable consequences: conversation can proceed only on the basis that the participants share a set of beliefs, that is, certain things must be known to all parties; others may be known; some will have to be explained; questions may be asked for clarification; difficulties will be negotiated or cleared up somehow; people will be understanding and tolerant; and the various processes that are involved will be conducted decently. If only one participant in a conversation refuses to subscribe to these beliefs and to conduct himself or herself accordingly, the others will become irritated, confused, or frustrated, and may well abandon any attempt to continue what they have begun.

Since most participants in a conversation usually do share a certain amount of background knowledge about 'proper' behaviour and the 'right' way to do things, much of what they say can be understood if we, too, are familiar with the knowledge they share. Their references to places, times, and events, and their accounts and descriptions are related to what they know and what they believe the others know. A participant in a conversation must believe that he or she has access to the same set of reference points that all the other participants have access to; all he or she needs do in conversing is use those points for orientation, and listeners will comprehend. And such a belief is largely justified. What is hardly ever necessary in a conversation is to begin at the very beginning of anything and to treat everyone and everything as unique and somehow without antecedents. In a trivial sense every occasion is unique, but procedures exist which minimize novelty and maximize normality – accepted ways of asking and giving directions, rules for regulating who speaks to whom and about what, and basic principles for conducting yourself, for example, with complete strangers.

A conversation between familiars offers a very special mix of knowledge. There are matters in it which the parties know but are reluctant to refer to directly, although they may allude to them if necessary. There are matters which are in the conversation by reason of the fact that they are deliberately avoided – their absence is conspicuous. And then there are the actual topics of the conversation. However, these topics are not introduced logically, as it were, but rather in a variety of ways according to the needs of the individuals and of the occasion, with each participant willing to let a topic emerge as seems natural at the time in the expectation that its various bits and pieces will hold together.

In general conversation with others it is ordinary, every-day, 'commonsense' knowledge that we assume they share with us. In certain circumstances, as between professionals, we can also assume a sharing of specialized knowledge. We must always take great care when we refer to items outside these shared areas. We cannot rely on others knowing what we know. They may not even share the same assumptions about what it means to 'know' something. A physicist's knowledge of matter is different from a lay person's, and an actor's view of character is unlikely to be the same as that of a psychiatrist. Explanations may well become necessary, and they may not be easily provided. Briefing is one kind of explaining behaviour in such circumstances. But a recurrent difficulty is knowing just how much to say on a particular occasion and then judging how successful we have been in saying it. This is particularly crucial if we then proceed to treat this 'new' information we supply henceforth as part of our listeners' everyday knowledge. It may not be easily in-corporated into existing knowledge, as anyone who has ever taught well knows, for it is one thing to teach something and quite another to learn it.

Repetition and checking up therefore become a very necessary part of conversation. They are demanded by the general requirement of language and communication that you must always say more than you minimally need to say so that you will not be misunderstood. The person you are talking to also must have checking devices to indicate whether you are being understood: for example, certain kinds of gestures or glances, which, because of the puzzle-ment they show, require you to offer some further expla-nation; outright questions; some kinds of denial behaviour; and so on. In other words, as a speaker you are not free to indulge in a monologue, disregard those who are listening to you, and assume you are being understood. You must work to be understood and you must be sensitive to your audience. One consequence is that sophisticated public communicators are much more likely to seek other ways than formal speeches in order to get their views across to an audience which, by its nature, cannot ask for clarifications – a president's 'fireside chats', press conferences, staged interviews, and appearances before favourable groups or friendly committees. We should note that some systems of government make it easier for their leaders to do this kind of thing than others: we have only to compare the papacy, the American presidency, the British premiership, and any one of many strong dictatorial leaderships.

What should be apparent from what we have said is that successful conversations exploit many of the same principles that underlie all forms of social existence. There is really nothing 'special' or unique about conversation in that sense. To get through a week in your life, you must be prepared to accept things for what they appear to be and put your trust in that appearance. You must also assume a certain regularity and continuity of existence. To do otherwise is to be paranoid or act antisocially. When disaster strikes and the 'normal', consistent world vanishes, people often find themselves unable to cope with the changed circumstances of their lives. They no longer have the necessary reference points on which to pin their existence. Conversation is a form of 'coping' behaviour which relies heavily on just those same sets of assumptions that allow us to drive to work safely, drink water in a restaurant, cash a government cheque, and even go to sleep at night. Saying *Hi* to Sally and expecting Sally to say *Hi* in return is much the same kind of thing, or asking a stranger *Excuse me, do you have the time?* and getting the reply *Yes, it's ten to four.*

Without routine ways of doing things and in the absence of norms of behaviour, life would be too difficult, too uncertain for most of us. The routines, patterns, rituals, stereotypes even of everyday existence provide us with many of the means for coping with that existence, for reducing uncertainty and anxiety, and for providing us with the appearance of stability and continuity in the outside world. They let us get on with the actual business of living. However, many are beneath our conscious awareness; what, therefore, is of particular interest is bringing to awareness just those aspects of our lives that make living endurable (and even enjoyable) just because they are so commonly taken for granted.

Further Reading

Linguists have usually placed the analysis of conversation within the sub-discipline of sociolinguistics. For an overview of concerns in sociolinguistics, Trudgill's *Sociolinguistics: An Introduction to Language and Society* and Hudson's *Sociolinguistics* are recommended. Other useful books are Giglioli's *Language and Social Context: Selected Readings*, Gumperz and Hymes' *Directions in Sociolinguistics: The Ethnography of Communication*, Labov's *Sociolinguistic Patterns*, Laver and Hutcheson's *Communication in Face to Face Interaction*, and Robinson's *Language and Social Behaviour*.

For ethnomethodology, see Garfinkel's *Studies in Ethnomethodology*, Leiter's *A Primer on Ethnomethodology*, and Psathas' *Everyday Language: Studies in Ethnomethodology*; for cognitive sociology, see Cicourel's *Cognitive Sociology: Language and Meaning in Social Interaction*. The ethnography of speaking is the concern of Bauman and Sherzer's *Explorations in the Ethnography of Speaking*, Saville-Troike's *The Ethnography of Communication: An Introduction*, and Sudnow's *Studies in Social Interaction*. Watzlawick, Beavin, and Jackson's *Pragmatics of Human Communication: A study of Interactional Patterns, Pathologies, and Paradoxes* is a basic text on the theory of human communication.

A basic introduction to discourse analysis is provided in Coulthard's *An Introduction to Discourse Analysis*. Other useful books on the same topic are Brown and Yule's *Discourse Analysis*, Coulthard and Montgomery's *Studies in Discourse*

Analysis, Edmondson's *Spoken Discourse: A Model for Analysis*, Gumperz' *Discourse Strategies*, and Stubbs' *Discourse Analysis: The Sociolinguistic Analysis of Natural Language.*

Various books by Goffman are highly recommended for the insights they contain into the human situation: *The Presentation of Self in Everyday Life, Interaction Ritual, Relations in Public: Microstudies of the Public Order, Frame Analysis: An Essay on the Organization of Experience*, and *Forms of Talk*. On the subject of 'face', see his 'On Face-work: An Analysis of Ritual Elements in Social Interaction'. The 'normal appearance' of the world is discussed in the papers in Garfinkel's *Studies in Ethnomethodology*, his own paper, 'Studies of the Routine Grounds of Everyday Activities', and his paper, co-authored with Sacks, 'On Formal Structures of Practical Actions'.

Levinson's *Pragmatics* is a good, wide-ranging introduction to many of the issues that must be considered in relating language to use; much of the text is concerned with aspects of conversation.

2

Locating an Agenda

When you begin a particular conversation, you undoubtedly have certain expectations about it. It is very unlikely indeed that you see somebody – anybody – and just open your mouth and let your words spill out as they happen to come. It may be the case that some people do behave this way, but we soon learn not to pay much attention to what we hear from them, as it is not likely to be very important. In contrast, you almost certainly will have a number of assumptions about what kind of conversation you are likely to be embarking on and what kinds of matters will be 'proper' within it. But, of course, your assumptions may well need to be changed as a particular conversation progresses and as various topics are introduced and treated within it. Nevertheless, if the conversation is to be perceived as a genuine interchange, each part must have its own kind of coherence and credibility; it must sound right; an emotional reaction must seem genuine; a question or a request must appear properly motivated. While it may often be difficult, if not impossible, to explain exactly how speakers create this feeling of authenticity, most of us find its absence rather easy to detect. We also know that while some people never seem to experience any difficulty in persuading others of the credibility of their words and deeds, others rarely succeed in doing so.

Embarked on a conversation, you must fairly quickly start making judgements about what you can accomplish as you begin to 'read' the other person. This is particularly important when he or she is either a total stranger or someone you do not know well. You must make tentative judgements about the kind of person you are dealing with. Your views are likely to be heavily influenced by the kind of language he or she is using. Is he or she assertive, quiet, talkative, polite, rude, or what? How does he or she deal with ideas and information, both old and new? Some people employ a kind of free association, spinning off whole series of loosely, and sometimes randomly, connected ideas. Others employ more logical frameworks. Still others insist on dogmatically fitting everything into a pre-existing framework. Then there are those who personalize everything: they are unable to stand apart from any issue or event, but insist on seeing it solely in relation to their individual circumstances. And exaggeration, posturing, tentativeness, scepticism, over-simplification, obfuscation are just a few of the other characteristics that you might observe rather quickly to be part of another person's way of dealing not only with you but also with your joint conversational endeavour. What is not at all uncommon is that another's behaviour soon becomes quite predictable; after a short while you know how he or she will react to almost anything someone says. All you must do is mention a topic or venture an opinion and you can be fairly sure what he or she will do with it: give you a political speech; relate it to immediate personal circumstances; use it to display a biting wit; deliver a boring monologue; question your assumptions; dismiss it as obviously 'wrongheaded' or 'uninteresting'; and so on. We cannot escape making personality judgements of others, nor should we. We need to fit people into certain 'slots' in order to deal with them. What we must do is guard against judgements that are premature and unwarranted, keep in mind the possibility of error, and allow for revised assessments. The problem with judgements of this kind is that they tend to become self-confirming; they may be difficult to change or even to revise just a little because they blinker us to see only evidence that appears to support them and to ignore matters that do not.

The kind of language a speaker uses can offer us a key to his or her personality. For example, it may sometimes have an allusive, even metaphorical, component. If we recognize this component, it may help us to predict the kinds of topics with which we think the speaker feels comfortable, the kind of framework within which he or she is likely to approach ideas, and the bounds within which he or she seems prepared to place issues. In this way we can attempt to establish the kind of mental and conversational set the other has. As a conversational partner, you may find it easy or difficult to relate to what you have discovered about how the other presents himself and his ideas. Do you have a similar set? Is his one you can easily key into? Or is it just too different and difficult for you to relate to and react meaningfully with? Another variation in such special uses of language is to resort to the kind of jargon that is typical of much professional, technical, and pseudo-professional and pseudo-technical communication. Allusive, metaphorical, or technical language has the advantage of helping those who use it to communicate with one another about the range of topics covered by that language, but it has serious drawbacks too. It can blinker those who use it: they may see the world only through the language of their narrow interests and find it difficult to relate to others who do not share their 'world view'. Technical talk is fine in its place, but that place is not everywhere, and such talk has few uses outside the *bona fide* place of employment.

Sometimes you find yourself in situations which cause you to wonder why you are present. You go to a party and find everyone is interested in topics that have no interest for you and in discussing them in terms you cannot relate to. You wander into a ceremony the structure and language of which mystify you. Someone gives you a book 'that might interest you', and, after turning a page or two, you start questioning either the sanity of that person or his or her view of you. In no case can you relate to the situation, either to the circumstances or to the language. The vast majority of people learn to avoid recurrences of the experience; they can make no contribution nor do they wish to, for in most cases it would be just too hard or alien a task to acquire the necessary skills.

You must 'present yourself' in a conversation, and part of that presentation is the way you choose to display yourself to others and how you view your relationship with the rest of the world. In fact, every encounter with another person requires you to come to a decision about how you want to appear in that encounter, that is, how you wish to present yourself to the other or others. This requirement is obligatory even though you have met the other person on innumerable occasions, and even when the last occasion was just moments ago. Every encounter is unique, or at least novel, in that respect. Each party to the encounter must also make that same decision for himself or herself. Consequently, one important feature of every encounter is the need that each participant has not only to establish a personal presence or 'face' but also to figure out what presence or face every other participant is trying to establish. You even incur an obligation to help out the other participants in this task – a very important point if a conversation is going to appear to be successful: we usually accept the presence or 'face' each party tries to create for himself or herself; we rarely question or attack it; we go along with it unless there is a very good reason for not doing so. You might wonder what Bob is up to, but to question or confront him about how he appears to be trying to present himself – his motives, his agenda, *Who do you think you are?* – would seriously breach the sense of cooperation that must prevail if the encounter is to be used to accomplish anything of significance. Such a move would also open the way for Bob to retaliate and question the presence you yourself are seeking to establish.

As a participant in a conversation, you must also nicely judge your degree of involvement in it, both its topics and its participants. You must place yourself somewhere on a scale ranging from complete emotional and personal detachment from any topic discussed or from any other discussant, to strong passion and commitment to either ideas or personalities, or both. Every participant may choose much the same point on the continuum, but it is also possible for different individuals to choose quite different points. Here it may be difficult for the group to sustain what should be a cooperative endeavour: the differing levels of personal involvement may quickly threaten the harmonious relationship that is necessary if there is to be a genuine group activity. Dissatisfied participants will agree that either 'bad' or 'inappropriate' behaviour has destroyed whatever goodwill they might have brought with them, and after a while discussions of 'behaviour', of who is responsible for what, may pre-empt discussion of any other topic. We should not be surprised when the rational fails to communicate with the emotional and the intellectual with the visceral, and each blames the other. Their styles are incompatible, and the key to effective communication must be sought elsewhere.

Taking part in a conversation requires of you a considerable amount of self-monitoring and self-regulation. You must not only look out for and look after others but you must also look after yourself and guard your own interests. Others will provide you with some help because of the very nature of the activity, but it can be only a limited amount of help. As a participant, you are faced with a seemingly endless array of choices: for example, to speak or not to speak at any moment and to say one thing rather than another. What you say, how you behave, and how you react to others establish your 'presence'. So you must constantly monitor and regulate your saying and doing. Moreover, that presence is not fixed. It is not something you quickly establish and then forget about. It must be continually demonstrated and recreated. Each person has a unique presence, and one, too, which must inevitably vary from occasion to occasion. That presence has important social and cultural consequences for the individual: you must establish it and exercise it somewhat differently according to circumstance. You are not the 'same' person in every circumstance: sometimes you may be a son, at others a father; sometimes a customer, at others a golfer; sometimes a student, at others a bystander. You may also have multiple presences, for you can be at the same time both a son and a father, a customer in a golf shop, or a student who witnesses a campus disturbance.

You must also be prepared to shift your 'presence' momentarily. You and your spouse are having a heated argument, the telephone rings, and it is an old friend calling after some time. You are the president of the United States talking to reporters and your young son somehow manages to wander into your office. You are driving home from a party with some boisterous friends when you notice a policeman who is pulling you over. You are caught glancing into someone's lighted window while walking the dog. In each case you must establish who and what you are in order to carry on in the new circumstances; in each case another or others will judge the performance you choose to give and may judge it harshly or not.

Having identified who you are and what the particular occasion is, you are then in a position to establish some kind of agenda for yourself suitable to that occasion. The agenda will include not only the topics that you feel should be brought up, but also those that could be brought up if necessary as well as those that are best avoided or evaded. Some of these latter topics you know, or suspect, to be taboo, or to be embarrassing, painful, or inappropriate either for one individual or for the group as a whole. They are therefore not to be put on the agenda. If you do happen to introduce a topic that seems to discomfort others, you should know how to reshape it to make it acceptable or even to drop it if necessary. To pursue a topic that discomforts others is to be boorish and insensitive at the least. To pursue certain topics at length may be equally inappropriate: only certain aspects may properly be discussable because of individual sensitivities, uncertainties, and ambiguities. Not to recognize these in the determined pursuit of 'the facts' or of 'the truth' is acceptable only in narrowly prescribed circumstances – for example, trials and official inquiries – and even then it is circumscribed by definite bodies of rules concerning what is and what is not evidence and the procedures that one may properly use to gather it.

One characteristic of a relationship that is faltering, for example a failing marriage, is just this insistence by one party that the other must discuss certain topics. *Why do you keep bringing that up?* may be the second party's justifiable complaint in these circumstances. In general, we remember bits and pieces of the past, recalling most things vaguely and leaving to historians the task of proposing more elaborate reconstructions. A failing social relationship is not likely to be conducive to a searching review of the past, particularly when the purpose of the reviewer is often to recommend to another a road not taken and deplore the one actually taken. A different agenda seems called for if failure is to be avoided.

The very language we choose to use also enables us to work out things about ourselves as we use it: who we are and what exactly we are doing. It is part of the process of 'self-creation'. Not only do we use language to communicate factual information, but we also use it to express our feelings and to do a variety of other things. In a very real way language helps us to work out what we are feeling, what we are doing, how we are doing it, and how we must seem to be doing whatever we are doing. Our words provide us with a kind of feedback into our actions, thoughts, and feelings, and allow us to achieve a certain amount of objectivity about what is happening to us and around us. We not only observe others and their language and behaviour; we also observe ourselves: our own acting, doing, behaving, and talking. Language allows us this kind of distance from ourselves, while at the same time continuing to be an essential part of that self. It enables us to have an agenda while at the same time serving as an item on that agenda.

What we do when we talk is express ourselves through language while creating part of ourselves in that very expression. Language is means as well as end. Talk comes so quickly to our tongues that sometimes we surprise ourselves with what we say, sometimes to our pleasure and at others to our discomfort: *Wow, did I say that? – that was good!* or *That was a terrible thing to say!* The relationship between thought and language has long interested and puzzled a variety of scholars. Without seeking to answer the various puzzles, we can say that much of the relationship is symbiotic, just as is much of the relationship between language and personality. Just as by their deeds ye shall know them, so by their words too.

Language does all of this within what we must call a

'system', but this system is really a collection of systems. There is very obviously a grammatical system which all speakers of a language must observe: you must put the words you use into a definite order if you are to make sense when you speak. And there is a system of sounds, that is, agreed ways for pronouncing those words and sentences. But there are also systematic ways, as we shall see, for carrying on conversations with others, certain expectations that the parties must share and certain 'rules' they must observe. And there are other systematic characteristics too, such as the patience and goodwill a participant must bring to any conversation if it is to be successful. Unless you are willing to exercise systematic tolerance toward others, you will not get very far in your interaction with them.

Such tolerance is necessitated by the fact that there is a considerable amount of imprecision and vagueness in conversation, and participants continually rely on one another's tolerance of that fact. They refer quite casually to fragments of information that may, or may not, be known to all. They use words like *this* and *that* constantly but not always clearly, so that it is difficult at times to know exactly what a speaker is referring to. Even when they do offer accounts or explanations or attempt to stick closely to a very specific topic, they fall back on expressions such as *something like, that kind of thing, roughly, sort of, kind of,* or *more or less.* Consequently, the listener is left to fill in many of the details. In this way, of course, if you yourself are the listener, you are compelled to take an active part in constructing the message that the other person is trying to communicate. That person gives you only certain facts, not always coherently, and to these adds admissions of vagueness. Consequently, much of the burden of figuring out what is being said falls on you, the listener, and you must be patient, for you undoubtedly do the same kind of thing yourself in similar circumstances.

An example of this kind of impression is the following conversation. As A is about to leave the house, she mentions something to B:

A. I've got that meeting I told you about.

B. What meeting?
A. The one to go over the accounts.
B. Oh, that one. So when will you be home?
A. A little late, I suppose.
B. How late?
A. Six-thirty perhaps. Maybe a little later.
B. Oh!
A. You know, when we get through. It shouldn't take that long. But . . .

From A's remarks B concludes that A does not really know what time she will be home, so he eventually tells A not to rush home; he will eat out that evening. This apparently was the message A intended, that B should indeed do that; she finally leaves, remarking *I'll see you later this evening then*.

Conversing requires considerable patience. You cannot insist that speakers make everything they say completely explicit all the time, or conversation will become a laborious undertaking. You must tolerate unclarity and ambiguity. You may seek to resolve these on occasion, but, if you do, you must do so gently. You cannot stop the other every time something is not clear; such behaviour will completely obstruct what is happening. It will not be welcome by the other, for it is not what he or she should expect. You must be prepared to wait and see whether things said later will clear up earlier uncertainties. You must gently ferret out what it is you need for clarification and, in doing so, take great care to avoid direct confrontation about omissions, unclarities, and even contradictions. The other person may even make a remark which seems quite extraneous to the topic in hand, for example, make an observation, ask a question, or even direct a request to you, none of which appears relevant to the immediate circumstances. You can certainly ask for clarification: *Why do you say that?* Or you can take the more usual course, accept the interpolation at its face value, respond appropriately, and wait to see what happens. Your expectation in such circumstances would be that there will be some kind of later clarification: the reason for the interruption will become clear as the conversation works itself through. However, if it appears that the other person is going to bring the conversation to an end without providing such clarification, then it is possible for you to ask for an explanation of an earlier unclarity: *By the way, what did you . . .?* And you may reasonably expect that the other will provide a satisfactory explanation. A refusal to do so would not be in order.

When we listen to someone tell us about something, we do not usually expect a completely detailed, thoroughly organized, and totally explicit account. Indeed, we might find such a performance quite intolerable. In its attempt at completeness, it would remind us of the way legal documents are written. What we usually find instead in accounts are occasional gaps, sudden leaps, a lack of explicitness, and a considerable and sometimes pervasive unclarity. We are constantly asked to suspend our disbelief, to wait for items to be clarified, and to think back to earlier details so as to make sense of later ones. So, essentially, when you listen to someone give an account of something, you yourself are partly responsible for the coherence of that account; you cannot rely on the speaker alone, but must 'help' him or her. Only in rare cases are accounts adequately and coherently presented – for example, accounts by such 'professionals' as story-tellers, newsreaders and certain salesmen – and one obvious mark of such accounts is their fluency, their very lack of hesitation, tentativeness, and uncertainty.

The meaning of a conversation, therefore, is something that is negotiated during the course of the conversation rather than directly expressed. What is going on, what is meant, depends on what has gone before, what is currently happening, and what may or may not happen. It is not fixed, but subject to constant review and reinterpretation. However, at each point in a conversation the parties to it must have some view of where they are in order to make sense of what is going on, but it is not a view that they can or should hold rigidly for, if they do, misunderstanding is likely to be the consequence.

As we saw earlier, a certain indirectness rather than directness seems also to be the norm in speech. We rarely attempt to make fully explicit what we have to say but rely on the intuitions of others, their common sense, and a general idea about what we assume everybody knows and expects in order to get our points across. We tend to avoid the naked use of power or position and are generally reluctant to indulge in plain, blunt speaking in the form of either unequivocal commands or confrontational questioning. Such behaviour violates the basic assumptions we hold about mutual trust and decency, and threatens the very conditions that must prevail if there is to be the kind of exchange that conversation normally requires. However, the price we pay can be high. There is always the possibility that our words will be misunderstood, that the intent of an utterance will be misconstrued, and that hints and partially disguised promises or threats will go unrecognized. But it is a necessary trade-off, for effective communication requires the various participants to be gentle with one another, even though that very gentleness can sometimes lead to failure.

There are times, of course, when directness is called for: sometimes you just have to say *No*. However, some people find it very difficult to refuse others, particularly in cultural settings which seem to give one party 'rights' over another. In one such case a woman tried to refuse to do something for her ethnic group – the discussion was in English because some English speakers were present – by making remarks such as *Well, it may not be a very good idea, Perhaps we should wait*, and *Shouldn't we get X to do it*? Finally, she agreed to do something she did not want to do and later complained as follows in private to her house-mate:

A. So I said 'Yes'.
B. But why, if you didn't want to?
A. Well, I can't say 'No'.
B. But if you don't want to do something, just say so.
A. It's not easy.
B. But you can do it if you want.

To B it is quite a simple matter to say *No*; he has to be able to do so, for he could not do his job otherwise. But for A to say

No to 'authority' figures in her cultural group is an extremely difficult task. However, A's next remark shows she sees the humour of the situation as well as its drawbacks:

A. Why do you think I'm living with you?
B. Oh!

In listening to someone explain something or give some kind of account, we must make the best of what we hear. We assume that what we are listening to makes sense and that there is a certain order to the events that the other is describing, even though that order may not be immediately apparent from the description we are being offered. We tend to tolerate any bits and pieces that do not quite fit and constantly seek to make them fit. We are likely to be hesitant about questioning too much so as to seek clarification, fearing that too much such behaviour will indicate either disbelief or rudeness. The result is that we may well put quite a different interpretation on events than the speaker intended; certainly we are not likely to interpret them in exactly the same way. What we must do is construct a plausible interpretation from data that someone else selects for us and presents to us in an idiosyncratic manner. It would be remarkable indeed if the result was that both parties achieved exactly the same view of the events. A third person forced to view it through the eyes and reports of either will see it differently again.

When we try to make sense of accounts that others give us, the assumption that guides us is that an account is coherent if we can but find the pattern that lies behind what we are being told. We wait for clarification of uncertainties and interrupt only if the confusion becomes intolerable – which it sometimes does. On some occasions, regardless of the amount of effort we expend or tolerance we exhibit, we still can make no sense of what we hear. We are forced to abandon any hope we may have of understanding what is being said to us: nothing fits; a 'crazy' world emerges from the other's account; or all initial credibility is lost for some reason. However, the general principle that guides us when we first begin to listen is that a genuine account will emerge, not that what we are being told will turn out to be nonsense. It is therefore fair to say that we enter conversations with others not as sceptics and cynics but as potential believers who may be quite reluctant to become disbelievers.

We also know that we should not take everything we hear literally, because we ourselves have had much experience in using language to express what we mean indirectly and obliquely rather than directly and unambiguously. So when a child comes downstairs in the morning and announces *I have a pain in my stomach*, we may be reluctant to believe what we hear. We may start asking questions about what is happening at school, homework possibly not done, or some other possible anxiety-causing factor. Likewise, we know that *I have a headache* may be true, but, on the other hand, it may be an excuse for not doing something. We are aware that it is quite often very difficult for speakers to come right out with words that directly and boldly state their intentions and that attenuation and even complete avoidance are commonplace. Nor should we expect people to do otherwise, because one of the basic principles of communication is that you cannot, and should not, always 'tell it like it is'.

Of course, at any time in a conversation there exists the distinct possibility that one of the participants misconceives what is happening. He or she may think that something has been agreed to or that a question that has been asked has been answered, but he or she may be quite mistaken; this may be one of the consequences of the general lack of directness that characterizes so much conversation. You proceed through a conversation not as you would through an exercise in logic but rather in the manner in which you might try to find your way through a maze. You must be prepared to check, recheck, backtrack, hypothesize, and live with uncertainty for a while. If you are unwilling to live this way, misunderstanding would seem to be the inevitable consequence, unless you choose to play the confrontational game. Furthermore, if your hypotheses are incorrect about what is going on, you can be led seriously astray. Many of use have had the experience of seeing summaries of meetings we have attended, summaries which make us wonder whether we actually did attend because they characterize events other than in the way we experienced them.

We may even be led astray by the imprecision of certain very common words, words whose meanings can be determined only in relation to the contexts in which they are used. But since those contexts may never be made fully explicit or may be differently viewed by speaker and listener, here too the result can be misunderstanding. These words give an appearance of great precision: *here, there, now* and *later* are good examples. But we must interpret them with caution. *Here* is not just one clearly identified place of a certain size. If you are in Toronto talking on the telephone to New York and say *It's cold here*, you probably mean that it is cold in Toronto. On the telephone to Paris, the *here* is likely to be interpreted as referring to a much larger geographic area than the city of Toronto, possibly to eastern Canada or the northeast of North America. But, if you are talking to someone within the city of Toronto and use the same sentence, it is likely to bring a response like *Is there something wrong with your heating*? Your listener is likely to interpret *here* as referring simply to your house or office. As listeners, we must tolerate this kind of basic imprecision in language: we must constantly tie the words we hear to the contexts in which we hear them, for it is only in this way that we can make sense of what is said to us. Deprived of contextual support, words are little more than just words, as meaningless as any that appear in books devoted to the study of grammar.

Even the commonly used *we* can cause us problems. It can be used inclusively so as to include both the speaker and the listener: *We should hurry up or we'll miss the bus*. It can be used exclusively so that the listener is not included in the activity: *We are just about to leave, so can you call back tomorrow?* Or it may be ambiguous, so that the listener cannot be sure which interpretation is intended. It can also be used as a solidarity marker, that is, as a way for the speaker to identify himself with the listener, as in a teacher's *We'll begin the test now* or a doctor's *How are we feeling today?* It can even be used to regulate the listener (*We don't do that kind of thing here*), as a request for help or understanding (*We seem to have a problem*), or as an indicator that the listener is not to get involved (*We can do without your help*). Or again it can be ambiguous, so that the listener must guess at the speaker's intent.

Individual words and even complete utterances must be interpreted not just in relation to words and utterances pronounced in their immediate context but also in relation to everything in that context: who is speaking; who is listening; what roles are being played; what is the situation; what is the agenda; what is the history of and future prospects for this particular relationship; and so on. Each context is different; each is unique. But there must be only a finite number of ways of dealing with any situation, or conversation would be an impossible, completely unpredictable activity. It is not. But it may still be an extremely difficult one in many circumstances!

A conversation not only requires you to work out who you are and to some extent what you are doing, but it also demands that you perform. It is a piece of theatre. There is a real sense in which each of the participants in a conversation plays out a part in an ongoing action or drama. Each consciously or unconsciously plays a role. Each must have a sense of both character and event. Each must choose a self or 'face' to present and relate to the selves and faces of others. What is remarkable about this kind of theatre is its fundamental improvisational nature. Each scene or episode is a new creation unless it is particularly marked as a ritual. We must have learned rules or principles for constructing such scenes, for otherwise they would not be the reasonably coherent entities they are. And, in following these rules or principles, we know that we must not be too 'theatrical', that is, we must not draw the attention of others to the rules we are following. We must act out the parts we choose to create for ourselves, but we must not over-act them.

While you must play your chosen role with a certain amount of detachment (or awareness), too much distancing from it may prove to be just as ineffective as too great an involvement. You have to be comfortable in the role you choose: you must be seen to be playing it properly rather than playing *at* it or mocking or parodying it. This is particularly necessary in roles that are ritually prescribed: they must be performed with every appearance of sincerity or the ritual becomes a mockery. Here it is not even possible for you to stand back just a little. We can compare such situations with role relaxation on less ritualized occasions – shifts from formal to informal from superior to colleague, from tenant to neighbour, and so on. In such shifts boundaries between roles are likely to be flexible and fluid, but on grand ceremonial occasions queens are always queens and footmen always footmen and there is never any relaxation or mixing of roles. Hence arises much of the appeal of those stories that claim inside knowledge of the private worlds of public figures, worlds in which a queen can have a relationship with a gamekeeper or a Lady Chatterley take a lover.

Staying in a role can be quite a delicate affair, for even an apparently trivial matter can flaw a role if one is not secure. A new radio or television announcer may get quite upset when something goes wrong in the studio and he or she is left to improvise. A misplaced page in one's lecture notes can be very stressful for a neophyte teacher or lecturer. Forgetting what you were going to say after managing to get the floor in a meeting can be quite embarrassing. In each case experience may eventually tell you how to manage the situation so as to stay in role. Perhaps one of the best examples of role maintenance in difficult circumstances was shown when Queen Elizabeth carried on perfectly normally when someone fired a starting pistol near her while she rode on horseback in procession through London. She never faltered in her role, one she has now played with great success for over three decades.

We can see, therefore, that a conversation is not simply *about* something, nor is it merely a series of somethings, such as topics. A conversation *is* something. It is a performance, a kind of show in which the participants act out as well as speak whatever it is that they are doing. Each must present himself to the others. Each must at every moment decide who he is and what he is doing, where he is and what he is saying, has said, is about to say, or does not wish to say, and how all the foregoing is related to all the other things done and said, being done and said, and possibly to be done and said. Each conversation, therefore, is a scene – or a succession of scenes – constructed in the very playing by actors who create their roles as they play them.

It is very rarely that any of the above becomes a conscious activity for the participants: we do not constantly see ourselves as actors on the stage of life. It is quite possible, too, that we are better able to observe the 'performances' of others than those we give ourselves. Indeed, some kinds of highly esteemed work focus on classifying performances given by others, for example, counselling and the various psychotherapies. What we do not do is wander through the world like Rosencrantz and Guildenstern, wondering what strange world we inhabit and what kind of performance is expected of us. What wandering and wondering we do is at a far less conscious level, and much of what we might do is pre-empted by the need to get on and live – to accept the world as it seems to be and to fit into it as best we can, dealing with what comes along in tried and trusted ways. Not to do this is to create for oneself a character which may not fit at all well into the currently accepted scene.

A conversation is also like a scene in a play in that it is a discrete event in a larger ongoing process. It is a coherent unit with each participant acting out a role, each sustaining the others, and the whole having both a begining and an ending. It is a unit with a set of internal conventions which the participants observe and which any others who might happen to overhear or overlook what is happening may observe too. Each participant is conscious that he or she is participating, if not acting, and that this performance will be viewed in relation to past performances and possible future performances. Consequently, in acting through a particular scene, he or she must consider that larger span and plan the various details of the performance accordingly.

However, in general, as we have indicated, that planning is unlikely to be conscious planning. Conversation is generally completely unrehearsed. It is essentially spontaneous, in that you create its content and any structure it has in the course of playing it out. Occasionally bits and pieces may be planned, but rarely can a whole performance be plotted out in advance. Of course, you can take care in choosing a particular time and occasion to say something, for example, to make an announcement. You can even rehearse the actual words you intend to use. But often such a deliberate act is highly 'marked' and it quickly becomes very obvious to all who hear it that you are performing some kind of set piece, whether it is making an announcement, delivering a sales pitch, providing a rehearsed excuse, or seeking a deliberate confrontation. And once the set piece is over, conversation quickly reverts to its more naturalistic and relaxed characteristics.

In some situations it is easier to identify appropriate roles to play than in others, and some roles we find it easier to play from training, practice, or observation. When we can easily identify a role we can play, we may find it much easier to converse with others than when we must work out a brand-new role. Take, for example, meetings between strangers; eating in a restaurant; shopping; waiting in an outer office; selling (or buying) something; sitting next to someone in a theatre; and so on. Most of us know the 'proper' role selection and behaviour in such circumstances and are familiar with all the appropriate details. We do have expectations about how people should behave in certain settings and we know that others expect the same of us. However, these expectations can be quite demanding for someone who must play many roles in succession and change quickly from one to another, or who must be seen as playing several roles concurrently.

These demands are also extremely severe on someone trying to adapt to another culture. It is one thing to know the language of another group and quite another to know how to use that language appropriately to play a role. It is easy to collect examples: the question-asking and -answering styles of students from cultures which favour indirectness rather than directness; a peremptory *Bring me two rice* to a waiter, from someone who could say that in his native language without offending the waiter (or the people with whom he was eating) but not in an English language environment; the extreme formality of colleagues who come from a different part of the world, carrying over into English a 'position' - oriented rather than 'person'-oriented manner of dealing with others, and the 'Let's negotiate it' approach to everything, when, as we know, that approach could no more apply to everything in the country of origin than it could in the new society, nor indeed in any other. Such cultural differences can result in misunderstanding, conflict, and even charges of racism. A society undergoing rapid social and cultural change is therefore likely to exhibit a considerable amount of ambiguity about roles and how particular roles should be played.

During the course of a conversation your role is unlikely to be completely 'fixed' unless the occasion is a very formal one. Instead, you are likely to be called upon to play a variety of roles – some, as we have said, concurrently – and you must accord others the opportunity to change roles too. One moment you may be a friend, the next a professional colleague; now a dutiful son, then a professor; and so on. As conversation shifts, so roles will shift, and, particularly if several people are present, you may find yourself experiencing problems with role conflict and role shift. Social events designed to 'mix' people may be unsuccessful if the participants find it difficult or impossible either to shift back and forth among different roles or to forget for a while certain roles they insist on playing. Certain 'characters' are so called simply because they have chosen to freeze themselves into a single role, usually one which amuses others in some way!

A role is a complex matter and many factors go into its make-up and interpretation. A speaker's attitude to others, the topics on which he feels free to converse, his appearance, gestures, tone of voice, and choice of words, the particular grammatical structures he favours, and the way he sequences longer utterances all combine to fix an impression in others. They will judge him to be either arrogant, diffident, sarcastic, cold, warm, light-hearted, serious, or whatever, to be making certain claims about himself which they may regard as justified or not, and to be acting or not acting his part well. They may even find the role that he has chosen peculiar in the circumstances: for example, a very esoteric role where a more commonplace one is required; an overstated role when an understated one seems called for; or playing the fool when a certain seriousness is necessary. You cannot avoid giving a 'dramatic' performance; what you must try to do is give the one you intend and one which is appropriate to the circumstances.

A certain amount of self-monitoring is necessary, as in most aspects of daily living. You must be constantly attentive to what you are doing and who is observing you. Your role in any situation requires behaviour specific to that situation, and you must see to it not only that you exhibit it but that others acknowledge its correctness. Whether the situation is as commonplace as walking along a street or eating breakfast, you have to define it and comport yourself appropriately within it. You do this by watching yourself behave and observing how others judge that behaviour. So a certain distancing from the self is necessary. When you see someone totally involved in a role, you also see someone who appears impervious to what others say or do, and someone who is no longer monitoring his behaviour, so completely carried away has he become. In such circumstances you may feel wary because of the lack of just that right amount of detachment you have come to expect from those who can play a role but not forget their audience.

The difficulties of dealing with a self-absorbed person are many. We use language for a variety of purposes, and one of these is communication. In the technical sense, we achieve communication only when, in an exchange between A and B, A learns something from B that A did not already know, or vice versa; if an exchange between A and B reveals nothing new to either, then no communication took place. With rigid, dogmatic, blinkered people you do not communicate – you just listen and, when you speak, you do so to no effect. They are completely caught up in what they are doing. Of course, the result has been the occasional 'saint'; unfortunately, too often, it has been the opposite.

The 'acting' in conversation is a special kind of acting, one that should come naturally to us. That is, we should have learned how to do ordinary things and produce a 'natural' appearance in doing them. We should have learned how to present ourselves in many different circumstances, how to fill the roles expected of us, and how to play new roles. Occasionally, we do become conscious of our acting – for example, if we must dissemble or lie – and we are likely to feel somewhat insecure in our roles when we do so. Many people – perhaps the majority – find it difficult to stay calm when they are experiencing inner turmoil, to knowingly mislead another, to pretend feelings they are not experiencing, or to give a normal appearance to what they know is a very unusual occasion. In such circumstances things done normally, casually, and without a moment's thought as part of everyday activity must be deliberately enacted, so that everything takes on a new significance. It should come as no surprise that many people are hopeless at dissembling; whereas they can act out their 'normal' selves to perfection, they cannot act out a self at variance with their norms nor can they easily use words to express a false intent. The principles of good, decent behaviour have them in their grip. In contrast, the confidence man exploits these same principles to the fullest extent possible for his own ends.

There is one respect at least in which talk as unconscious theatre can become talk as deliberate theatre. It can be deliberately played for the benefit of a third party. A private argument can be extended to become a performance put on for the benefit of spectators – either to inform them or involve them in some way. Conversations can go public. Of course, once the spectators have been brought into the action in this way then the public theatre that was temporarily achieved becomes a kind of private theatre once more. A conversation may be designed or conducted to be overheard, but once it is overheard and involves the new party then new roles must be subscribed to by *all* parties. The play now has a new, enlarged cast of characters and is in that respect a different play; it is no longer being performed to entertain others, for the others have become part of the action. We must note how reluctant many people are to become involved with others in this way: there is a tendency to resist being 'dragged in', whether it is into a quarrel between neighbours, while watching a police officer make a difficult arrest, or witnessing a political demonstration, or attending certain kinds of social or cultural activities which violate our feelings about what we agreed to see and do – and thereby not to see and do.

Re-composing yourself to play an unexpected role when you find yourself in an unforeseen situation may not be very easy. You go to the theatre to find yourself not observing others but actually participating with them when the players directly involve the audience in their drama. A magician or comedian chooses you by chance as stooge or 'victim'. Or walking along a street on the left bank in Paris, you find yourself the object of a mimic's attention. Or your secretary says to you *Can you come along to the lounge for a minute? Someone wants a word with you* and you find a group assembled there to wish you a happy birthday. Some people cope better than others with this kind of predicament; indeed, a few even seem to glory in it, for how else can one account for the fact that certain kinds of public spectacle depend on people volunteering to make fools of themselves? But for the majority, performing is not an end in itself, nor is performing in roles over which one has little or no choice something lightly undertaken.

One aspect of the theatrical component in conversation that we must not overlook is that which involves ritual. Certain conversations have large 'frozen' chunks in them. For example there is likely to be a much larger ritualistic interchange among strangers brought together for a meeting and between friends meeting after a long separation than there is among people who meet regularly and often. Such ritual is necessary in the first case to establish a working relationship so that everyong can decide how he or she may relate to everyone else. It enables basic contacts to be made: physical, if hands are shaken; names to be shared; and a few ritual topics to be brought up (weather, mutual contacts, shared background, and so on). When friends meet after a considerable time apart, the ritual concerns of family, job, mutual friends, current circumstances, and so on are used to re-establish contact. Sometimes these ritual concerns in fact achieve just the opposite effect: running through them reveals that a gulf now exists between the two participants, possibly one that cannot be bridged, and saves both the embarrassment of attempting to re-establish the earlier state of affairs. They can once again part, on completion of the ritual, without being required to deal with each other on matters of substance, having realized that little possibility any longer exists for regenerating the previous relationship – *My, how Sally has changed!*

'Getting down to business' in conversations requires varying amounts of time. Little time is required in certain circumstances: *Do you 'ave the time?*, *Got a match?*, *Excuse me, where's the post office?*, *Is this the employment office?* The business is over as soon as the request is answered and no further preliminaries are necessary. But a meeting involving a number of participants, some of whom are strangers to each other, requires considerably more time. It can involve such matters as introductions, seating rituals, deciding on some kind of chairperson or leader, and perhaps even agreeing to a formal agenda. People have to feel comfortable with one another, so there can be no rush into business that requires early decisive moves before they have had the opportunity to sound one another out. Hence, many such meetings have highly ritualized beginnings: minutes to be approved, old business to be discussed, prepared statements to be made, written reports to be filed, pre-circulated documents to be read, and so on. These give the participants time to feel comfortable, so that when an important topic is introduced they can make a contribution if they wish. Without such time people may feel rushed or coerced and, even though they may agree with the course of action adopted, they may not feel any satisfaction about the agreement. Or they may feel that a decision has been made arbitrarily, objecting not to the quality of the actual decision but to what they see as the inadequate preparation that preceded it.

As we have seen, conversation makes extensive use of routines, of ritualistic and stereotyped topics and patterns. The consequence is that many interchanges serve little function other than what has been called the 'phatic' one, the indication of social solidarity. They function much like mutual grooming behaviour in the animal world, showing only that the various parties acknowledge that they have a social bond which they have agreed to maintain. Hence, what is most likely to impress you if you read transcripts of recorded conversations drawn from everyday life is that not much of importance ever gets said. Indeed, most conversations are so banal that they must have some other function than communication. They are part of the theatre of everyday life, commonplace and unremarkable in one sense but extraordinary and intriguing in another, in that they require people to exhibit such finely tuned skills and provide us with so much evidence of basic human goodwill.

Further Reading

For a variety of interesting observations on how people judge certain characteristics of speech see Giles and Powesland's *Speech Style and Social Evaluation*. Gumperz' *Language and Social Identity* also deals with a number of broad issues concerning the relationships between language and social factors. Much of Goffman's work concerns the 'theatrical' aspects of daily living (*The Presentation of Self in Everyday Life*, *Interaction Ritual*, and *Relations in Public: Microstudies of the Public Order*), but his paper 'On Face-work: An Analysis of Ritual

Elements in Social Interaction' is of particular interest here. The use of language for 'phatic communion' is discussed in Malinowski's 'The Problem of Meaning in Primitive Languages'.

3
Cooperation and Playing the Game

Conversation is a social activity, one that always involves two or more people. Talking to oneself is not conversation, whatever else it is. Conversation is therefore a cooperative endeavour. One very simple and clear illustration of this fact is that, once talk has begun, most conversationalists assume that they have undertaken a definite obligation to keep it going. If they intend to discontinue it, they must do so gracefully. Keeping it going also requires the various parties to 'work' so as to seem that all get some satisfaction out of the activity. Endings become a particularly delicate matter. They cannot be arbitrarily imposed by one party on another; they must be negotiated in some way. If for some reason you are forced to end a conversation prematurely, you are required to offer an apology of sorts. If you 'break off talks' with others you make a very strong gesture of non-cooperation, for you deliberately choose to violate the normal assumption that talk will prove to be mutually satisfactory and beneficial to all parties. Cutting talk short is therefore a clear indication of failure or disagreement. Which nations are talking to which others has become a rather precise indicator of the general good health of the world. Whether talks are beginning, continuing, foundering, suspended, about to be broken off, or soon to be resumed is always a newsworthy item. There is a feeling that while there is talk there is a certain amount of safety and hope, but without talk only the fear of ugly possibilities. This is but another instance of language used for *phatic* ends, to keep channels of communication open and reduce uncertainty.

We may also ask ourselves why silence during a conversation creates as much embarrassment to the participants as it sometimes does. It does so because silence signals a failure to keep alive what the participants regard as this essentially cooperative venture. All seem to suffer because the failure is felt to reflect on the participants, both collectively and individually. When a period of silence occurs in a conversation, you can almost sense that everyone involved is searching for a way to fill the hole that has appeared. There is a kind of collective embarrassment and it is not unusual to notice an increase in tension. Sometimes more than one voice will break the silence and the conversation will start up again. When a new topic seems on its way to being established, the hole is filled, and the momentary pause is no more than an embarrassing memory, there is a noticeable reduction in tension, a collective acknowledgement that the day has been saved and that the threat that silence had posed to the group has been successfully removed.

Cooperative behaviour is also sharing behaviour. You cannot monopolize a conversation: you must offer others the opportunity to say something even though they may decline that opportunity. Everyone has some right to speak – or not to speak as the case may be. Constantly to interrupt another person is a partial denial of this right. An even more severe denial is to refuse to let another speak or to question his right to speak. Consequently, the power to control the right to speak is a considerable one. Its extreme form is censorship, but it also reveals itself in such places as courtrooms and classrooms where someone in authority controls who speaks, and on what matters. One interesting fact about the principles that operate in conversation in general is that they tend to ensure the rights of people to speak and be silent as they choose, rather than to deny those rights.

These rights vary from group to group and culture to culture. Some cultures favour silence in certain circumstances, for example, when there is some uncertainty in the relationship, as with the Western Apache; others favour large amounts of talk but may restrict the topics, for example, the !Kung bushmen. Still others may favour using language for certain competitive ends, such as the Subanun of the Philippines or many black people of the Americas. In some circumstances older people may have precedence over younger people in speaking, and those holding certain offices may have special rights that no one else has. Each group will have its own rules about who gets to speak, to whom, when, what are proper topics, and how these topics are to be discussed. Learning another language is not just learning how to say something in a new way; it is also knowing what can be said and exactly how to say it 'right'. It is knowing the principles that native speakers observe when they speak to the other native speakers: in this sense you can speak French (or any other language) successfully only when you are prepared to 'be' French.

You can generally exercise your right to speak or to be silent without being challenged. And even when two or more people are gathered in a situation in which communication seems necessary and one person attempts to initiate a conversation and the other or others refuse, you cannot say that there was absolutely no communication. Refusal to converse is itself a form of communication. Somebody who refuses to participate or who withdraws after initial participation is consciously – or subconsciously – making a 'statement'. You will undoubtedly come to some conclusion about that person and what has happened or is happening if you are the 'offended' party. It is an interesting legal principle in certain systems of jurisprudence that an accused cannot be compelled to testify in his own trial and that this refusal must not be held against him. Just how jurors react to such refusals is not at all clear; in ordinary life we are accustomed to seek reasons, generally prejudicial, for a failure to speak when speech is expected: someone is hiding something, or is disturbed, or is uncooperative, and so on. It would be remarkable if jurors were completely uninfluenced by their 'normal' interpretations of such events.

The cooperative nature of conversation reveals itself in another somewhat peculiar way – participants may mimic each other quite subconsciously. One person may even begin to sound like another through adopting certain speaking mannerisms, for example, a regional accent. This behaviour may prompt the question *Are you mimicking me?* More subtle will be the achievement of a shared speech tempo as the participants adjust their speech rhythms to harmonize with one another. Physical mannerisms may be copied too, for example, posture, fidgeting, and coughing. In some cases there may even be a kind of epidemic of speech and behavioural characteristics, as a whole group (for example, a classroom) becomes infected with a general communicative style or tone: volatile, lively, languid, bored, and so on. Thus, cooperation is achieved in a somewhat unexpected manner.

It is also possible to look at this as some kind of synchronization of speech activity. Good conversationalists tend to match each other in such matters as the tempo of their speaking, the kinds of words they select, the grammatical structures they employ, and the general focus they choose in dealing with topics. This kind of synchronization at once creates and expresses a certain empathy between the parties. For example, it makes answers to questions feel like 'real', genuine responses, and it is partly responsible for the warmth and understanding that the parties believe to be characteristics of such a conversation. When such synchrony is lacking, and it can be lacking for many different reasons – dialect differences, different ways of presenting information, of expressing requests, of asking favours, and so on – that kind of empathy between the parties may be entirely lacking. Each party may feel dissatisfied, even irritated, and each may believe that the other is being difficult or uncooperative and that the conversation is futile. Such breakdowns are often quite noticeable when the parties come from different ethnic, social, or educational backgrounds; in such circumstances conversation can become disjointed, sometimes unproductive, and occasionally unpleasant.

Taking part in a conversation requires your cooperation and participation even when you are not actually talking or intending to talk very much or even at all. You are in a sense always 'at risk', even in a group conversation in which you have little or no intention of making a contribution. There is always the risk that one or the other speakers will address you or select you to speak. Being so addressed or selected can result in considerable embarrassment to you if you are not attending to what is going on. So if you want to be involved – without actually desiring to speak – you must still cooperate by listening, on the off chance that you may be called on to say something. You must listen to find out at least two things: whether you might be asked to speak and the topic you might be asked to speak on. Inattentiveness is usually regarded as failure to cooperate. For example, teachers deplore inattentive behaviour in their students. Boredom is, of course, a clear sign of inattentiveness and reveals itself through many characteristics associated with uncooperativeness: fidgeting, lack of concentration, day-dreaming, and so on.

It is not always possible to be sure that the other person is attending to what you are saying. It is quite easy for him or her to provide feedback signals, particularly the little *Mmm*s which sometimes indicate 'I'm listening' without actually listening. In the following conversation A had heard several such 'acknowledgements' that B was listening, or so he thought, until the following exchange:

A.   . . .So we'll go on Thursday then?
B.   What?
A.   We'll go to the ballet on Thursday and the opera on Friday.
B.   What do you mean?
A.   You weren't listening. I said we'll have to change our ballet tickets.
B.   Why?

B had been providing A with signals which A interpreted to mean that B was listening and could take up the conversation at any point. However, B had not been listening and had been treating A's words as phatic rather than informative. To her A was merely indulging in a series of pleasantries, being sociable rather than informative. Her *Mmm*s meant no more than 'go on speaking'. In the circumstances, of course, A could be excused for misinterpretation. Much of the language between closely bonded people is phatic rather than informative. One of the difficulties that can result is that if the emotional bonding weakens, the pattern of not really listening to the other, because so much of what has been said has been phatic, can be carried over to attempts to be informative. The result, of course, is the charge that the other does not listen, but really it is a different kind of listening that is being demanded.

There are two ways in which any conversation can be spoiled. If one party violates the principles of good behaviour, the other will feel that what should be a pleasant cooperative venture has become either antagonistic or unproductive. That party is therefore likely to want to abandon it. Likewise, if all the work of keeping a conversation going is thrust on to one participant, he or she is likely to feel that it is too much of a burden to carry very far, for it is just too tiring to carry on a conversation with someone who offers little support or feedback. No benefits seem to accrue or the costs vastly outweigh the benefits, so giving up the effort avoids any further waste. You can get very little out of hostility and antagonism – except a painful ulcer or a headache – or out of 'talking to a brick wall' – except frustration. In neither case do you find the support you need to continue. There is a failure of cooperation. Cutting your losses and moving on to something else may be your wisest course.

As we saw with the example about changing the evening for attending the ballet, persistent claims that the other is not attending to what you say are likely to reflect a change in relationship. Unfortunately, once a pattern of not listening to the other has been established, it may be difficult to break. Marriage counsellors seem to spend much of their time trying, not often with much success, to get couples to listen to each other. When listening ceases, talking does not necessarily cease with it: much of what is described as 'nagging' is essentially an imbalanced situation with much talking by one party and little listening by the other. Sometimes the result is that the parties talk right past each other: both talk but neither listens. Occasionally neither talks. In all cases conversation has broken down: cooperation has vanished and the lack of verbal harmony merely reflects the underlying personal discord.

Confrontation is, of course, the opposite of cooperation. When you confront another person, you deliberately choose to challenge some of the basic principles on which normal communication depends. You are saying that you do not trust the other, you are questioning the other's statements, and you are possibly disputing his honesty. To some extent you are assaulting the other's presentation of the world and declaring it to be false. We can contrast this with what we must assume happens in normal circumstances, where we indicate a basic trust in the other's statements, we accept his views as being both worthwhile and honestly held, and we may even try to help him present them in a coherent and reasonable manner. Although we might not agree with what we hear, we do not directly challenge the actual presentation. However, when you confront another person, you assault him. You assert that your views must take precedence over his and you deliberately seek an admission that he is either deceiving himself or deceiving you and possibly others too.

Most of us use confrontational tactics quite rarely, since they are a harsh and somewhat desperate way to achieve objectives that we may often obtain by milder and more subtle means. In fact, we can note that one pervasive characteristic of cooperativeness in conversation is that speakers generally try to avoid saying unpleasant things of almost any kind to each other. We avoid taboo subjects and things that cannot 'decently' be mentioned, and we resort quite often to euphemisms in order to do so. We spare others' feelings. Indeed, it is more usual for us to understate than to overstate, and we tend to give others the benefit of the doubt: *That's OK* ('It's not very good'); *She manages quite well, all things considered* ('She's having a difficult time'); *It seems to be getting better* ('I don't notice any change'); and *John is not the best teacher in the world* ('John is a very poor teacher'). We also expect the same kinds of behaviour from others. Those who insist always on 'telling it like it is' are likely to run out of listeners quite soon: how do they know any better than we ourselves how 'it is', and even, if they do, what right have they to tell us? Missionary zeal may have its place in society, but that place is not in everyday, run-of-the-mill conversation. Digging for 'the truth' or expounding on it at length are highly 'marked' activities best kept for suitable occasions.

While conversation must be a cooperative endeavour if it is to exist at all – lack of cooperation, as we have seen, kills the activity – we should not infer that it cannot be used for ends which may be inimical to future cooperation: to jockey for position; to score points; to put others down; to build oneself up. Consequently, individual utterances may have a tone to them which signals both cooperation and some other attitude, such as, 'I'll answer your question but you cannot be very bright if you ask such things' or 'That's a clever observation and remember *I* said so.' In this way an individual 'selfish' agenda may exist alongside a collective 'cooperative' one, and it is often the tensions between the two that become interesting, particularly to observers. Dramatic art actually makes this phenomenon quite central to its being.

We can see how the absence of cooperativeness lies behind the effectiveness of certain kinds of language used to inhibit, break up, or break off conversation. The existence of expletives and their very form – short, direct expressions of a 'rude' nature – is explicable largely in terms of the general convention that conversation is a cooperative undertaking. Terse, explicit expressions such as *Get lost!, Damn you!, Why don't you shove off!* indicate a strong reluctance on the part of those who choose to use them to observe the niceties of social behaviour. Indeed, they are a conventional signal that normal decencies will not be observed. Paradoxically, therefore, in that sense they are also part of the very system of conventions that they explicitly attack.

Resort to abusive terms and obscenities generally provides a very clear violation of the cooperative principle that is basic to speech, and signals that communication is not to occur or has broken down. But this is not always the case. In some groups abusive language actually functions as a solidarity signal, so that its absence would be remarkable and would occasion comment. It is said that one can tell the urgency of an order in the lower echelons of the armed forces by the amount of four-letter words used in giving the order, with the relationship an inverse one so that *Get your rifles!* is more urgent than *Get your — rifles!* Abusive language may also be employed as a signal of intimacy between familiars who use it to show a certain type of solidarity; parents are often dismayed by the 'dirty' talk of their children as the latter pass through (as most of them do) this stage in their social (and verbal) development. It may even be humorously employed on occasion, as when certain ritualistic insults are exchanged, whether among black children in large northern urban centres in the United States or among the children discussed by Opie and Opie in their monumental study of the lore and language of schoolchildren in the United Kingdom. So in a sense the wheel comes full circle: whereas for most of us and on most occasions 'abuse' signals a failure of cooperation, for some and on some occasions it is the special mark of cooperation and every bit as important to its users as the technical language of a profession is to its practitioners.

Conversation is a finely tuned activity. What is particularly remarkable about it is that it does not depend on the subtle manipulation of very few devices. Rather, the devices are quite numerous and their combinations extremely subtle. Confusion and difficulty might seem to be the natural consequences of this diversity, but our common-sense view of most conversations – that they are not very interesting as examples of 'creative' endeavour – indicates how easily we manipulate the complexities and navigate ourselves through large areas of potential difficulty. We owe our success in no small part to the fact that we enter most conversations with good intent. We have a strong bias toward making a particular conversation work; we are willing to go along with others; we know the conversation is likely to be one of a series so we cannot 'close doors' with impunity; and we are prepared to believe that others share our views.

An interesting question is how we achieve the cooperation necessary to conversation. The answer appears to be that it is through having learned how to play the particular game that conversation is. As a result of learning a language, we have learned control of a highly complex system of behaviour. It is that learning which we put to use whenever we open our lips to say something. But just exactly what it is we have learned – what that particular ability is – is the central issue that linguists (that is, those scholars whose major preoccupation is trying to figure out why languages are the way they are) see as central to their discipline.

Language is an extraordinarily complex medium. Those who make a career of studying how language works will tell you how difficult it is to explain just how any part of any language really functions. Communication too is a complex endeavour. If, when two or more people attempt to engage in conversation, every possible utterance had an equal chance of occurring in every circumstance, there would be no communication. It would take the participants just too long to figure out what was happening – both what to say and what was being said – to make any meaningful exchange possible. Fortunately, both human languages and the process of communication are highly redundant: that is, most possibilities can be eliminated from consideration because they cannot occur in particular sets of circumstances. Furthermore, the grammatical structures of all languages require that certain kinds of information must be repeated, and the social requirements of language use demand that speakers and listeners share some assumptions about appropriate linguistic behaviour. Grammatical redundancy, the linguistic demands of particular situations, the necessary observation of conventions, the careful reinforcement of words through certain accompanying physical activities, the shared backgrounds of participants, all serve to delimit what can occur in a particular conversation, and, in so delimiting, make meaningful interchange possible – without, of course, guaranteeing it. It is never the case that 'anything goes' in language or that anything can happen, just as it is not the case that 'anything goes' anywhere else in the natural world. There are always constraints of some kind that operate to limit possibilities, and in one sense scientific endeavour is all about forming hypotheses about how behaviour of any kind is constrained, or 'lawful', to use another way of expressing the same idea.

None the less, the choices available to you at any one moment in a conversation are considerable. What, for example, is the appropriate response to a question asked of you? Or of a request that another has made? Or even to a simple statement? You have so many choices available to you that it is almost impossible for an observer to predict which one you will choose. Any rules or principles that we might construct to describe conversation must be phrased in very general terms and be concerned with broad issues; we can never hope to predict behaviour in highly specific terms. The instances mentioned above must also allow for no response at all. But in that case the originator of the question, request, or statement faces a dilemma: how to proceed further in the conversation. Any rules we construct must allow us to characterize in some way the options – probably considerably reduced – that this negative countermove creates for the original speaker. As move follows move in conversation, we need to find some principles that distinguish possible moves from impossible moves, and perhaps 'good' moves from 'bad' ones.

As we have observed, good behaviour in a conversation is cooperative behaviour. Each party agrees to abide by certain conventions, one of which is that you recognize the particular circumstances in which you meet and quickly establish what kind of relationship you are in: doctor–patient; former classmates; neighbours; cab driver–passenger; customer–shop assistant; and so on. Having done this, you can then set certain limits to, and constraints on, your behaviour and, by doing so, reduce the risk of offence and enhance the possibilities for cooperation. A second convention is that you agree to hear out the other or others as circumstances require, for only in this way can you yourself expect to get a hearing. On occasion, the circumstances will require very special kinds of hearing out – a courtroom, for example – but propriety demands no less. What this amounts to, in effect, is that you will be respected by others only in so far as you show them the respect that is due to them. Since conversations are usually voluntary as well as cooperative exchanges, they require the parties not just to work, if they are to be successful, but to do this work for a combination of both altruistic and selfish reasons.

Conversation involves a kind of trade-off between public benefit and personal profit: you have to give in order to get. If you do not provide others with responses, feedback, and support, you will find them reluctant to reciprocate. What you must do is judge how much you are prepared to give in order to get what you want. Sometimes a conversation becomes burdensome because you feel you are getting nothing for what you are giving: it becomes *a waste of time, frustrating, exasperating, maddening*, and so on. (When it is all gain and no give, you might not be quite so aware!) Any attempts to force you to give, in certain circumstances, might find you resisting stoutly: you keep your lips sealed; you refuse to testify (and take the consequences); or you invoke some doctrine of confidentiality or privilege. Sometimes it may not be at all clear which motive is stronger: the private selfish one or the more public and altruistic, but almost invariably the claim will be the latter, as in the Watergate affair.

Since communication must occur in an endless variety of circumstances, there must be some easily recognized principles to follow to prevent chaos and achieve order. If anything were possible, there would be no recognizable devices for beginnings and endings, no procedures for filling in the middles, no rules about who could say what, when, and how, and no means, indeed, for even deciding what anything might mean. Actually only a very few things are possible, and it is these few that are the concern of those who seek to explain what happens when people converse: the rules, procedures, principles, maxims – call them what you will – that people apparently follow in order to communicate effectively with each other.

One simple way of convincing yourself that some such rules exist is to ask why it is that when you find yourself in another culture or among a group of people who are strangers to you, but not to one another, you may find it difficult to understand what is going on. You fail to recognize the signals to which the others are reacting and find few or no clues to the conventions that appear to regulate their behaviour. Things happen without you knowing why they happen: agreements are made without your understanding; beginnings, changes, and endings occur and you discover them, as it were, only after the event. Familiar clues from your own culture are absent and those clues that are present escape your attention. What you lack is access to the system of rules for behaviour that the others are following. It is not the same as the one you have learned, so you must either learn to recognize and use it or be prepared to remain an outsider.

Learning a new language from a textbook or in situations far removed from contexts in which the language is used offers you no assurances that you will actually be able to converse with speakers of that language. Many of us have had the experience of meeting people from other countries who have been well schooled in certain aspects of English but who cannot get through the simplest conversation. Many of us who have learned a foreign language have also learned it in such a manner that, faced with using it to order a meal, we ask the waiter if he speaks English! More than one classical scholar has expressed private doubts about whether the extensive knowledge gained of classical Greek and Latin would have been of much use in pursuing the simple daily activities needed to survive in ancient Athens or Rome. In each case there is a recognition that an essential part of being competent in a language is knowing how those to whom the language is native use it in going about their ordinary lives – a competence which, though it may be described in part by trained observers, may be acquired fully only by becoming a participant in the community of users.

In recent years linguists have often said that languages are what they call 'rule-governed' entities. By this they mean that when you know a language you know a set of rules for producing sentences in that language. You may not know how to describe that set of rules – linguists themselves have trouble describing those that speakers of English use – but the fact that you speak in grammatical sentences is clear evidence of your 'knowledge'. Some social scientists have tried to characterize certain aspects of social behaviour in similar terms – that is, through rules – in the belief that it is only because human beings are on the whole willing parties to rules and conventions that we have whatever social harmony that exists. In that broader social context, then, the rules and conventions for language use comprise merely a special subset of the rules and conventions for general social behaviour.

The principles or guides to behaviour that govern conversational practice are not the rigid laws that characterize theorizing in the natural sciences or that are employed in mathematical systems. They apparently may on occasion even contradict one another: you must choose the principle that seems most likely to achieve whatever objective you have, all the while realizing that you could have chosen to follow some other principle. For example, to challenge another person is to violate a basic principle of cooperative behaviour. But it may be necessary to challenge him if he is being obscure, or is threatening or misleading you. You need not be cooperative in such circumstances. If your territory is infringed on or if there are obvious violations of truthfulness or common sense, you will have to choose which principle to follow in any response you care to make. Do you cooperate and go along with the other person, do you seek clarification of his or her intent, or do you offer a direct challenge?

The principles we follow in conversing allow communication to go on in an orderly manner. For example, they enable one speaker – and usually only one speaker – to have the floor at a time. They allow for changes of speaker, for interruptions at appropriate points, and for a conversation to be brought to an orderly end. Such principles enable us to exhibit a basic tolerance toward and cooperation with others, which is the basis of all social bonding and all social behaviour. To that extent, then, they are inherently rational in origin. Without them social life as we know it would not exist, and we would have to invent some such principles for regulating who can say what to whom, when, and how.

According to the philosopher H. P. Grice the general 'cooperative principle' that operates in conversation has very specific consequences for speakers and listeners. In speaking, you must observe this principle and try to do certain things – follow certain maxims, if you will. You must offer the other, or others, as much information as is necessary for the particular purpose at hand – not too much nor too little, but just enough. You must try to be truthful; consequently, you must avoid stating deliberate falsehoods and making statements for which you have little or no evidence. The comments you make must be relevant to the topic under discussion and they must appear to be adequate to the occasion. And, finally, you should avoid obscurities and ambiguities and make sure that what you say is both brief and orderly. Grice acknowledges that you may either violate or ignore these maxims on certain occasions, either to mislead or to be uncooperative. On some occasions, too, you must choose to be guided by one rather than another. In addition, you may use one or more maxims so as to 'implicate' something: that is, you can deliberately say too little or too much, deliberately be irrelevant, inadequate, obscure, ambiguous, and so on. Your listeners will probably recognize your exploitation of the maxims and you may indeed communicate in this way quite effectively what you mean to communicate – which will be something more than (or even quite different from) what the words are usually used to convey.

Perhaps the basic concept behind Grice's maxims is sincerity: in order to communicate with others you have to assume that they mean what they say and in turn they must be led to believe that you mean what you say. And anything which does not quite fit has to be made to fit by 'implicature'. This principle, for example, explains our reaction to rhetorical questions such as *Is a whale a bird?*, *Can you believe she's a murderer?*, *Are we going to stand for that?*, *Was Hitler a saint?* Such questions are not genuine, capable of either a *yes* or *no* answer, so they are not sincere. They are answerable only in the negative, so they are not questions but a 'marked' way, that is, a special way, of making a negative statement, and making it strongly. But it is the hearer who must infer that fact through the process of implicature, which requires him or her to infer that a question of this kind asked in such circumstances cannot be answered except negatively – it is 'loaded'. Therefore, it is the rhetorical effect which is important.

Grice's maxims are an attempt to explain certain principles that seem to lie behind most conversations. They are not intended to describe every aspect of a specific conversation. For example, people are not as direct and forthright with others as the maxims would describe them as being. Indeed, as we have seen, indirectness is probably more typical of conversational utterances than directness. However, the maxims are important in that they describe a kind of foundation for conversational interaction. In practice, the participants in most conversations use the maxims inferentially and indirectly. They 'know' that some such system as Grice describes provides the foundation they need for communication; if it did not, conversations could not even begin (nor for that matter could any human language be acquired); but they do not exhibit this 'knowledge' directly in what they say on any particular occasion. Rather, we can infer that it exists from what people say and from what they choose not to say. It is the consistency of human behaviour in conversation that makes this task possible. Certain kinds of things happen repeatedly and the inference we should draw from this fact is that people are behaving systematically. It is our task to describe that system, and Grice's proposals are a major attempt to do so.

One of Grice's maxims is that you should be as informative as is necessary for the occasion – no less and no more. But *enough* requires you to make what is essentially a subjective judgement. How do you judge how much is enough? Must you tell all you know? Apparently not. It would almost certainly violate the cooperativeness principle if you were to tell all, for your listeners are likely to know something about the matter at hand. Then there are taboos to be observed, privileged information not to be divulged, codes of ethics to be subscribed to, and principles of decency to consider, and all of these require of you various kinds of concealment. The problem therefore must always be to tell enough so as not to mislead others, but not too little nor too much – and where you must draw the line between the two is not at all clear. If you say too little, you may appear 'to damn with faint praise' and, if you say too much, your enthusiasm or verbosity may 'protest too much'. Of course, you may deliberately intend one of those consequences and exploit the maxim in such a way that your listeners understand your intent rather than take what you say literally. To say of a co-worker with whom you have shared an office for five years that *John is always punctual and makes a good cup of coffee* when asked what kind of worker John is, is certainly not going to be taken as a strong recommendation of John's abilities. Nor is effusive and obviously exaggerated praise likely to achieve a much better effect – perhaps you just want to have the whole office to yourself!

If your contribution to a topic is considerably less than what the others consider would be a reasonable contribution from you, they may well wonder why you are behaving in such a way. They will surmise, correctly or not, that your action is deliberate and that they are to consider as your total contribution not only what you said but what you declined to say. Since conversation requires you to make a constant series of choices, your choice not to say something that you might well have said or even on occasion that you should have said becomes a very significant one. Of course, in another respect you have chosen to conceal the truth or to tell only part of the truth – you have chosen not to tell the *whole* truth. And since the cooperative nature of conversation requires us to believe that it is the whole truth that is spoken, our discovery of the partial nature of what we have been told could lead to a charge that we have been deliberately deceived.

Still, telling less than the truth and telling a lie are not the same things. While the assumption behind most conversations is that the parties are telling the truth – to the best of each's knowledge – some concealment is nevertheless likely. As we have indicated, certain things may not be said which probably could be said, but they are allowed to remain concealed for one reason or another. However, telling deliberate falsehoods is a serious violation of trust. We know that many people find it very difficult, if not impossible, to tell untruths; they are so conditioned to this requirement of normal social behaviour that prohibits deliberate lying. Forced to lie by circumstances, they are easily seen to be dissembling – they may even at times seem to be dissembling when they are not lying, when they are merely attempting to conceal something by telling less than the whole truth. The practised liar, the 'con man', for example, works this general expectation about truth-telling to his advantage. Everything he does has the aura of conviction – he exudes truth. His victims cannot resist the allure of this 'truth': they do what he wants them to do, to their eventual regret. The 'normal' conditions of life exploited skillfully by his practised mouth lead them to their downfall.

Some actual bits and pieces of conversations can be used to show how we operate with something like Grice's maxims in mind when we listen to others. For example, in two of the following three circumstances one person was misled by the other because not enough was said. In the third the person offering an observation was only partially informed, as we shall see. In this first case, B understates his qualifications:

A. Do you have a degree?
B. Yes, a BA.

It turned out that B also had a PhD which he was concealing because he felt it was irrelevant to the job for which he was applying and would make him appear to be 'over-qualified'. However, when A found out about the degree, he reported that he wondered 'what else B was hiding', a rather ungenerous interpretation of what had happened, one might argue. In the second case, a son A spoke to his father B as follows:

A. Oh, I bought a duvet on Saturday.
B. That's nice!

Later, B learned that A had bought it from a store in which A's sister worked. B found out about this a few days later from his daughter who told him that A had been in and bought a duvet. At their next meeting B mildly protested to A about not being told everything. A's response was interesting: *I didn't know whether [X] wanted you to know she was working part time there.* Since B did not indeed know she was, this explanation proved acceptable even though A had not seen his sister for several months until he bought the duvet and B thought that a report of A's seeing his sister might have taken precedence over his report of buying a duvet. The third instance is somewhat different. A novelist and occasional book-reviewer said of Shiva Naipaul, the novelist, that he should *not be confused with V. S. Naipaul, despite the fact that both are Trinidad-born, Oxford-educated novelists.* That is true. But they are brothers! This fact was surely unknown to one who could speak in such a way of them. The reviewer's statement would lead one to believe that the Naipauls were quite unrelated and only accidentally have similar backgrounds.

Other examples can be given of utterances having different meanings from what they 'say'. *If he finishes, he finishes; if he doesn't, he doesn't* and *It'll either happen or it won't* are obvious tautologies. They do not tell us anything we do not already know, so they must intend some other effect than communicating information. Likewise, the sarcastic *You can do what you like* said by one spouse to another states something obvious, and it is that which gives it the effect it communicates. Saying too much is apparent when a manager walks out of an inner office and addresses two secretaries in the outer office with the words *I wonder if I could possibly drag one of you two away from discussing your soap operas just long enough to type this letter.* The manager does not have to say all this to get a letter typed, so some additional effect must be intended. Intending the opposite effect to what the words actually express is seen in remarks like *Wow, isn't she sweet?* and *He's a real star, isn't he?*, said in the first case of someone bad-tempered and hostile and in the second of the worst student in a class.

Finally, we can see how responses to questions must sometimes be treated to make them relevant:

A. Is Mary home?
B. Well, the light's on.
A. OK, then.

A interprets B's response as relevant to the question: if the light is on, then Mary is at home. In the next case A asks B about a colleague:

A. How's Fred today?
B. All's quiet on the western front.

A knows Fred, not the easiest of colleagues, has an office on the west side of the building. B knows A knows that: his answer, therefore, is taken by A as a genuine one to the question that was asked. (It is not, however, as we must recognize, the kind of answer one would practise to such a question in a class in English for foreign students. Yet it is just such oblique answers that we do use in our dealings with others, relying on others to implicate the meanings we intend.)

As we have discovered, one of the skills you must acquire in learning how to use language in a socially acceptable way is to know just when you can 'tell it like it is' and when you can not. You must learn to accept a little bit of evasion, as well as some failure to be completely explicit and accurate. And you yourself must be prepared to act likewise on occasion. You must also be prepared to tolerate a considerable amount of uncertainty and ambiguity; people do tend to be vague, imprecise, non-committal and equivocal. And you must also be prepared not to question this general climate within which people go about the business of communicating. If you constantly draw the attention of others to these 'inadequacies', insist always on setting them straight, and persist in 'calling a spade a spade', you will end up isolated and labelled 'anti-social'. Of course, you can always then talk to yourself or to your faithful Fido! Language exists not to communicate absolute, elegant, unadorned truths. It *may* do this – as in the language of mathematics – but it is above all a social instrument used by rather fallible beings for a multiplicity of purposes, of which 'telling the truth' and the search for 'the truth' are but two, and not necessarily the most important ones.

While it may not be possible to list definitively the various functions that language serves in our lives, because a single utterance can do many things, we can be sure that each of the following is necessary. We can use language to give information to, and get it from, others: *The train's on time*. It can also be used to express feelings: *Damn!* and to control and direct others: *Stand up!*, *You must tell the truth*. Social bonding or 'phatic communion' is important: *Nice day!*, *How's things?*, *Good to see you*. It has a heuristic function too, as in scientific investigation: *Two plus two equals four*, *If A, then B*. And it offers us the possibility of creating one kind of artistic work: *To be or not to be*, *All the world's a stage*. Different proposals have been made concerning how many such functions language serves, but everyone who has thought at all about the matter agrees that the conveying of information is but one, and while this is a very important function, probably more attention might be paid to some of the others if one is to be achieve a balanced view of what people use language for in society.

One of the things you must do in conversing is to give some kind of appropriate length to the various exchanges that occur. Someone met frequently, you can greet with a simple *Hi*, *Hello*, or *Good Morning*. Someone met less frequently will require a few more words. Someone you have not seen for a while deserves much more from you: a mere *Hello* would seem 'cold', but at the other extreme, an overlong conversation might indicate a warmth of feeling that is no longer present. What you must do is to quantify your remarks according to circumstances. We learn to judge how others feel about us from the quantity of their remarks as well as from their content or quality. We also assess whatever quality they have (*We must get together again soon*) against this quantity.

Speaking about anything involves you in making choices, not just the obvious ones to do with selecting this word rather than that one but also choices concerning just how much to say on any topic. If you say too much, you may appear to be a bore or to be obfuscating an issue; if you say too little, your remarks may puzzle others by their brevity or you may appear to be concealing something, or seem unnecessarily abrupt, even rude. And even within the quantity of words you choose, you must make further choices: you must decide the proportions of the various bits and pieces, how important is each particular, and how much of what you say is already known or not known to others. Consequently, a 'simple' question asked of you may actually be very difficult to answer, particularly if the audience awaiting the reply is a mixed one, that is, the members have very different background knowledge on matters relating to the question. Indeed, it may sometimes be almost impossible to answer such a question so that everyone is satisfied with the answer. Some will find you say too much, others too little. Called upon to speak to a heterogeneous audience, you may have the same problem: how can you hold everyone's attention and find a unifying theme? Making a direct appeal to the emotions rather than to the intellect is often one recourse in such circumstances – persuasive orators sometimes appeal strongly to the emotions, in an attempt to obviate this difficulty.

One of the greatest difficulties teachers face in their work is this differential knowledge and ability in their students. No matter how well 'streamed' or selected a class is at the beginning of a new term, it soon begins to lose its homogeneity. Since most teaching is still done by means of 'talk and chalk', language plays a critical role, but the language of the teacher cannot possibly satisfy everyone in the class. To some it may be too hard, to others too easy. Teaching is not only a special form of conversing with others – it is an especially difficult form, if for no other reason than that the teacher must 'converse' with a large heterogeneous group of listeners. Good teaching requires one to be good at a particular kind of conversation; it is a skill not easily acquired because of the special demands it makes, and it is not a skill one can readily practise outside classrooms, since it is very rarely appropriate to any other circumstances.

Most of the moves we make in conversations would not be made if we did not assume that they would be followed by responses whose nature we can predict. We greet others in the expectation that they will return our greetings. We apologize and expect that our apology will be accepted. We make statements which we assume others will believe. We offer someone something in the expectation that our offer will be accepted, unless it is one of those clearly marked, deliberately over-generous offers which we assume will be refused. We also expect that our feelings will be recognized and our beliefs considered by others in framing what they say to us. In these and other ways we trust that others will take us seriously as we go about our joint conversational endeavour. And we lead others to expect that we will take them just as seriously. It is this trust in the fact that appearance and reality are the same that guides us in dealing with others. It is, as we have seen, this same trust that enables us to deceive others and others to deceive us when appearance and reality turn out to be very different.

Many kinds of utterances in conversation appear to require responses of very specific types: a greeting usually calls for a greeting in exchange, a question for an answer, and an invitation for a response. Likewise, challenges, threats, offers, warnings, requests, and complaints call for certain 'uptakes' from those to whom they are directed – usually, we would expect, some kind of acknowledgement, acceptance, or refusal. But, of course, you can also ignore them by not acknowledging, accepting, or refusing. The consequence is that you have various options when, for example, someone makes a request of you: you can comply, refuse, or simply just ignore what was said to you. And, in complying, refusing, or ignoring, you have a variety of devices available to indicate the 'strength' of your response. It is in this way that conversation is at the same time both predictable and unpredictable – certain patterns of behaviour exist but within these patterns there is still a vast number of choices available to you.

As we have just indicated, there is a general expectation in conversation that certain kinds of utterances occur in pairs: greetings; questions and answers; requests and either compliances or refusals. Consequently, any response to a greeting, question, or request will be interpreted in relation to this usual paired relationship and will be judged by the initiating speaker to be either an adequate or a deficient second member of the pair. A greeting not returned may cause bewilderment; a question response to a question will leave the original question unanswered – and still to be answered – but the question response itself will be assumed to be relevant to that eventual answering; and a request that is apparently ignored may be treated as a request that has been taken under consideration, and you may expect that, if it is to be refused, some indirect indication of refusal will later be provided.

Silence itself is a potent communicative weapon, and the pairing of utterances in conversation is so strong that you can regard a deliberate breaking of the paired relationship by a failure to supply the second member of the pair as a deliberately uncooperative act. You may proceed to seek an explanation. Consequently, an ignored greeting, a refusal to answer a question, a disregarded request or apology – that is, any situation in which the pairing is not completed – will cause you to wonder what is going on. Since one of the strongest constraints in conversation is being violated – the constraint that an item of type A must be followed by an item of type B – you cannot just completely ignore the resulting silence, that is, the absence of B after A. You must regard this silence as speaking at least as loud as any words that might have been uttered, and you might seek to know the reason for it. Of course, if you are a persistent questioner, one who greets everyone indiscriminately, and an unreasonable demand-maker on others, you may often find your words greeted with silence. In such cases it is you who are violating the code of decent behaviour as you intrude on others constantly and, in doing so, appear to them to be over-demanding and therefore to that extent somewhat uncooperative.

There are, however, certain situations where silence is actually expected. One does not talk at classical concerts, during piano recitals, on certain ceremonial occasions, and so on. But silence expressed as inarticulate behaviour may also be appropriate in settings where there is actually quite a lot of talking going on. You can be inarticulate, that is, silenced, with rage, grief, surprise, shock, joy, or whatever. That is, silence can be the accepted expression of some kind of deeply felt emotion or be used to give the appearance of such deep feeling. It is even possible to make the silence itself a topic so that words like *I just don't know what to say* are used on certain occasions: bereavements, presentations, confrontations, and so on.

Effective conversation makes use of other kinds of routines too. Many of these have to do with the use of space, movement, and gesture. People stand either near each other or at certain distances, or they sit in certain arrangements. These distances and arrangements change with circumstances, and various factors, conscious and unconscious, are involved. There are routines to help people establish themselves in appropriate positions: routines for taking off and hanging up coats; arrangements concerning where one is to sit or stand at a party or in a meeting; offers of hospitality (*Would you like a drink?*); and so on. There are routines for beginnings and endings of conversations, for leading in to topics, and for moving away from one topic to another. And there are routines for breaking up conversations, for leaving a party, and for dissolving a gathering. In a few cases the routines are so fixed that they have become almost ritualistic, with formal ways of signalling almost every part of an activity: the business of the law courts and of church ceremonies offers clear examples, but visits to the doctor's surgery and to the bank manager are only less formal instances. Routines reduce anxiety and diminish the possibilities of misunderstanding. However, once everything is routinized to the point of ritual, they stifle creativity. It is difficult, though, to imagine how life could be lived without some routines, for social harmony apparently requires that certain things happen consistently in order that certain very basic human expectations be fulfilled.

Sometimes routines are so unconscious that others have to draw your attention to the ones you yourself employ, because you are not aware of how systematic certain bits of your behaviour may have become. We quickly become familiar with the habits, idiosyncrasies, and routines of others; our own tend to remain hidden from similar recognisition. One instructor found that he was beginning his evening classes with certain routine expressions: *Well, it's seven, I see, Right, it's time to begin again, OK, anything I need to know about before we begin?* These utterances served to bring the class to order and get the evening's activities started. There was little variation from class to class in the actual words used, and the effect was always the same: the instructor's words marked a clear transition for everyone involved from the non-teaching to the teaching situation. Likewise, the ending of the class was likely to be signalled in a routine manner: . . . *and that's why they regard the linguistic variable as so important.* [Pause] *Right, before you go out into the cold, next week we are going to talk about . . . so read . . .*

In one way any conversation is like a game of chess: it has an opening which is followed by a series of moves, the middle game, and it comes to a conclusion of sorts. However, the rules are by no means as explicit as those of chess, but, as we have seen, 'rules', 'principles', 'maxims', 'conventions' of some kind do exist to guide the 'players'. The moves are also not as discrete as those in chess, but they are nevertheless still identifiable as separate moves. The middle game too may often seem to be quite confused. But just as participants in a chess game are required to plan ahead and anticipate some kind of closure, so too must you as a conversationalist constantly take a 'prospective', or future-oriented, approach to your task. In a conversation too, just as in a chess game, there is sometimes an obvious winner (and therefore an obvious loser), but there is also quite often neither a winner nor a loser, the game having provided the parties to it with little more than another opportunity to hone their talents.

Of course, conversations, like games, are not always successful – there are 'good' ones and 'bad' ones. Bad conversations can have a variety of causes, such as when one party fails to play by the rules, or when no empathy is achieved. Misunderstanding is not infrequent, as we can see from the currency of such expressions as *Can't you take the hint?*, *He didn't get the message*, *I can't seem to get through to her*, *But I didn't say any such thing!*, and *He doesn't seem to know when he's not wanted*. The norm, however, is not misunderstanding but some measure of understanding, and it is just how those levels of understanding are achieved that is our concern.

Conversations are generally neither structured in advance nor are they entirely 'free form'. Upon analysis they do seem to have structures of certain kinds; yet these structures are usually apparent only retrospectively. What structure a conversation has is created by the participants in the very process of their conversing, as they observe the basic principles of conversing. If this is the case, then it follows that the participants in conversation must know what is permissible and what is not: that is, they must be aware that, if the conversation is to succeed, they must do certain kinds of things and not others. Those who study conversational structure attempt to state precisely what these things are.

The data required to help them in their search for principles exist all around us. Every conversation offers another instance, but not all instances are equally valuable. 'Talk shows', for example, are not particularly useful. You can learn very little from them, except perhaps what it is like to 'manage' talk for others in situations in which one person is acknowledged to be that manager and the talk is for the benefit of non-present listeners. Such shows do not provide you with genuine interchanges between two or more participants. A does not talk to B in order to listen to B, but so that others may listen to both A and B for the purpose of admiring how clever (sophisticated, witty, amusing, informed, and so on) A and B are. This is talk for an audience on largely prepared topics, and talk 'managed' so as to gain the greatest possible effect. It is talk as deliberate theatre, even to the extent of being broken up by staged entrances and exits, scene changes, and breaks for extraneous activities. All this is not to say that real talk never displays such characteristics. Real talk too may be staged-managed and performed for others; it too can easily become a performance rather than just a simple conversational event confined to the actual participants with little or no thought given to external appearances.

Further Reading

One of the earliest attempts to analyse conversation is found in Soskin and John's 'The Study of Spontaneous Talk'. More recent and insightful attempts can be found in Moerman and Sacks' 'On Understanding in the Analysis of Natural Conversation'; a number of papers authored by Sacks: 'An Initial Investigation of the Usability of Conversational Data for Doing Sociology', 'Notes on Police Assessment of Moral Character', and 'An Analysis of the Course of a Joke's Telling in Conversation'; Schegloff's 'Notes on Conversational Practice: Formulating Place'; Speier's *How to Observe Face-to-Face Communication: A Sociological Introduction*; and Sudnow's 'Temporal Parameters of Interpersonal Observation'. (Note that Sacks' unpublished works and even his lecture notes have been widely disseminated and are often referred to by scholars.)

A 'rule-centred' approach to conversation can be found in a variety of places: Cicourel's 'Basic and Normative Rules in the Negotiation of Status and Role', Ervin-Tripp's 'On Sociolinguistic Rules: Alternation and Co-occurrence', Gordon and Lakoff's 'Conversational Postulates', Grice's 'Logic and Conversation', and Keenan's 'The Universality of Conversational Postulates' and 'The Universality of Conversational Implicatures'.

Basso writes on the importance of silence in 'To Give up on Words: Silence in Western Apache Culture'. The use of insults in conversation has been discussed in various places, but see specifically Dundes, Leach, and Özkök's 'The Strategy of Turkish Boys' Verbal Dueling Rhymes', Labov's 'Rules for Ritual Insults', and Mitchell-Kernan's 'Signifying and Marking: Two Afro-American Speech Acts'. Opie and Opie's study is entitled *The Lore and Language of Schoolchildren*.

Schenkein's *Studies in the Organization of Conversational Interaction* contains a number of especially interesting papers on various aspects of conversational organization, and Coulmas' *Conversational Routine* deals fairly extensively with a number of common conversational routines.

4
Beyond and Behind the Words

What you actually say and what your listener (or listeners) will believe you to be saying may be rather different. What you say may be 'unsaid' by how you actually convey your words in the non-verbal 'envelope' that accompanies them. Likewise, on occasion the intent of what you say may go unrecognized by your listeners. There is often considerably more to a message than the actual words that were uttered; there may be matters of importance both beyond and behind those words.

The verbal part of any conversation is, of course, extremely important. You are likely to remember what is said – or at least the content – for a while. But you will notice and remember other things too. You will form certain impressions of events that are happening alongside the talking; how the various participants are using their bodies; how they are gesturing; where their eyes are focused; and so on. You will be aware that this non-verbal part of a conversation either complements what is being said or sends its own messages of doubt or even denial of the accompanying words.

Suddenly dropped into a foreign culture, you may find yourself very uncomfortable because your awareness does not extend to everything that is happening in that culture. You may know basically how to say things in the new language, but not only may you not know how to say things properly, you may lack any knowledge of the non-verbal behaviour that should accompany the utterances. Your gestures may be all wrong when you attempt to speak French; your requirements for eye contact may be inappropriate when you try to teach members of another ethnic group; your favoured distance for informal talk may be too distant for the Arab to whom you want to appear approachable; and your posture and movements may appear to be too rigid for those who have acquired more relaxed way of using their bodies. You may misunderstand others in such circumstances, and almost certainly you will be misunderstood. Part of our stereotyping of people from other parts of the world arises from the interpretations we give to their non-verbal behaviour. They may not actually be 'sly', 'pushy', 'passive', 'emotional', 'unsociable', and so on, but that is how we are inclined to interpret their non-verbal behaviour, judging it against the norms that apply in our own culture. This is a dangerous mistake, but one that is commonly made. We tend to assume that non-verbal behaviour, so much of which is unconscious, is universal, and we do not realize that most of it is in fact learned and therefore specific to the cultural group in which it is found.

Non-verbal behaviour serves a variety of purposes, and we may be able or unable to control it according to particular circumstances and the specific type of behaviour that is involved. One kind of non-verbal behaviour involves the use of parts of the body such as the face, hands, and arms. You can use these to make gestures which are themselves quite explicit 'statements': for example, you can stick out your tongue at another; you can nod assent; you can 'give someone the finger'; and so on. Such gestures often completely replace speech and have a strong communicative import. They are also deliberate, learned, and generally quite unambiguous within the cultural group which employs them. You certainly cannot avoid this kind of non-verbal behaviour and are generally quite aware of your own and other peoples use of it.

Another kind of gesture is also a learned gesture – but one that shows considerably more variation according to the cultural group of which you are a member – and that is the kind used to supplement and illustrate speech: for example, hand movements, body postures, facial expressions, and so on. These gestures may not be used as consciously and deliberately as the first kind, but, like the next kind, emotional displays, they can be 'put on' by or they can be genuine. Emotional displays make use mainly of the face, but the body can become involved too. In learning how to use language and how to behave, you learn how to express emotions 'properly'. Not much direct teaching is involved, except perhaps negatively: *You shouldn't do that.* Anger, joy, fear, and so on are signalled, quite often fleetingly, and we learn to express such emotions and to recognize them, often without being at all conscious of what exactly it is we are indicating or what we are reacting to.

There may be large quantitative differences between cultural groups in emotional displays. What is an appropriate display for one group may be quite inappropriate for another. Anyone who has spent some time at a large international airport is likely to be able to testify to that face. It is interesting, for example, to compare the arrival or departure of a charter flight from or to London with one from or to Rome at Toronto's Pearson Airport. On such occasions British and Italian emotional displays are quite different; you could not possibly confuse one group with the other! But the conclusion that some parties draw from this kind of observation, that the British are unemotional (*But you never show your feelings*) or that Italians are too emotional (*You should see the way they go on!*), is false. All we can be sure of is that each group has different expressive norms; probably, underneath, the depth of feeling in the two groups is pretty much the same! It just comes out differently.

Two other kinds of non-verbal behaviour are largely involuntary: one is the feedback signals we give to others in a conversation (the *Yeah*s and *Mmm*s which show our attentiveness), and the other is the way in which we do certain very basic things like breathe, eat, scratch, handle objects, 'groom' ourselves, and so on. Both signal certain information about us to others, and while there is a considerable amount of learning involved in each kind, the actual behaviours are not easily described. What we do know, however, is that we can find it very difficult to communicate with others who do not give us the kinds of feedback we have come to expect or whose techniques and manner of self-presentation are very different from our own.

It goes almost without saying that many movements and gestures have little or no communicative importance in isolation from words or social context. People must breathe, eat, and move the various parts of their bodies in order to stay alive. However, not everyone does these things in the same way as everyone else. And everyone must continue to do many of them while conversing. What we react to in communicating with others are often fine shadings of movement and gesture: how a particular person is breathing at a certain time; how a hand moves abruptly or a finger straightens just a little; how a particular part of the body is positioned (the head, for example); how the small muscles of the lower jaw are set; and so on. We learn to react to the finely tuned movements and gestures of others and we also fine-tune what we ourselves do with our bodies. In fact, the tuning is usually so fine that we are not at all conscious of just what it is that we are doing. We are told 'the camera never lies' but do not quite believe it when we see certain pictures of ourselves: did I really look like that on that occasion?

In talking, we make use of both sounds (that is, sounds in addition to those which we necessarily must make to pronounce the words we are using) and gestures in order to reinforce what we say. We can snap our fingers, crack the knuckles, and slap a leg, we can tap on a table or a desk, or we may even make direct physical contact with another through hand touching or back slapping. Gesturing without accompaning noise can involve us in various kinds of nodding and hand waving, as well as placing our hands on particular parts of our own body. We can scratch or rub various body party, twiddle thumbs, and handle objects in the environment. We may also extend this behaviour to touching others: putting an arm around a shoulder; grasping a hand; and more intimate fondling. Even our aggressive displays – rude gestures, punching, throwing objects, and so on – fall into the same broad category of body actions which supplement what we say in words.

Movement and gesture reveal their importance in other ways, too. People who are enjoying a conversation with each other will tend to adopt somewhat similar postures and may even mirror each other's behaviour as they copy certain characteristics. We can contrast this type of empathetic behaviour with what happens when two complete strangers are forced together, for example, to share a table in a crowded cafeteria or a seat on a bus. In such circumstances they are likely to differentiate their behaviours as much as possible: to sit facing in different directions; to avoid eye contact; to immerse themselves in some activity with almost excessive enthusiasm (for instance, eating, reading, or gazing out of a window); to attempt as much physical separation as possible, even possibly by building a 'barrier' with a newspaper; and so on. The goal apparently is to reduce the number of attributes which they appear to share, so as to signal to each other and also to others that this is indeed not a 'pair', not a relationship freely entered into, but rather one compelled by circumstances.

The way in which strangers deal with one another, particularly in circumstances which crowd them together, is of interest. Not everyone behaves like the British or Japanese, who, herded together on to crowded tube trains, try to minimize as far as possible in one way or another any kind of contact with others. Travelling on the subway in Mexico City is a much more lively affair, as is riding on a crowded bus in many parts of the Third World. The ride becomes a kind of group experience; people are drawn toward one another; and boundaries are lowered rather than raised. Travel in such circumstances can become a very rewarding experience for someone from a boundary-raising culture, but it can also become disconcerting if you lack the means for dealing with strangers in this way.

The eyes also play a very important role in conversation: who looks at whom, how, and for what length of time. You may find it difficult to talk to another person if there is no eye contact at all, or very little – some telephone conversations will prove difficult for this reason – but, if you perceive the kind of eye contact the other person provides you with as being evasive, or if he or she seeks to dominate you or to resist you by insisting on too much direct and even unblinking contact, you will also feel very uncomfortable. The amount of eye contact that is permissible varies considerably among cultures and even within a particular culture. Who may look directly at a king? Who may stare at whom? You may stare at a film star or celebrity but he or she may not return the stare. Who may return a look, particularly between males and females? We must learn exactly how and where to look while we speak, because to use the eyes inappropriately is to subvert whatever we might intend to say: a statement you regard as sincere accompanied by a shifty look will convince no one.

It may even be best to consider that we use the eyes in conversation to perform acts of some kind. In speaking, you choose to look or not to look and either to look away or to sharpen your focus of attention, just as you choose a particular word to use or to disregard something that you hear. Language choice is part of language use, and the kinds of behaviour you employ to accompany your language choices are part of the total meaning that you convey. You can choose not to look at something, you can 'disregard' things in your environment that you prefer not to see, or you can do the opposite: 'look into' something, 'eye' a prospect, or 'give full attention' to what is going on. Part of the language with which we describe what happens when Ilsa meets Pierre often concerns how they relate visually to each other: *Ilsa saw Pierre about something*; *Ilsa stood staring at Pierre*; *Ilsa gazed fondly at Pierre*; *Ilsa ignored Pierre's gesture*; and so on. And just as gestures can speak louder than words, so can the eyes proclaim feelings we have not put into our mouths.

On meeting others, we sent out signals to say whether we want to enlarge on that contact or not. What you do with your eyes is extremely important in signalling your intent. To look at someone for any length of time is in a sense a kind of violation of that person. So we tend to fasten our gaze only on those who we think would welcome it or on those who are quite unaware of the attention they are getting, for example, people at a distance. If the gaze is returned, we have created a possible opening for talk, and if both parties smile in addition, talking may come that much easier. But if the gaze is not returned, the other's head is deliberately averted, and the lips are compressed, we see very clear signals of avoidance: the other person is either a complete stranger and is reminding us of this fact, or is someone we know who on this occasion is discouraging us from initiating an exchange. From someone we know very well, such behaviour might appear to be a deliberate snub.

Even between intimates engaged in a conversation, prolonged mutual gaze is not the norm. It is more characteristic of lovers 'lost in each other' than of any other kind of pairing of intimates. Mutual gaze tends to be brief and intermittent, a checking device that the other is 'with you' rather than a basic condition necessary for participating in a conversation.

In certain circumstances one party in a conversation or a spoken exchange may attempt to demand of the other that the gaze be mutual and prolonged. In a power relationship such a demand may be hard to resist. (In some power relationships, such as officer to inferior in the army, the requirement may be quite the opposite – *Don't you dare look me straight in the eye!*) What happens in such a case is that the normal comfortable gaze relationship is violated. Gaze becomes an issue in the conversation itself instead of an associated, somewhat peripheral, activity. So the demand for mutual gaze, or its avoidance, becomes an instrument of threat and an expression of inequality between the participants.

Gaze is also important for signalling when you are prepared to give up your turn in a conversation. If you want Sarah to speak after you speak, you will look at Sarah as you finish what you say. This gaze is Sarah's cue to pick up the conversation. However, if you want George to speak and want to discourage Sarah from attempting to speak, you will studiously avoid eye contact with Sarah as you cease speaking. If, while talking, you decline to gaze steadily at anyone and instead let your eyes glance here and there, you are probably signalling to others that you do not wish to be interrupted. Others, however, may seek the floor. They may try to 'catch your eye', but only if that device fails and you refuse to accede to what they consider their legitimate claims to be heard will they feel free to interrupt you. Once having gained the floor, however, a new speaker will tend to avoid returning gazes until he or she has established the right not just to begin to speak but continue speaking. On occasion a person just stops speaking without looking directly at one of those being addressed or without indicating. in some way who is to speak next. A period of silence may follow in the absence of a clear signal as to how the conversation is to continue, that is, who is to carry on with the topic in hand.

Some conversations are able to proceed with a minimum of eye contact. Instead of looking at each other the participants fix their gaze on an object in the environment: another person, a piece of paper, a television screen, and so on. They can then talk to each other, but, in looking at someone or something other than the person being addressed, they severely limit the possible topics of conversation. They must talk about what they are looking at or tie in what they want to say with what they see as the object of their joint attention. The gazing at a third party or object can be useful, for it can enable you to sound out another's views – for example, when the parties are not familiars – without directly having to look that person in the eye. If you find you have some common areas of agreement, then the greater intimacy which eye contact provides becomes available to you.

In the following conversation recorded in a small art gallery we can see how the two speakers used objects in the environment to negotiate mutual gaze and initiate direct conversation:

A. [to B, but looking at a picture] It's pretty, isn't it?
B. [looking at same picture] Yeah, really quite unusual.

A. [gesturing and pointing vaguely to right] I think I like that one over there better.
B. [looking in direction of A's pointing] Which one?
A. [shifting gaze back and forth between B and picture] That one.
B. [finally looks directly at A] Mmm!

Actually, nothing much came of the resulting very brief conversation about the new picture. After looking at it and offering a comment, B turned away from A, deliberately averting his gaze in doing so, and closed off A from any further spoken contact. For A the 'neutral' gazing had opened up a conversation, but B was reluctant to carry on with it and used gaze, among other things, to put an end to A's approach.

We can see how useful this neutral kind of gazing can be if we consider what level of comfort can, or should, be provided in a waiting room. Certainly not that of a family's intimate living space – that space brings people together in relaxed, trustful settings. A waiting room, on the other hand, draws strangers together. They must keep their distance and maintain their public appearances. They must not be forced to gaze on one another if they do not want to do so; hence, the custom is to provide a selection of reading materials to engage the eyes and to arrange the chairs in such a way as to minimize face-to-face contact. Waiting rooms are essentially neutral settings designed to help people not get involved with one another; instead, they must be comfortably isolated from one another. If there is any involvement it tends to be directed toward some object that is recognized to be common to all: a receptionist, a notice board, a loudspeaker system, and so on. If A wants to speak to B, some characteristic of that object will quite often provide the starting point for the conversation, offering as it does a common focus of attention: *What did she say?* rather than *What's your name?*

In some conversational settings the opportunities for using gaze as a signal are considerably diminished. We know how important it is for formal talks to have clear endings. Those

that stop abruptly or keep limping on without a clear conclusion can embarrass both speakers and listeners. The kinds of
gazing behaviour that could be used to signal an end to an
ordinary conversation cannot be used here, so speakers must
have recourse to some other device, usually a rhetorical one,
to bring matters to a conclusion. If a speaker mishandles that
device, he or she must look toward the chairperson for relief,
or else the chairperson becomes anxious about the event
getting out of hand.

Hesitant speaking is accompanied by less eye contact than
fluent speaking. Fluent speech demonstrates the speaker's
control over the topic and a certain amount of assurance in
dealing with an audience. It may also be difficult to interrupt
because of the speaker's use of certain rhetorical skills, so that
breaking into it requires a very deliberate violation. In contrast, hesitant speaking almost invites interruption. Consequently, in order to avoid having to give up the floor, the
speaker must try to reduce as much as possible any chance of
interruption. He or she cannot do it by sheer flow of words,
and looking at others directly is likely to indicate that they
can speak. So, if you are hesitant, the best course of action for
you is to hold on to the floor once you have gained it by
almost refusing to acknowledge the presence of others: if you
do not see them, in one sense they are not there to interrupt
you; if they want to interrupt you, they must use more than
their eyes to gain access to the floor – they must actually
interrupt you and appear somewhat rude in doing so.

The amount of gazing in a conversation is also directly
related to the distance between the participants. It is difficult
to gaze for long periods at someone who is extremely close to
you: such behaviour is too personal and too intrusive. Except
between lovers it is likely to create considerable discomfort.
The further you move away from the other the greater the
permissible amount of continued looking. The distant eye is
less dominating than the close eye: there are other things you
can see alongside it. Of course, there are few restrictions
possible on gazing at distant people and objects: also, people
at a distance are unlikely to be aware that they are being

looked at. There is a whole gradation in possible gazing behaviour, and we must learn various tolerances. They may, of course, be violated, if necessary, to achieve a particular objective: you can stand 'eyeball to eyeball' in mutual confrontation; you can stare when staring is otherwise not permissible (*Who are you staring at?*); or you can even refuse to look closely at something quite distant just in case you might be caught looking, even when the chances of being caught are virtually nil.

In addition, a particular gaze may indicate much about how the person gazing views what he or she is involved in. Showing attentiveness or lack of interest both rely heavily on what the eyes are doing. The 'rapt attention' of an audience is indicated by the way all eyes are focused on a speaker or a performer. In contrast, inattention is likely to be signalled by both fidgeting and wandering gaze. Teachers often monitor what is happening in their classroom by checking up on where individuals are looking, and a fair number of their directives concern what should be looked at (or gazed upon): *Let's look at page ten again, OK, pay attention now, John, if you could just look this way for a moment, Why don't you come out here where everyone can see you?* Likes and dislikes are revealed through the eyes as well as through verbal comments and physical movements. Honesty, sincerity, embarrassment, anger, unease find themselves partly reflected in eye behaviour. They eyes can give you away or lend credence to what you are saying. In a practised 'performer' they can be used to deceive, that is, to lend credence to statements which the speaker knows to be false. The eyes, therefore, communicate in their way just as the tongue does in its. The result is that sometimes appearance and the reality that underlies that appearance may be somewhat different.

However, one paradoxical fact about communication is that you learn to recognize what people are really doing or saying even though they are apparently doing or saying something else. For example, although the form of a particular utterance addressed to you may be clearly that of a statement, you may recognize its intent to be that of a request for you to do something or respond in a certain way. You must react to the intent of what was said, not just the form in which it was said, if there is to be no misunderstanding. Nor is this phenomenon unique to any particular language; apparently it is a 'universal', a feature characteristic of all languages and their speakers, to say what they mean by conveying meanings both beyond and behind what their actual words alone communicate. People everywhere say things whose full meanings you can appreciate only if you are sensitive to the circumstances in which they are used: the total physical, social, and psychological setting. In other words the total meaning of an utterance derives from its context as well as from the actual grammatical form it takes.

A simple illustration may be helpful. The relationship between a question and a proper answer can be a complex one. Questions have purposes, one of which is to seek information, but that information may be about matters well beyond those indicated by the superficial form of the question. A question such as *Where have you been?* might be prompted by any one of a variety of reasons: a simple request for information; an expression of surprise; doubt about what the other has been up to; and so on. A whole variety of answers is possible, depending on what you perceive to be the intent of the question: *Acapulco, The doctor's, Out for a walk, Nowhere, There was a delay on the underground.* And then having replied like this, you cannot be sure what the response to your reply will be. That response itself depends on so many factors: the real intent of the original question; your perception of that intent; the original speaker's perception of that intent; the various fits between actual and perceived intents; concurrent gestures, facial expressions, and movements; and some decisions as to how the two parties are to deal with this complex mix of factors. We have all undoubtedly had the experience of an exchange of remarks quickly getting completely out of control, finding that after as few as three or four moves a 'simple' opening remark has led us into a quite unpredictable, and sometimes most unfortunate, outcome.

Much that is said in conversation is so ambiguous as to be virtually incomprehensible outside the framework in which it occurs. Sometimes there is such scope for ambiguity that it may be necessary to provide or to seek explicit 'disambiguation' so that the intent of a remark cannot be misconstrued. In an unequal power relationship the superordinate may simply tell a subordinate *That's an order* so that there can be no doubt of the intent of a remark. Or the subordinate may ask *Is that an order?* When there is some uncertainty about the intent. Nor should it surprise us that on certain occasions one or other party may demand the explicitness of a written affirmation of intent. It is very unusual indeed in our society to find matters which bind people in important or lasting commitments conducted in the medium of speech alone: instances such as the conduct of certain financial transactions in the City of London must be regarded as exceptional, requiring unique circumstances in which one's word is indeed one's bond.

It is often necessary to be quite explicit about the nature or function of an utterance so that a listener is left in no doubt as to its intent. The 'marking' for intent can be as obvious as *Once upon a time*, the sure signal of a fairy-tale. Or a misinterpreted remark can lead you to make a clarifying statement: *That was a joke* or *I'm only kidding*. Reporting something for which you have little evidence so that you are doing no more than passing on a rumour, you can preface what you say with an introduction like *I've heard that*. You can indicate a change in tone from light-hearted and casual to something more purposeful with a well placed *seriously*. A confidence might follow a preparatory *confidentially*. Such overt signals are fairly commonplace: they indicate that the speaker is very conscious of the need to provide listeners with explicit indicators of the intent of what is being said. Of course, sometimes a speaker may deliberately exploit these overt indicators: not everything following a *Once upon a time* need be a fairy-tale – a political satire can begin this way – and a comedian's *seriously* can provide the lead into a further outbreak of hilarious remarks.

In helping you to indicate to your listeners the intent of your utterances and your attitude toward your subject matter, 'marking' or 'framing' what you say can be very useful. A prefatory *honestly* or *frankly* indicates your feeling of sincerity about what is to follow. The much condemned *hopefully* is also used in this way. Words like *fortunately* and *unfortunately* convey another kind of opinion about what you are saying. Framing, a kind of context-setting procedure, enables you not merely to report on something or pass on information but to add a further dimension to what you say, a dimension which, superficially at least, is intended to help your listener interpret your remarks.

There are certain types of utterances that are very clear as to the intent of their speakers. The intent is overt since it is part of the very structure of the utterances, and this clarity of intent results in these utterances being not so much sentences as acts of some kind. They do not report anything, nor can they be said to be true or false; they can be said only to be either appropriate or inappropriate, according to the circumstances in which they are used. The philosopher J. L. Austin described such utterances as 'performatives': for example, *I hereby pronounce you husband and wife*, *I name this ship* Liberty Bell, *We find the accused guilty*, or *I sentence you to three years in gaol*. To be appropriate, a performative must be part of some conventional procedure, like marrying, naming ships, pronouncing a verdict, or passing a sentence in court. It must be uttered in appropriate circumstances: only certain people can marry others, name ships, pronounce verdicts, or pass sentences, and they can do so only in very narrowly prescribed settings. The procedure itself must also be carried out fully and correctly: a marriage ceremony may be deficient in some respect; the champagne bottle may not break on the ship's hull; the judge may refuse to accept the jury's verdict of guilty when a juror protests disagreement; a particular gaol sentence may exceed the judge's authority. Performatives are very special kinds of utterances when they are fully and properly executed, that is, when there is no doubt that you have witnessed or been a party to a performative act.

There are, however, also many varieties of inexplicit performatives, utterances which are acts but to some extent veiled: a request expressed in the form *It's hot in here*; a promise hidden behind a simple declarative *I won't mention it*; or a warning concealed in the statement *The dog bites*.

In the appropriate circumstances you can use certain verbs to perform acts. Following the first person, *I*, used in the present tense, and with a complement that is appropriate to the circumstances, verbs such as *accept, advise, applaud, appoint, beg, compliment, confess, consent, deny, deplore, dispute, exercise, forbid, guarantee, guess, hypothesize, insist, judge, nominate, predict, prohibit, promise, propose, question, resign, suggest, surrender, urge*, and numerous others may be used to perform the acts of accepting, advising, applauding, appointing, and so on: *I accept your offer*; *I advise you to go immediately*; *I applaud your decision*; *I appoint you to be my legal adviser in this matter*. Such utterances are not statements or reports of any kind: they are acts that do what they say they are doing. The utterances must be evaluated in the context of their delivery as valid deeds (if properly executed) or as invalid ones. In this way promises are made, confessions are uttered, denials are issued, and so on. You cannot carry on much of the business of everyday living without using utterances of this kind.

There are many explicitly performative verbs which we can and do use. We have mentioned those that are associated with very specific legal and social sanctions. Certain performative acts, once completed, may not easily be undone: for example, the acts of marrying or of signing a promissory note or swearing an oath. But there are also many ways in which you can use language – and verbs in particular – to perform somewhat ambiguous acts. Whereas if you say *I promise I'll go*, you are indeed making a *promise* – indicated by the use of the explicit performative verb *promise* – the roughly equivalent utterance *I will go* – but without an explicit performative verb – may be understood either as promissory in nature or as merely a simple statement of future intent. If, after saying to someone *I'll give you £5 if you do it*, that person does whatever *it* refers to and you do not pay over the money, the complaint *But you promised!* seems entirely justified.

There are various kinds of indirect performatives. *I wouldn't do that if I were you* is usually not just a bit of advice you offer another person but rather some kind of threat, in that you appear to indicate some outcome that will be prejudicial to your listener if whatever he or she proposes to do is actually done. Likewise, *I'll be there at eight* will be taken as some kind of promise, *Look, don't say anything and he'll forget all about it* is a piece of advice, and *How about a drink?* is an offer. In each case there seems to be a fairly clear performative intent even though none of the utterances has the trappings of the explicit performative.

With other than explicitly performative utterances, we can appreciate that while you may be certain about what was said on any particular occasion – that is, you may be able to repeat the exact words that were said – you may nevertheless find it impossible to say for certain what the words actually meant. If part of meaning is the intent that lies behind the words, then the meaning of an utterance will be obscure to the extent that this intent remains hidden from view. And since some part of intent *must* remain concealed – lying as it does entirely within the mind of the speaker – the meaning of an utterance requires a certain amount of guesswork. Some people are better guessers than others in that they are more capable of divining the intent of those with whom they are talking. We sometimes compliment them for this 'intuitive' ability.

Sometimes the form and the intent of an utterance are very obviously different. *Waiter, there's a fly in my soup!* is a statement, a special kind of statement to be sure, but one that explicitly draws a fact to someone's attention. A reply such as *Oh, yes!* followed by neither remedial action nor apology would be quite unacceptable. The intent of the statement is a request to the waiter to do something about the offending fly (and soup), and not only to do something about it but to offer a suitable apology. In this example the difference between form and intent is readily transparent. But other cases are much less clear. Since you must respond to the intent of utterances and not simply to their form, and since the intent is often masked, in trying to figure out what lies behind a remark you may choose the wrong interpretation.

In deciding the intent of an utterance, you must search out the motivation of the speaker: what is he or she apparently trying to do? You must, of course, find some evidence for your beliefs about that intent: exactly what is there in what you hear that leads you to believe that one thing is intended rather than another? You must assume that some choice of words or characteristic of their delivery, some accompanying gesture, or some other bit of behaviour provides the clue to intent – the clue which, if recognized, opens up to you the full meaning of the utterance. If you cannot find a clue, you must remain in the dark about motive. If you find the 'wrong' clue, you may misinterpret. Of course, even if clues are not readily apparent, you can still reduce to a considerable extent your uncertainty about the intent of what was said. Certain possible clues were definitely not present; consequently, you can eliminate a number of possible meanings – the utterance could not have meant this or that. In conversation participants respond not only to what was said and what that appears to mean, but also to what could have been said and was not said.

Sometimes we may find ourselves confronting another person on the subject of the intent of his or her remarks. You find yourself saying *You should say what you mean* or asking *Do you really mean what you said?* Such remarks indicate that you notice some kind of gap between the actual words the speaker uses and the intent you perceive behind those words. The first says that you perceive an intent that was not fully or properly expressed in the words; the second that you perceive an intent in the words but one unsubstantiated by other appropriate evidence. What is of interest in each case is why you perceive the discrepancy: what are the signals you are reacting to so that you find yourself saying what you say? Is it something in the appropriateness (or inappropriateness) of the words spoken, in the tone of the speaker's voice, in a gesture, in his or her posture, in the circumstances of the utterance, or what? Certainly there is something there that causes you to react as you do to seek an explanation of the speaker's intent.

In cross-cultural situations intent is sometimes particularly difficult to decide. The significance of a particular remark may completely pass us by, just as we may be mystified by someone who phones or calls on us and does not appear to have any reason for doing so. On other occasions, not necessarily cross-cultural, we may realize the other's intent but only a while after the event: *That's what he meant, Oh, I never guessed!, I wondered at the time what it was all about, I couldn't figure out what she was getting at.* Intent is not at all transparent, and it is this opacity which should warn us not to take what we hear literally but at the same time alert us to the fact that we may still misunderstand the other if we postulate the wrong intent. A particularly interesting case of postulating the wrong intent is the following. After having paid off a rather large mortgage (some unexpected funds suddenly having become available), a houseowner received a notice from the mortgage company reminding him that a payment was overdue. He called the company and spoke to the representative who had signed the notice to point out that the mortgage had been paid off completely, anticipating the offer of an apology. That was the intent of his call. However, the representative merely acknowledged that he should not have sent out the notice but, though prompted to offer an apology (albeit indirectly), declined to do so. He seemed completely unaware that in the circumstances an apology was called for, and that the houseowner's remarks were addressed largely to the end of having him apologize. Needless to say, the houseowner found the call somewhat unsatisfactory, expressing his feelings as follows: *I'm glad I don't have to deal with that guy again; he can't be very bright if he didn't know he should apologize.* His intent in making the call had been completely missed.

As we have discovered it may not always be easy to communicate what you intend to communicate: you may say the wrong thing, or not enough, or too much. Your performance may subvert your intent. But then again, speaking can be an act in its own right and may be largely a kind of performance itself – its intent may be to deceive or conceal. What can appear to the casual onlooker to be a failure of intent may actually be a brilliant execution of a carefully disguised intent: people do play the fool, deliberately act incompetently, purposefully over-react, and so on. However, if you feel that your intent is being subverted by your poor performance, you may also attempt to overcome the failure by choosing any one of a number of strategies. With a foreigner a usual device – but quite often a completely inaffective one – is to raise your voice and speak slowly. In general, though, repetition, rephrasing, and supplying additional information or explanation are devices that you can use to clarify intent: *Let's get this straight*, *That's an order*, *I repeat*, and so on.

Sometimes the intent of a remark is perhaps all too obvious. For example, a sarcastic remark is one which means the opposite of what it says: *You're a real genius* ('You are an idiot') or *How brilliant!* ('How stupid!'). You understand such a remark to be sarcastic because of the circumstances in which it is uttered: they do not warrant a compliment but do possibly demand a critical comment. Consequently, you understand the intent or 'implicature' of the remark. In one respect sarcasm is not as nasty as a bold statement about the inadequacy or deficiency that occasioned the sarcasm: *You're an idiot* and *How stupid!* are rather offensive. Their sarcastic equivalents avoid the strongly negative words *idiot* and *stupid* in favour of – superficially at least – the positive words *genius* and *brilliant*. But what the speaker gains in avoiding the negative he or she can well lose in choosing the sarcastic aproach. Sarcasm is the tool of those who want to appear to be wiser or superior, and it is this sense of superiority (consequently, of the other's inferiority) which is likely to be passed on. Consistently sarcastic people are unlikely to be very popular: the superiority they claim is either not warranted or, if warranted, decency and good manners seem to require that it be demonstrated in some other way.

Since we can never be absolutely sure of the intent of any utterance, we must be careful to distinguish between any literal interpretation we give that utterance and what the speaker does or appears to be doing by saying what he says. A speaker's words may have the grammatical form of a statement, but function as a request. They may be positive when taken literally but actually be entirely negative in the context in which they are delivered, the negative feeling coming from what the speaker is concurrently doing or from the juxtaposition of the statement with other remarks. Given that utterances taken out of context are virtually meaningless, subject to all kinds of interpretations, it is somewhat surprising that courts of law allow literal meanings to be valued as highly as they are: 'Did someone say "X"?' seems to be the concern rather than 'How did someone say "X"?' or 'What did you believe someone to mean by saying "X"?' The answer to the first question is regarded as hard evidence, whereas the answers to the second and third are much less highly valued. Yet in real life you must act constantly on this latter kind of information and intuition. To interpret everything said to you quite literally and not to search for a speaker's intent would be to put yourself under a serious handicap both in conversation and in everyday living. So also would be to insist that you must yourself tell everything 'like it is' and that others must do likewise.

The various parties to a conversation may not necessarily interpret what is happening in the same way. For example, one may look much further below the surface of the words than another, searching for intent and motivation in what we may possibly regard as an abnormal way. One instance is the kind of interchange that occurs in a psychiatric interview in which one party, the 'patient', is asked to speak freely about certain aspects of life, and the other, the 'psychiatrist', listens. The latter treats what is said within some kind of theoretical framework derived from the discipline of psychiatry, while the former just talks. The result is a very definite imbalance of involvement so far as the two participants are concerned. Of course, that imbalance is what psychiatric interviews are all about. A psychiatrist carrying the same kind of behaviour over into normal life would soon be challenged, unless, of course the other party felt reasonably comfortable in the role of patient.

The intent a psychiatrist reconstructs for a psychiatric patient is a highly theoretical entity. It can be almost 'too deep for words' so that its very existence can be seriously debated, for not everyone believes in psychiatric explanations, or in particular ones. *What does X really mean?* is a question we all must ask ourselves constantly in conversations. We usually do not get terribly serious about finding answers and content ourselves with simple surface explanations. We do not tend to probe deep, to create fancy hypotheses, or to risk offending others. Again, this is largely because of the trust factor in conversation: we accept things for what they seem to be and for what they are presented as being unless there is very good reason for doing otherwise.

Working as we must with both the words and the perceived intent of the speaker, and trying to weigh one with, even possibly against, the other, we are forced into what Gregory Bateson has called a 'double bind'. The words have one value but the intent may have another, each possibly at odds with the other. How do you decide between the two? The predicament can most easily be seen in relationships between powerful people and subordinates. A dictator's comment *Jones is a threat* may be interpreted (and meant) as a command to a subordinate to get rid of Jones – Thomas à Becket was apparently such a victim. The statement can later be denied as having any such intent; indeed, it may actually not have such an intent. However, the subordinate may not know, and, if he or she is in no position to question, may be left completely at the mercy of events: *Jones is still around; why?* or, if things turn out badly, *I didn't tell you to get rid of Jones.* Our world has seen numerous instances of this kind of behaviour. A more familiar circumstance to us is marital or domestic disputes. These can take on the same feature of double-binding, as one party is forced to make decisions about what 'message' to react to from the other, only invariably seeming to respond to the wrong message – the typical 'I'm damned if I do, damned if I don't' situation.

From the fact that we can often not be sure what is really intended by a particular remark – perhaps not even the speaker knows – derives one of the great attractions that literary works have for us. We can view literature as a species of 'frozen conversations' and can argue the varieties of intent we find there almost *ad infinitum*: Shakespeare's intent in writing *Hamlet*, the prince's motivation, the meaning of 'To be or not to be', and so on, and so on.

Further Reading

A clear, simple introduction to non-verbal behaviour is contained in Knapp's *Nonverbal Communication in Human Interaction*. A popular treatment is that of Morris' *Manwatching: A Field Guide to Human Behaviour*. Other treatments are Duncan's 'Nonverbal Communication', Hinde's *Non-Verbal Communication*, Kendon's *Nonverbal Communication, Interaction, and Gesture*, Key's *Paralinguistics and Kinesics: Nonverbal Communication*, La Barre's 'Paralinguistics, Kinesics and Cultural Anthropology', and Ruesch and Kees' *Nonverbal Communication: Notes on the Visual Perception of Human Relations*.

Gestures and movement are of particular concern in Green's *A Gesture Inventory for the Teaching of Spanish*, Kendon's 'Movement Coordination in Social Interaction' and 'Some Relationships between Body Motion and Speech', Morris, Collett, Marsh, and O'Shaughnessy's *Gestures: Their Origins and Distribution*, and Scheflen's *Body Language and the Social Order* and *How Behavior Means*. The function of gaze is dealt with in Argyle's 'Non-Verbal Symbolic Actions: Gaze', Argyle and Cook's *Gaze and Mutual Gaze*, Goodwin's *Conversational Organization: Interaction between Speakers and Hearers*, and Kendon's 'Some Functions of Gaze Direction in Social Interaction'.

There is now an extensive literature on speech acts. In particular, the following provide useful information on this

topic: Austin's *How To Do Things with Words* and *Philosoph-
ical Papers*, Cohen's 'Speech Acts', Cole and Morgan's *Syntax
and Semantics* (with its collection of articles on this topic),
Hancher's 'The Classification of Cooperative Illocutionary
Acts', Searle's 'What is a Speech Act?', *Speech Acts: An Essay
in the Philosophy of Language*, 'Indirect Speech Acts', 'A
Classification of Illocutionary Acts', and *Expression and
Meaning: Studies in the Theory of Speech Acts*, and Strawson's
'Intention and Convention in Speech Acts'.

The use of language in doctor–patient relationships is the
subject of Cicourel's 'Language and Medicine', Coulthard
and Ashby's 'A Linguistic Description of Doctor–Patient
Interviews', Labov and Fanshel's *Therapeutic Discourse:
Psychotherapy as Conversation*, and Pittenger, Hockett, and
Danehy's *The First Five Minutes: A Sample of Microscopic
Interview Analysis*. For the double bind see Bateson, Jackson,
Haley, and Weakland's 'Toward a Theory of Schizophrenia'.

5

The Importance of Context

If we were to attempt to say what any utterance in a conversation meant and, in doing so, ignored its context of use, we would be forced to conclude that its meaning would be vague and ambiguous. It is just impossible to say what most utterances mean, or what their intent is, without having some knowledge of the situations in which they occur. That context includes not merely the linguistic one, that is, those utterances that precede and follow the utterance in question, but also the surrounding physical context, previous conversations between the participants, relevant aspects of their life histories, the general rules of behaviour the parties subscribe to, their assumptions about how the various bits and pieces of the world function, and so on. Only by acknowledging that all these factors contribute to the meaning of a particular utterance in a particular context can we hope to understand what is going on when one person says something to another.

From time to time certain linguists have proposed that we must study language apart from context, so that we may be able to describe language as an entity separate from anything else in the natural world. But this is a dubious proposition. It would be like trying to study the cardiovascular system as a completely separate entity from any other part of human or animal anatomy, as though it had some completely independent existence and no function or purpose except its own existence. An alternative, and much more fruitful, proposition is that any truly insightful study of language requires us to examine the contexts in which language is used. But that task is not without its difficulties, for to perform it we must be able to differentiate clearly between language and context. Since language also creates context, helps structure reality, and is inseparable from its use, what language is and what language does are therefore two closely related facets.

It is context which creates possibilities for interpretation and helps remove the multiple ambiguities that utterances would have if they occurred in isolation. That context obviously includes previous utterances or following ones, so the language surrounding what is said provides some of the clues we need. An utterance may make reference to the external world in the way it names objects and participants and indicates places, positions, and times. Thus, by referring to the physical context, we can clarify, for instance, many of the *he*s and *she*s and *here*s and *there*s. Then, too, speakers and hearers share a knowledge of the world around them, have some idea of what is 'common knowledge', and observe conventions about what can properly be said to whom and on what occasion. In this way they also narrow the possibilities for misunderstanding.

A very simple example of how meaning is dependent on context involves the use of certain kinds of words that can be understood only in relation to the contexts in which they are used. Philosophers describe such words with the technical terms 'indexicals' or 'definite descriptions'. In addition to the personal pronouns (*I, you, he,* and so on), there are the demonstrative pronouns (particularly *this* and *that*), certain adverbs (*here, there, now,* and *then*), and proper names (*John, Mary,* and so on). You must use such words carefully in conversation because, carelessly used, they can create ambiguity for your listener, who will be left unable to fathom precisely who or what you are referring to. *Do you see that man over there?* may lead to a response such as *Which one?* or *Where?* rather than *Yes* if there is more than one man in view, or to the person to whom the question is addressed misidentifying the man who is to be looked at. We can easily imagine the incongruity of using an indexical expression in completely inappropriate circumstances if we consider how meaningless it would be to say on the telephone of a particular object that *It's* SO *big* or *It's* THIS *big* (with the usual accompanying gesture indicating size). Almost as meaningless are those notices sometimes posted on the doors of shops that are closed, for instance, *Back in fifteen minutes* (compare *Back at 1 p.m.*).

We are also obliged to locate objects and actions in time and space for others. To do so we make use of reference points known to both parties and assume a common orientation to these. A and B are discussing the location of a book over the telephone:

A. Where is it?
B. It should be in my den on the bookshelf where I keep my reading glasses, the shelf above the receiver. It's got a red cover.
A. Just a minute.

Or again, a conversation concerning the location of a street which makes use of known geographic reference points in the city:

A. Do you know where I mean?
B. I think so.
A. Two blocks west of Spadina at Bloor, a one-way street running south.

Time is the subject matter of the last example:

A. When then?
B. How about next Thursday?
A. The twelfth, not the fifth?
B. Right!
A. That seems fine.
B. OK, let's say the twelfth then.

In this case the extra checking appears necessary because of the use of the word *next*; not everyone has exactly the same interpretation of *next* when used in conjunction with particular days and time spans.

Every conversation has a location in both time and space. Often, too, the participants have a history, sometimes long sometimes short, of previous conversations with each other to draw on: they know what it is like to deal with each other.

Every move in a new conversation becomes part of that history and continues the total historical relationship. The participants' location can influence how each deals with the other; as the conversation takes place, other events are transpiring which may intrude on both its content and conduct. Then, too, each participant is *uniquely* located in both time and space, and is not exactly the same individual as he or she was yesterday or, if at the office, as at home. We largely ignore this unique characteristic of particular encounters because one overriding principle that appears to guide us in dealing with the world is that people and objects do not really change from moment to moment and place to place. However, we cannot completely ignore the fact that changes really do occur, if we wish to fully comprehend what is happening on a specific occasion. Finally, there will be a difference between what we can describe as the 'objectively real' situation that prevails in a particular encounter, and the various subjective realities which that encounter has for its participants. Each conversation is a unique event, but it is most unusual for you to leave a conversation with the feeling that you have indeed participated in a unique experience. The opposite is much more likely to be true: you will almost inevitably experience it as a quite commonplace activity and not at all remarkable.

In order to understand fully any particular bit of conversation, we must ask ourselves a set of basic questions about it. We need to know who is talking to whom. We must be concerned with the where and when of the utterance, that is, its location in place and time. We must also examine the content of what is said and the precise manner in which that content is communicated. The specific choices of word and phrase must also interest us, particularly as they relate to the topic or topics under discussion. And, finally, we must try to discover what a particular utterance achieved, that is, its effect on others. Not only must we understand these matters fully if we are to know what is happening, but in a very real sense the speaker and listener too must conduct much the same kind of analysis. Only by doing so can they communicate effectively with each other. They, of course, generally perform this task subconsciously and nearly always instantaneously.

One of the leading analysts of conversational structure, Emanuel Schegloff, has pointed out that the feelings we have about the 'rightness' of the various bits and pieces of a conversation are governed to a considerable extent by its immediate circumstances or context. These circumstances require us to have some fairly clear idea of who the participants are, of where we are, and of what we are doing. All the participants should share this knowledge to a considerable extent, for it provides them with a necessary centre to that conversation, a kind of critical orientation. They can then relate all the other details of the conversation to this centre. Truly effective communication, of course, presupposes that all parties to the conversation have much the same feeling about this centre. We can readily observe that if we do not know who we are talking to, if the general conversational setting is ambiguous or in some other way unclear (for instance, a phone call from a stranger), or if the purpose of the conversation is quite obscure (as in a Kafka novel), we must attempt to seek the information we lack if we are to proceed effectively. In contrast, conversations between intimates show little effort spent on such concerns, since the participants share all this information.

One possible reason for your not understanding or misunderstanding an overheard conversation between strangers is your lack of information about what it is that they know. You lack knowledge of the 'centre' of their concerns. They know who they are and what they are doing, but, as a casual observer, you are not privy to such information. But something like the opposite can happen to. What is particularly interesting is either the amusement or the difficulty you may experience in overhearing a conversation when you actually have better or more information on the topic than the participants possess. It is sometimes very difficult indeed to resist the temptation to interrupt: to give better street directions; to correct a serious error; to issue some kind of warning; and so on. Moreover, it is not at all clear what your responsibility is in such circumstances, because you must weigh the violation that an interruption is against any repair in knowledge you can supply. If the repair is of little significance, the others may well resent the interruption; however, if it is a considerable repair, they may welcome it, or if you do not offer it and they later find out, they may consider you to be negligent.

We have mentioned that the physical setting in which a conversation takes place is important. For example, in whose territory does it take place? Who goes to whose office when near equals are involved? How does a subordinate's visit to a superordinate's office differ from a visit of superordinate to subordinate? When is a neutral location called for? What happens when unequals meet accidentally on neutral ground, for example, at the theatre or on a planned informal occasion, such as a company picnic? The meeting place will be an important factor in how each party views the other, and will influence what each feels he or she can say to the other. Topics unmentionable in one situation will be accessible in another and ways for discussing them will also change. But it may be a serious *faux pas* to attempt to carry over the casual exchanges with superiors at the annual Christmas party to the first working day back at the office in the New Year.

The context of a conversation includes, as well as the actual space in which it takes place, the ways in which the various participants choose to make use of that space. Which seat do you choose on a bus or in a classroom? What 'right' have you to that seat and how do you control the space adjoining that seat? You cannot sit down next to someone on an almost empty bus unless you know that person – to do so would be to perform a very threatening gesture indeed. A seat occupied at the first meeting of a class seems to become the occupier's 'property' for the following classes. How do you best arrange space for the occupants of a classroom, a living room, or an office? The arrangement will help determine how those who must use the space will behave toward one another. And, of course, those in charge of the seating arrangements at dinner parties, conferences, committee meetings, and negotiating sessions must often give very serious attention to the matter. To be an effective participant in encounters where space is particularly important, you must know what others have done and can do with that space and what you may do with it – if necessary, how to change the space and allocations within it in ways favourable to you without violating the feelings that others may have concerning their rights in the matter.

When we enter another person's space, for example another person's office, workshop, or house, we quickly form an impression of that other from the way he or she has arranged that space. Is it clean or dirty, open or cluttered, arranged to be used or just to be viewed, welcoming or inhibiting, and so on? We see such space as somehow expressive of the person who inhabits it or who is responsible for it. If 'clothes make the man', so does the space he occupies. Sometimes we find ourselves forced to occupy space which is not what we would choose and about which we can do little. A teacher assigned to teach in a poorly lit room either standing on a low platform or separated from students confined to fixed, tiered seats may find himself thoroughly defeated if his preferred teaching approach is casual, relaxed, and highly dependent on easy-going discussion. In such a case space can undo, even negate, the best chosen words. Your space can defeat you, turn you into a voice crying in a wilderness, in this case one that others have sent you into.

We can see clearly from the following example that language use must be related very closely to the immediate physical circumstances. If your car has broken down in bad weather and a passing motorist stops and asks *Do you need any help?*, you will probably answer *Yes*. Your expectation would be that this is not a theoretical question asked simply out of some kind of intellectual curiosity. It would strike you as particularly perverse if, on hearing your reply, the other motorist just drove away. Has the motorist gone for help? Was he or she just getting some cruel pleasure out of the incident? Or what? The normal expectation you would have about *Do you need any help?* in such circumstances is that it is a direct offer of help. You are, of course, free to refuse that offer, but once it is made, and accepted, then the help should be provided. To seem to offer help and then withdraw it would be a particularly nasty act. The context has provided the participants to the exchange with information that requires no mention but establishes the background for the remarks they make to each other. The remarks have a 'normal' interpretation *in that background.*

Not only does context provide many of the clues we need in order to interpret an utterance correctly, but many utterances need certain kinds of contextual support in order to be convincing. Angry words, for example, require certain kinds of associated signals: sharp gestures, a flushed face, loudness of voice. Anger without these is 'cold' and 'malevolent' – and particularly nasty in most interpretations. When you listen to someone speak, you judge the words you hear against their surroundings. Do the two match or do they conflict? Does the performance ring true with your expectations about such performances? And, if it does nor ring true, why does it not and how is the performance then to be judged? Is what is being said too good to be true, too hollow to be convincing, too dishonest to be accepted, or is it, on the other hand, just right? And even if it is just right, is it so because it is an exceedingly clever performance rather than an honest one? Occasionally you find the opposite situation: a completely honest performance can be so bungled that you call the speaker's honesty into question. Unfortunate indeed is the person who, because of certain mannerisms or appearance, can never find his or her words accepted at their face value. Certainly such callings as bank manager and politician would appear to be closed to such a person.

We regard the non-verbal signals that accompany speech as powerful indicators of the intentions of speakers. They help listeners to understand how the words that are being used are actually to be interpreted. These signals can therefore interact with the words you use in subtle ways: they can reinforce the literal meaning of what you say or they can subvert, or even deny, that meaning. You can use such signals to provide a kind of feedback to what others are saying: agreement or disagreement, empathy or hostility, boredom or interest, and so on. You can also use them to manipulate the channel of communication. Is communication to be easy? Is it being closed off by one party? Can it be entered into by third parties? Non-verbal signals help to establish and maintain a general tone about the status and roles of the participants, indicating such matters as who is in charge, who can do and say what, and what can or cannot happen. Such signals are not merely the trappings of a stage that has been set for a particular language performance, but form an integral part of the very action of that performance.

These signals are all around us and we are constantly reacting to them. We see someone we might speak to but she is looking at a magazine in such a way that she is telling us 'Do not disturb me', so we do not. We are at a meeting, it has not begun, but we know that it is to begin when someone who is sitting at the head of the table clears his throat while looking around at the assembled participants. We are in a lawyer's outer office and see her approach two secretaries and stop. They immediately break off their conversation. In all three instances a piece of non-verbal behaviour is communicating: absorption; 'time to begin'; and 'I want to speak to one of you.' In no case would it be easy to ignore the non-verbal message: to interrupt the reader; to delay beginning the meeting by continuing to chitchat with the person sitting next to you; and to ignore the lawyer's obvious wish to speak.

The way people use the space around them provides important clues to their behaviour. Some take over space just as they take over conversations: they spread themselves out and scatter their possessions around them. But there are other ways too of providing space for ourselves. We can 'reserve' space either formally – by reserving a table at a restaurant – or informally – by leaving a book on a chair. We can prohibit others from access to 'our' space by the use of certain gestures or movements. We can erect barricades such as desks and counters or we can open up space by deliberately moving around these or moving them out. We can come close to others or employ various strategies to retreat from them. What is important is that we should know at any particular time just how we or the other person is using space in relation to what it is we both want or expect. We also hope that the other's use of space will conform to our wants and expectations. When it does not, we may encounter frustration – if we feel we cannot get as close to the other as we would like – or feel threatened – if we feel overpowered in our own space. And, since different cultures have different concepts about the kind and extent of space that surrounds, or should surround, an individual, we face the prospect of cultural conflict when we must communicate with others who have very different expectations about how individuals should locate themselves in relation to one another.

People also use props during conversation. Some props are large pieces of furniture: desks, chairs, and tables. But many are quite small: books, newspapers, pens, pencils, spectacles, cigarettes, and so on. They are not used entirely casually, even if they appear to be used or manipulated almost absent-mindedly. They are used to support a particular performance and are actually an important part of that performance. Just as you choose certai words to say something, so you choose to chew on a pencil, take off your glasses, play with a paperweight, light a cigarette, and so on. Choice and timing are just as important in these matters as they are in selecting a particular combination of words, a certain intonation, an appropriate gesture, or any other bit of the total performance.

Using objects in the environment is tied in with the character you wish to project: the determined (or relaxed) pipe smoker; the nervous chain-smoker; the doodler; the fidgeter. Your clothes, gestures, and posture, and your relationship to the objects that surround you say something about you. They do not exist by accident; usually there is a considerable choice in the matter. Like the words you choose to use, they express things about you – they are an important part of you. To attempt to describe a person's words entirely apart from that person's persona is essentially to attempt to describe something living while ignoring its essential life force – to produce a photograph or drawing of something rather than the thing itself.

We are related to our surroundings in one other important respect, too: we must have names or labels for objects and actions in our environment. And our choice of labels reflects our view of the world. From time to time people have argued that it even controls our view of the world, for, they claim, we actually see 'what is out there' through the labels we have for the world that lies outside of us. That is perhaps why it is so difficult to communicate with someone who possesses a quite different set of labels from ours – for example, with someone who holds strong opinions on social, religious, political, economic, or other matters which differ markedly from our own. There is little or nothing to talk about because we inhabit different worlds. 'Lunatics' are often so designated because they have created special worlds for themselves, worlds which the majority finds unacceptable and deviant in ways that have come to be classified within systems of mental illness. A simpler example relates to how men view women: it makes quite a difference in many circumstances whether men see women as 'girls', 'dames', 'ladies', 'women', or 'persons'. This is but one instance of how the names we choose to use affect our perceptions of 'what is out there'. A further indication is in the constant creation of new names – sometimes for old things – in order to change our views about the world: a *Ministry of War* becomes a *Ministry of Defence*; a *caretaker* becomes a *building superintendent*; or certain events no longer *begin* but now *commence*.

Self-labelling is also very important. Each of us has a set of labels for himself or herself: we are doctors, mechanics, successes, fathers, sons, bosses, obliging, tough, stupid, witty, religious, old, and so on. We also change labels according to occasion. This kind of labelling provides you with categories within which you can live your life: it provides ways for you to decide who or what you are at particular times and on particular occasions and who or what others are. Carried to an extreme, it results in stereotyping, the process of acting out, or responding to, labels rather than acknowledging the realities that lie behind those labels. We turn thirty or forty and feel we must act our new age, without being very sure what that means. We tell our children *Big boys don't cry* or *Nice girls don't speak like that* without thinking through the possible long-term consequences of either statement. We regard all people possessing certain characteristics with suspicion, even dislike in times of hostility, and others possessing not so very different characteristics with admiration; and we sometimes see, if we live long enough, the two groups exchange positions. We live our lives playing roles in which we feel comfortable and putting others into roles that we can play against. Unfortunately, some people have only very few such roles available to them, for example 'good guys' and 'bad guys', 'capitalists' and 'communists', 'haves' and 'have nots', 'over thirties' and 'under thirties', and so on. In such circumstances labelling loses much of its usefulness, since it dangerously over-simplifies the inherent complexities of human existence.

Labelling is also part of the general process of social regulation. Societies have labels for different functions and for different roles: there is a label for everything. Indeed, much of a person's education is concerned with acquiring knowledge of labelling systems. The power to manage such systems is also a considerable one, the power to say who is a *deviant*, who are the *poor*, who is *ill*, what behaviour is *artistic*, *stupid*, *brilliant*, or *insane*, who is *employable*, what *work* is, and just what behaviours are to be rewarded, punished, tolerated, and so on. Language is used for social control, and the power to control language, as George Orwell brilliantly observed, gives you much of the power you need to control society. Many of use have lived to see people no longer *fired* but *made redundant*, *slumps* become *temporary downturns in the economy* or *seasonal adjustments*, and an *invasion* dressed up as *answering a request for military assistance*. There is a thorough debasement of language in all of this, one which has all too readily been accepted by the general public. Above all, *1984* was most alarmingly accurate in prophesying that this would be so.

One other subtle bit of contextual information we react to is that which the human voice itself provides. The voice carries much information about the speaker in addition to the actual words spoken. It is usually sexually indicative among mature speakers, men's and women's voices being generally quite distinguishable. Age, status, and some kinds of occupation are often marked by voice characteristics, although you can never be absolutely sure about these since each reflects a certain amount of learned behaviour. We do learn to use the voice to indicate something about our status, our calling (if we have a distinctive one), and even to some extent how youthful or otherwise we are or want to appear to be. And, of course, a speaker's emotional state – and sometimes an indication of his or her general physical health too – often comes through in speech. How something is said obviously involves much more than the exact words spoken.

But we should be aware, in responding to another person, of how far we may be influenced by characteristics of the voice over which he or she may have little control, for example, the particular dialect spoken. There are also characteristics over which a certain amount of control can be exercised, and we need to decide what these indicate in any particular circumstance: a very breathy delivery; excessive slurring; a very open, projecting 'stage' voice; whispering; rasping; hoarseness; lisping; a 'little girl's' voice; and so on. Some of these may impress us as being 'put on' and therefore influence us in how we judge any content the speaker is trying to convey. We might question the sincerity of the total performance. Others may appear to be just right and help convince us that the speaker's presentation is a genuine one in the circumstances.

The general context is important in setting the 'agenda' for particular conversations, both the general agenda for all the participants and the unique agenda each participant has for himself or herself. Not only do the participants in a conversation know (or not know) what others know and have certain beliefs about the extent of others' knowledge, but they have ideas about just how much they can say. What you can say (or must conceal) on any particular occasion is controlled by the agenda you have set yourself for that occasion, that is, your overall purpose, which, of course, you must partially work our during the conversation itself. This agenda will also be controlled by what you perceive the roles of the different participants to be and by their views of who has the right (or responsibility) to do or say what. Consequently, what you actually say is determined by the choice you make from among the many possible things you could say. To a considerable extent these choices are limited – not *any* choice is possible – but rarely to the extent that what you say is quite predictable to others. Ritualistic occasions provide the most common exceptions, but the main purpose of these is symbolic rather than communicative: it is more important that something be done than that something be said.

Your language is but one expression of your being. In fact, your being can be thought of as the total collection of ways you have of expressing your existence: language, appearance, posture, adornments, artifacts, activities and so on. It is something you must constantly recreate. You habitually do certain things and have certain things and come to be recognized by that doing and having. Sometimes a considerable amount of self-monitoring is required, of constantly being on the alert about what you are doing at a particular time and about how others are reacting to what you are doing. This is a particularly risky activity when either you have no fixed idea of how you seek to present yourself in life or, through circumstances, you are in a period of change. Since the language you use and how you use it are the most adaptable of your possessions – or potentially so – you must be especially alert. It was Eliza Doolittle's language that Professor Higgins chose to change above and before everything else when he sought to transform her from a women of the streets into a 'lady'. If you are not necessarily who you say you are, you are certainly in a large part what you are heard to be in those places and in those ways in which you choose to present yourself.

Further Reading

The importance of context in understanding what is said is the subject of Argyle, Furnham, and Graham's *Social Situations*, Lakoff's 'Language in Context', Halliday's *Language as Social Semiotic: The Social Interpretation of Language and Meaning*, and Hymes' 'Models of the Interaction of Language and Social Life'. Frake's 'Struck by Speech: The Yakan Concept of Litigation' uses legal disputes in an 'exotic' society to show the importance of context. Schegloff's 'Notes on Conversational Practice: Formulating Place' shows how a sense of place may be defined.

The use of space in human interaction is discussed in Hall's *The Silent Language* and *The Hidden Dimension*, Sommer's *Personal Space: The Behavioral Basics of Design*, and Watson's 'Proxemics'. Paralanguage is the topic of Birdwhistell's 'Paralanguage: 25 Years after Sapir', Crystal's 'Paralinguistics' and *The English Tone of Voice: Essays on Intonation, Prosody and Paralanguage*, Crystal and Quirk's *Systems of Prosodic and Paralinguistic Features in English*, and Trager's 'Paralanguage: A First Approximation'. Birdwhistell's *Introduction to Kinesics* and *Kinesics and Context: Essays on Body Motion Communication* and Gosling's 'Kinesics in Discourse' contain basic information on kinesics.

Edelman's *Political Language: Words that Succeed and Policies that Fail* shows how language can be used as a political and social instrument.

6

Getting Started
and Keeping Going

In one sense the biggest problem you face in a conversation is going from silence to speech at the beginning and from speech to silence at the end. Once actual talk is initiated it follows its own rules, but starting and stopping are not always easy, and, of the two, getting started appears to be the more difficult. After all, you can just stop talking – you can turn away and take the consequences. But getting started requires you to interrupt something – even though that something is only silence – and may also involve a breach of someone else's territory. Clear signalling of your intent becomes necessary very early, so that you can negotiate the opening few moments safely and not close off communication when it has only just begun.

There are plenty of restrictions to prevent or deter you from making free and easy conversation with just anyone at all. One of the most basic is a general restriction on speaking without good cause to strangers. You may also, politely or otherwise, decline to take up a conversational opening offered by a stranger. *Don't talk to strangers* is a fairly common instruction for parents to give to their children. It is similar to another restriction that is also quite general in conversation: *Do not speak until spoken to*. The existence of both such injunctions may actually cause one to wonder how any conversation at all ever manages to take place. Obviously, there must be strong countervailing forces at work that encourage us to take a chance and speak to others: social needs to be fulfilled; trust to be established; and work to be done. But it is quite apparent that for many people conversation is a difficult art and that a considerable part of the difficulty arises from fundamental inhibitions and prescriptions about initiating conversations, particularly with strangers.

There is also a considerable difference between refusing to respond to an attempt by a friend to initiate conversation and one that a complete stranger initiates. The second kind of refusal will very rarely incur criticism; in fact, it may be regarded as a wise move on your part unless the circumstances are completely innocuous (*Got a match?*) or require you to set aside some of the normal constraints on behaviour, for example, in a serious emergency. But the first kind of refusal – particularly if it is an unexplained refusal – is likely to lead to charges of moodiness or some other personal failing. That is, the injured party will regard your behaviour as antisocial in that you have apparently deliberately rejected an attempt to keep open the channel of communication that exists between you. There seems to be some obligation upon you to acknowledge, one way or another, people with whom you are acquainted. In villages and small towns with fixed populations this requirement may lead to a lot of routine exchanges, that is, a considerable amount of phatic communion. People moving from such environments to large cities may find these quite unfriendly, if for no other reason than that they no longer can enjoy this communion. They are strangers to other people and other people are strangers to them and, on the whole, one particularly does not speak to 'busy' strangers, as city dwellers often appear to be to visitors with a more rural orientation. In contrast, you can often tell who is a stranger in a small town by observing either his or her lack of opportunity to indulge in small talk or, if there is such talk, its qualitatively different content from that of the locals.

It may be very difficult in most circumstances to deal with complete strangers who intrude into our space. The classic example of such an intruder is found in the Western movie when the tall, silent stranger rides into town. His antecedents are unknown and he is uncommunicative. He is perceived as a threat to everyone so long as his motivation for being where he is is unknown, and the more taciturn he is the less able are the residents to guess that motivation. We can observe a similar phenomenon when a complete stranger gatecrashes a party, or when someone refuses to comply with the requirements of a ritual, or when an individual behaves bizarrely without warning or explanation. In each case there is a violation of the norms of the group, whose members feel threatened and tend to unite to deal with the intruder and the intrusive behaviour by rejecting the individual or by attempting to ignore the 'aberrant' behaviour.

If you must ever interrupt or intrude, you take on the responsibility of repairing the damage you do. You must initiate communication. If not, you merit a challenge: *Halt, who goes there?*, *What are you up to?*, or the milder challenge (actually disguised as an offer) in *Can I help you?* Passing a neighbour shovelling snow, you might be expected to say something (*Good morning*), but if you feel yourself to be actually intruding in some way on such an activity you might say *It's hard work* or *Will it ever stop?*, so identifying yourself with the other's task. In each case you establish some kind of bond with the other, and the world remains at peace. However, to ignore the person or the activity, or not to comment, could be perceived as mildly threatening, causing him or her to wonder what you are up to, what he or she might have done to offend you, and how the relationship between the two of you stands currently.

Opening up a conversation with a complete stranger is obviously a somewhat risky endeavour – there are so many unknown quantities. But then again the strangeness is not usually absolute. There are some 'knowns'. The actual circumstances of the meeting itself can provide their own topic for conversation. The extreme example would be two strangers washed up on a desert island. It would be hard to imagine them not talking to each other until they were properly introduced, or, if they happened to speak different languages, not trying to work out some system through which to communicate. Circumstances, then, provide an initial topic: fellow passenger on an aeroplane; other patients in a waiting room; students on a course; ticket purchasers in a queue. There is something to talk about in these circumstances, some shared concern that can be used to reduce the feeling of threat you sometimes experience when venturing into areas in which there are few readily identifiable signposts. Of course, there are other indicators, too, that can help you: the manners and appearance of others and, once any talk is begun, the skill and sophistication with which it is pursued.

But you still face the problem of intruding into someone else's privacy. How do you most easily do that? How do you know who the other person is and what his or her status is in relation to your own? And how do you assess the willingness or reluctance of the other person to respond to any opening moves you might make. But again the person you have met is not likely to be a complete stranger. Most occasions for meetings provide plenty of signs that you can respond to: a meeting on a cruise is different from a meeting on a city bus; clothes, posture, and personal grooming provide signals; and then, too, some people deliberately seem to close themselves off from contact – for example, by hiding behind a newspaper – while others appear to seek it. What is crucial to initiating a conversation is being able to assess accurately the context in which it is to take place and some of the more salient features of the other person, and to have command of the devices that will be necessary to keep the conversation going once you overcome the initial difficulties.

Seeking to interact with a stranger, you may try to attach some kind of label to him or her in order to gain a measure of control over the situation. On occasion that labelling is fairly easy because of the nature of the encounter: doctor–patient; salesperson–customer; teacher–student. But often the situation is not at all clear, so you must fairly quickly establish who is talking to whom. Hence the concern we have for knowing other people's names, acquaintances, addresses, and occupations. It is remarkable how much of the beginnings of conversations among strangers concerns matters such as these – and variations of them: *I didn't catch your name, Do you know X?, Where do you live?, What do you do?*

In particular, occupational information is often exchanged very early. In Western culture it is quite acceptable to ask very early of a stranger *What do you do?* whereas it is not possible to ask *How much do you earn?* You have an obligation to answer a question about occupation with reasonable honesty. Occupations do sometimes get a little elevated in status, but the vast majority of answers show a considerable degree of veracity. Because of the nature of Western society, occupation provides us with many of the clues we need in order to orient ourselves to others. We believe we know how society works and what to expect from people in certain positions, and these positions usually have occupational titles. To be told someone is a stockbroker, physician, plumber, actress, or waiter is to know – or so we believe – a lot about that person. (Age, like occupation, is also of great interest; for example, newspapers usually report both these details about individuals mentioned in their news stories.) Knowing what a person does allows us to fall back on stereotypes and to proceed to handle what follows in comfortable ways. We all know how much more difficult it often is to continue a conversation with someone whose job – and therefore whose background – we cannot identify than with someone who readily identifies himself as a model, television producer, or dentist. When we know what another person does, we are likely to feel that we have some possible topics of mutual concern that we can talk about in the expectation that, in talking about these topics, other possible topics will be revealed. So if the person we are talking to reveals himself or herself to be a dentist, we can assume certain kinds of knowledge and education and we can talk generally about these. In doing so, we might discover a mutual interest in jazz or science fiction or skiing, and so on.

Beginnings of conversation also often involve a process of mutual 'feeling out'. The parties may not be at all certain of how to introduce topics because they have little idea of how the other is likely to respond. They may be virtual strangers, quite unsure of each other's background. Hence they must proceed cautiously and attempt to find some common ground on which to manoeuvre. In such a situation conventional topics such as the weather, some remarkable feature of the surroundings, and so on get you started. You must open a channel of communication in this way before you can use it for other purposes. We can compare such a situation with several others that are quite unambiguous. There need be no beating about the bush or preliminary negotiations between two people on intimate terms (unless the subject itself is a very delicate or disturbing one), between a lowly subordinate and a senior official when the latter has summoned the former to his or her office on some urgent matter, or when fire breaks out and you must warn others.

In talking with a stranger, you are considerably limited in the topics you can broach. You must choose 'safe' topics and avoid controversial ones. 'Safe' topics also require 'safe' views, that is, the opinions you venture on these topics should not vary widely, if at all, from the prevailing 'common-sense' views, that is, those apparently held by the public at large. If you insist on presenting highly idiosyncratic views to complete strangers, you will soon be regarded with suspicion, bewilderment, or amusement, although they may find such views quite acceptable from a close acquaintance (when held along with many other 'normal' views). Most of us have learned to ignore people who go around with such messages as *Repent* or *The end of the world is near*. Some of us have even learned what to do with strangers who appear on our doorsteps with petitions they want us to sign:

A. Hello.
B. Yes?
A. I'm taking around a petition to . . . [The topic was one on which B had diametrically opposite views.]
B. I'm sorry but I don't agree with you and won't sign.
A. OK, then. Thanks for listening.
B. OK, goodnight. Watch the step!
A. Bye.

In this case B firmly but politely refused to sign and A wisely decided not to press the point. The pair then negotiated a parting. One can only surmise about how often people in B's situation actually end up signing petitions they do not agree with, or complying with requests made in similar circumstances, because they do not want to say *No* or 'argue with a stranger'. It is not surprising that many countries have a 'cooling off' law which says that you can change your mind after agreeing to buy something from a door-to-door salesperson; such a law apparently recognizes how difficult it sometimes is not to give in to rather than argue with and/or dismiss someone who approaches you in this way.

In meeting strangers, then, not only do we resort to ritualistic language and conventional topics, but we also usually seriously curtail the number of novel ideas we introduce into conversation. We may state an opinion which we have reason to believe the others are likely to share on some social or political event, for example, on a sporting event, a famous wedding, the rising cost of living, and so on. Later on we can express more individualistic opinions, if some conversational rapport is established. This kind of beginning allows each party to sound out the other to discover whether the conversation might continue for mutual benefit. You must continue to observe a basic principle, though: do not argue with strangers. You can listen to them and they may indeed tell you very intimate details of their personal lives or ask your opinion on just about any topic, but you must not go too far. You must not get too inquisitive – questions like *How much do you earn?* and *Do you beat your wife?* are therefore ruled out – and you should not draw attention to any contradictions or serious deficiencies in the accounts you are given of the other's affairs. A considerable intimacy is required before you can do this kind of thing, and even then it is best done rarely and with great caution.

A very important part of most conversations is 'small talk', one of the important functions of which to provide a kind of escape from potentially threatening or dangerous situations. For example, strangers finding themselves randomly drawn together on some occasion may feel uncomfortable with one another. Each individual is cut off from each other individual

- nothing unites and everything is potentially threatening. Small talk on unimportant matters provides a means by which the various individuals can establish some norms for behaviour, norms which first of all seek to ensure the safety of all and, only when that has been achieved, turn toward problems of bonding. Behaviour in a waiting room is a good example. Strangers in waiting rooms are brought together usually with an ulterior purpose (except in Kafkaesque situations), but they need to deal with one another as well as with whatever or whomever it is they await. Hence, appropriate small talk is likely to involve either non-threatening general topics or the whatever or whomever they will eventually have to deal with: a doctor, an employment officer, a social worker, and so on. In some such situations, if you try to remain aloof from the others you may be perceived as part of the threat of the unknown – your aloofness will separate you out from the shared concerns of the others, no matter how trivial those may be.

We can also note the kinds of topics people choose for small talk. Often these concern objects and events in the immediate surroundings – topics that are 'safe' by their very nature, for everyone is a witness to them. Numerous such starting points are available: the decor of a house one is visiting, a new dress, a child's behaviour, a household pet, or some other physical aspect of the environment (particularly, as we have indicated, the weather) can be made to serve this ice-breaking function. The comments that result allow for agreement to be reached on the topic, for strangers' voices to be heard, and for initial impressions to be gained as to what might or might not be suitable follow-up activities. At this stage you may feel that you can hit it off with the other person or, conversely, that there is really no point in pursuing any topic any further, your initial impressions having been quite negative.

On occasion some kind of what can be called a 'pre-opening' signal may be necessary before a conversation is begun. Two strangers brought together by accident may find it easier to begin a conversation if one of them makes some kind of move which leads to a shared appreciation of the setting in which they find themselves. A gesture that indicates how cold it is can lead to a remark about the weather at a bus stop. Closing a window or a door can be a preliminary move to a conversation in a waiting area. Looking at an object (a pet, a picture, some flowers) or incident in the environment can lead to a remark about what is being looked at, and that remark can serve as the opener to a conversation. People demonstrate a wide variety of ability in the skills necessary to do this kind of thing – some are much better at initiating conversations with strangers in this way than others, who may find it almost impossible.

A lot of conversations actually begin with what can only be called 'pseudo-apologies', expressions such as *Excuse me, Sorry to bother you, Got a minute?*, and *I don't mean to interrupt, but . . .* What appears to be happening is that the speaker feels he or she must immediately acknowledge the fact that speaking is equivalent to breaking into the space and silence that surrounds another person. Consequently, a kind of apology is necessary. In this way, the speaker repairs the intrusion with a little ritual. Once the person to whom the remark is addressed acknowledges that the intrusion has been sufficiently apologized for by providing some signal of acknowledgement – *That's OK, Yes, what is it?* – the intruder must state his or her business. A telephone call is a typical example, with the mechanical ringing of a bell the signal of intrusion. Once you have picked up the telephone and answered – in North America with a *Hello* or in England often with your telephone number – the caller must get on with the business of the call, although a few pleasantries might actually precede that business.

There are many other ways you can use to open a conversation. A stranger in the street may want directions, or change for a parking meter: the stranger must quickly apologize (*Excuse me!*) and state his or her business. Familiars may catch the other's attention by using his or her name or a familiar term (for instance, *John* or *Love*, or a more formal *Mr Jones* in some settings). A conversation may be opened by a request for a certain amount of time: *Do you have a minute?*, *Got a minute?*, *Can you spare a minute?* In special circumstances special pseudo-formulaic openings are available: a waiter's *Are you ready to order?*, a shop assistant's *Can I help you?*, or the somewhat patronizing words of some doctors, as in *And what can I do for you?* or *Well, what brings you here?*

A very common kind of opening between strangers gathered together for some kind of designated event – say a party – is to adopt a system of self-introductions:

A. Hello, I'm Sally Jones.
B. Hi, I'm John, John Smith.
A. I'm Beth's sister.
B. Oh, I work with Fred.

What we see here is a self-naming process which requires the first party to offer a name and then the other party to offer a name in response to the name that was offered. Here we can see how self-identification in relation to someone everyone at the party is presumed to know acts as a second prompt that requires the volunteering of a similar kind of information. At this point the conversation can go in a variety of directions. The two parties know a little about each other and they have established some common links. They can talk about Beth, Fred, her or his family, Sally's or John's work, the event that brings them together, and so on. The ice has been broken. Possible topics have surfaced. Real progress can be made in communication if the parties so desire. But, of course, many such conversations go nowhere at all because the process is mainly a ritual designed to make strangers comfortable in one another's presence, not to make them uninhibited conversationalists.

There is another kind of attention-getting device we can use at the beginning of a conversation, but it requires a certain familiarity between the parties. People working or living side by side use it. A *Good grief!* or *Well, I never!* uttered while you are reading a newspaper will almost cer-

tainly act as a signal for someone in your immediate environment to request an explanation: *What is it?* or *What's the
matter?* In such cases your exclamatory remark makes use of
the channel of communication that is readily available to you.
You can dispense with any preliminaries. Moreover, it seems
that someone in the environment is under an obligation to
take up the remark, for otherwise there would be no purpose
in your uttering it. Consequently, such remarks are very
rarely ignored.

Sometimes you may try to attract attention at the beginning of a conversation so as to guarantee that the floor will be
made available to you. You can, as it were, demand attention. In this case it is necessary to whet the appetite of your
listener, to put him in a situation in which he almost has to
insist that you continue unless he wants to appear to be
hostile or indifferent to you. Openings such as *Guess what?*,
You'll never guess what, Have I got a surprise for you!, and
*Something strange [peculiar, fascinating, interesting, etc.] happened
today* serve to bring responses like *What?* or *Tell me!* They
allow you to begin the account that you have in mind and
guarantee you the floor for a while at least. A reply like *Go
away!* or *Don't bother me!* would definitely squelch you, and
would on most occasions appear to be completely unwarranted.

Getting started in a conversation can be made easier when
the parties have a certain amount of familiarity with each
other. Indeed, it may be difficult to talk profoundly and at
length with a complete stranger. However, there is one kind
of conversation that occasionally takes place between strangers that does not fit this pattern. The conditions seem to be
that the individuals involved must be complete strangers,
that this will be a once-only meeting, and that they must
never expect to see each other again. After an initial ice-
breaking, each (or often just one) will proceed to talk quite
uninhibitedly on any and every topic that comes to mind,
revealing even the most intimate personal details in an almost
confessional way. Many of the normal conventions of speech
may be set aside: direct questions may be asked; opinions

may be offered in a most candid manner; no subject seems to be taboo. Such conversations are not frequent – indeed, they may be memorable precisely because they strike us as being so different from our usual conventional and inhibited 'normal' conversations. But even a casual inspection of them reveals how impossible it would be to conduct everyday life in such a manner. We cannot treat everyone as a complete stranger appearing once only and then very briefly in our lives. We are connected with others in so many ways, and living itself is a cooperative enterprise dependent on continuing contacts with others. Conversations have an existence beyond the present moment, for they must be fitted into both a past and a future as life goes on. If a one-time, confessional encounter with a stranger proves to be therapeutic for one or both participants, we must be thankful for that fact, but we should not claim that we could make life more honest if all encounters were to be conducted like this. One suspects that life would quickly become impossible if it had to be lived so nakedly.

Beginning a conversation also brings up the issue of how you address the other person. How you address someone in a conversation, particularly at the beginning, is a serious matter. Deciding whether and when to use his or her name, which name to use (nickname, first, last, and last with a title or without one), and what you may reasonably expect in return can cause anxiety. Many languages have extremely elaborate systems of address which require you, as speaker, to relate yourself in certain ways to the listener, for example, as older or younger, related or unrelated, superior or inferior, and so on. These address systems are mandatory and unavoidable. For example, Clifford Geertz has observed that speakers of Javanese find it nearly impossible to say anything without indicating the social relationship, in terms of status and familiarity, between the speaker and the listener. Such systems often highly constrain what can be said and even who can speak. They impose severe limitations on what we would consider to be very routine opportunities for normal conversation, often turning such activity into the kind of speaking we tend to reserve for very formal occasions, for example, talking to high officials and using ceremonial language.

Consequently, you must use terms of address with considerable care. Knowing when you can address your listener by first name does not come easily. The practice is certainly very different between Britain and the United States: North American practice sounds over-familiar to many British people. Likewise, a *What will you have, dear?* from a waitress may sound strange and make you feel uncomfortable, just as would someone addressing you as *sir* or *madam* when that elevated term seems unjustified. Languages with extensive honorific systems are particularly demanding in this way, but we must not overlook the fact that English has its own subtleties of address: its own uses of names and titles; its familiar terms (*dear, son, honey*); its diminutives (*lovey, cutie, baby, Freddie*); and its systems of reciprocal and non-reciprocal address. While North Americans may appear to be on more familiar and casual terms with one another than people in many other parts of the world, it is not the case that anything goes, as many newcomers both to North America and to English usage in North America have learned to their regret. A too early use of a familiar form of address can seriously mar what is otherwise a normally developing relationship. On the other hand, a refusal or reluctance to adopt a familiar form can freeze a relationship at a level of formality which inhibits further change.

Not only do we have some choice as to *how* we address others in conversation, but we can also choose to use such things as names, endearments, and titles either frequently or infrequently. In case of doubt we can even generally manage to do without them. In addition, we can place the name in various locations in utterances. Consequently, we can observe considerable stylistic variation and freedom in naming practices. In certain more formal settings – classrooms are a good example – the use of names has the additional characteristic of allowing a particular person to control who gets to speak and to guide some kind of collective activity. A teacher in a classroom can actually choose who is to speak next and make that choice stick by naming speakers. It is hardly possible to do the same thing in an informal conversation.

Not only can we choose different address terms for others, but we can also vary how we refer to ourselves. For example, on the telephone:

A. Can I speak to Mr Jones, please?
B. This is Mr Jones.
   [or]
   Speaking.

Leaving a message, we have such options as *Tell him that Dr Smith/Mr Smith/Bob Smith/Bob called*. Parents may often be heard speaking to their children, using expressions such as *Can mummy have a taste?* We seem also quite prepared to 'correct' what we see as lapses in another's use of address terms:

A. Excuse me. Do you know where John Smith's office is?
B. Professor Smith's office is just along the hall.

A particularly amusing case of this is the following exchange where A has knocked on the door and B, a male, has answered.

A. Hello. Is the lady of the house at home, please?
B. *I* am the lady of the house.
A. Oh!

When terms of address and names are used, there may be noticeable shifts within any conversation, from formal to informal and vice versa. A mother's shift from *Joan* to *Honey* to *Joan Smith* in a conversation with her daughter is likely to signal a considerable shift in her approach to her daughter, as topics either develop or change. In fact, the level of formality changes in the course of most conversations. The most formal interchanges occur at the beginnings and ends and the less formal ones in the middles. The level of formality is directly related to ritual and ice-breaking. The beginning of a conversation requires a considerable amount of care, and such care brings a greater consciousness of the proprieties that must be observed. Once topics are introduced a different kind of care is necessary, care in dealing with the topics rather than in handling the other participants straight in from the 'cold' of silence. So the level of formality can be reduced. Endings show some reversion to the beginning situation. The parties must re-establish the conditions, modified to be sure, that existed at the beginning, so the level of formality is likely to increase and be accompanied by an increase in the use of ritualistic closing devices.

Having managed to begin a conversation, we are faced with the task of keeping it going. A conversation is not just a random series of utterances strung together. Each conversation has its own shape, one 'cut' by the participants in the course of conversing. Keeping a conversation going requires, therefore, a set of skills of a different kind from opening that conversation. Failure to exercise the necessary skills will, of course, bring about a premature closing. The whole effort will have been abortive.

When we speak, particularly if we want to hold the floor for a while, we must assure ourselves that we indeed do have listeners and continue to have listeners. Moreover, we should try to see to it that our listeners are attending willingly. What we need is some kind of feedback, an assurance that what we are saying is having some effect. When we listen to others, we also feel a need to show we are listening, either to encourage the speaker or merely to be polite. So both speaking and listening require an acknowledgement that the activity of speaking is worthwhile and can be continued. Physical distancing, gestures, facial expressions, nods, and so on are very important indicators of attention. So, too, are certain spoken signals. *Mmm*s and *Uh-huh*s serve this function, as do certain words and the various intonations we can employ in uttering them: *Yes, Yeah, Well?, So?, And?. And then?, Exactly, Quite, Correct*, or expressions such as *I see* and *I agree*. To both speaker and listener these actions, noises, and expressions indicate approval of the act of speaking, but not necessarily, of course, of the content of that speaking. They indicate that one party is willing to give up the floor to the other in the expectation that at some later point the other will be equally as considerate. They are signs of good manners rather than of agreement, although they may sometimes be interpreted as indicators of the latter too – which, of course, they may or may not be according to circumstances.

Speaking involves you not only in listening to others but also in listening to yourself. You work out things as you speak, and part of that working-out process involves editing what you are saying as you say it. This 'self-editing' can lead you at times into a considerable amount of hesitation and backtracking. It takes considerable practice to be able to talk without a certain amount of this, and people who must learn to speak carefully and guardedly on sensitive topics must necessarily acquire this skill. When no self-editing is apparent in another's speech, we may be put immediately on guard, for the resulting speech is apt to sound rehearsed and insincere, the 'right' responses coming too easily and glibly to be completely convincing. Except on very special occasions, part of being convincing is showing conviction through appearing to work out what you are saying as you say it, that is, by deliberately appearing to be choosing your words carefully.

A kind of repair process is therefore part of normal conversation. You can repair your own contributions by hunting for the right word, by correcting and modifying what you say as you say it: *I mentioned it to him when I saw him on Tuesday – sorry, Monday.* But you must do just the right amount, or you may appear to be a bumbling, mumbling fool. Others may help you in your repair work and you can reciprocate by helping them: errors can be repeated, therefore questioned ('Did you really mean to say that?'), as in the following exchange:

A. I got it at The Bay last week.
B. The Bay? But we went to Eaton's.
A. Sorry. You're right. Eaton's.

Likewise, a statement can be rephrased as a question so that the original statement can be altered if necessary; or a shift of gaze or a gesture can ask you to recheck something that you have just said. Since self-repair, looking after your own errors, is more polite, more cooperative, than having someone else do the repair for you or allowing others to do it, we tend to encourage such kinds of repair. It is rather boorish always to be going about correcting others. But it is also difficult to resist when, for example, you try to converse with someone who stutters badly, for the need for repair may seem to create a formidable barrier to communication.

As a speaker, you must develop some kind of feeling about what is happening to your words. Are they being received by your listener and understood in the sense you intended? Are they boring the listener? Or are they just passing him or her by completely? We often interject expressions such as *you know*, *you see*, and *you understand* into our utterances. These are clear indicators of our desire that the listener acknowledge that we still have his or her attention. What is readily apparent from listening to many people speak is how frequently they use such expressions, a sign that they are not sure how effectively they are communicating and an indication of their need for constant reassurance. A speaker who is always sure that others will 'hang on his or her words' has little need – or should have little need – to sprinkle his or her speech with expressions of this kind.

To be a good speaker, then, you must be aware of your listeners and know whether you have their attention and are not about to lose it, particularly if you wish to keep on speaking. Sometimes you can do this by deliberately involving your listeners in your speaking, by directly referring to them. Expressions such as *And you know what I said?*, *Can you guess what I did?*, *Let's suppose*, and *If you ask me* serve this function. They ask for a kind of tacit agreement from your listeners that you are legitimately holding forth, but, nevertheless, seek approval or encouragement to continue. Even *you know*, *you see*, and *you understand* serve this function in part.

Speakers must be sensitive to their listeners' needs; they must try to become aware of any difficulties they are experiencing. But listeners owe speakers something too. They must respond in some way to a speaker if they expect that person to continue speaking. For example, a teacher trying to get certain points across to students must rely heavily on indicators of both attention and understanding if he or she is to perceive that task to be successful. If the students just sit like rows of dummies, the teacher has no way of knowing what is going on, whether what is being taught is being learned. In such circumstances teaching can be an extremely frustrating experience. Even straightforward lecturing requires positive signs of feedback from the audience, unless the lecturer is one of those who constantly send audiences to sleep without seeming to be aware of the fact or much caring about it.

If you are a speaker faced with the difficulty of giving your audience – or even a single listener – a longish account of any kind, you may not always be sure what kind of attention that audience is giving you. Questions, interruptions, nods of agreement (and of attention) can help you, but still you may sometimes find it necessary to resort to direct appeal to find out whether the audience (and this includes an audience of one) is still attentive. You may ask certain questions for this purpose: simple *yes–no* questions to which as little as an affirmative nod is an appropriate response, for example, *OK, so far?*, *Are you with me?*, *Do you get what I mean?*, *Got it?*, *Right?*, *Am I making myself clear?*, and *You see?* Hesitation or a look of puzzlement in response to such questions is a clear indication that something is amiss somewhere; consequently, you must clarify what you have been attempting to say through repetition or paraphrase, or you must ask some further question in order to discover what the difficulty is: *What don't you understand?* or *Where did I lose you?* The feedback from your listeners clearly signals that all is not well and the onus is on you to repair the situation. Otherwise you may well end up speaking only to yourself.

If you perceive that your listeners are having difficulty

following you, you will probably want to rephrase what you are trying to say. However, it may be a good idea to serve notice that you are doing this. You can even preface your explanation or rephrasing with a question (*You know what I mean?*) to give your listeners the opportunity to express their views on the matter. Any actual restating can be prefaced by expressions such as *What I mean [meant, want, wanted] to say, [Let me] put it another [this] way, What I said [I'm saying]*, or just simply *I mean [meant]*. If it is obvious that there has been some kind of misunderstanding or that a remark you have made requires modification, a 'correction' may be introduced by *Don't get me wrong*. On occasion a listener rather than the speaker may offer this kind of restating as a kind of checking out of what the speaker said. The listener can use a confirming device: *What you are saying is. . . , Do I understand you to mean. . . , Am I reading you right, when. . . ?, You mean. . . ?, I think you are saying. . .*, or *In other words. . . .* If the first speaker then confirms the restatement, that restatement rather than the original statement becomes the topic at issue, and the listener has achieved a certain control over matters that he did not possess before. It is now his restatement (one, presumably, that the speaker fully agrees to) that is on the floor for discussion.

Consequently, some talk in talking becomes talk about talking. We can call this kind of activity 'metatalk'. It is talk directed toward the activity of talking itself and the forms such talk takes: *What I'm trying to say is. . . , I just want to ask you. . . , My point is. . . , Let me repeat. . . , That word you used. . . , I'll try that again, I'm at a loss at what to say, That's exactly what I was trying to say.* This kind of activity also keeps conversation going, serving as it does to clarify the structure of the conversational activity itself and so contributing to the coherence of that structure. But there may be some reason to believe that this is a highly stylized kind of activity – it is certainly the kind of activity people learn about in debating clubs and practise in public forums where rhetorical skills may be prized even more highly than the actual content that is being communicated.

Listeners have available to them a variety of ways in which to signal their attentiveness to speakers. Their movements and gestures as they listen are important. But many signals involve the use of language. Some expressions, such as *Yes, Mmm, Surely, Quite, I see, Yeah*, and *OK*, do not even interrupt the speaker's flow of words. Completing a speaker's sentences is also possible. Such completions may keep the flow going, but they also sometimes indicate a desire to take over the conversation because they can be used quite easily to engineer interruptions. As well as being able to interrupt to seek clarification or to restate a point, listeners can even confront without at the same time attempting to shut off the speaker. You can thus keep another's flow of words going while indicating a serious interest in what is being said. Your involvement in what is happening cannot be doubted.

In this way, by supplying solid evidence that what is being said is being closely attended to listeners can very definitely help speakers to continue speaking. But, of course, a listener can employ similar manoeuvres in order to take over the topic: this 'shadowing' behaviour may be a prelude to an attempt to carry on with the conversation by simply replacing the speaker. The presumption appears to be that in just carrying on with what the speaker is saying you are doing no more than speaking on his behalf. You are not challenging or interrupting him and you are not being uncooperative. Indeed, you are just helping him out, so the possible offence is minimized; you might even be considered to be doing him a favour!

Another kind of monitoring behaviour, but one which can produce ambiguous results is the interjection of various kinds of observations into what a speaker is saying. Often these interjections are clichés, aphorisms, or platitudes, that is, trite observations which the listener makes about the content of what he hears. They show attention and mild involvement, and quite often they seem to be supportive of the point of view the speaker is expressing. But a speaker would be wise not to overvalue this kind of attention signal, for it is almost valueless so far as its content is concerned. That content shows a mind that is unoriginal and uncritical, reveals advice which is tailored to the superficialities of the occasion, and seems to offer a degree of involvement in the speaker's cause that the listener is unlikely to feel. The kindest interpretation the speaker should put on this sort of material is that it shows some awareness on the listener's part but really very little commitment to a shared point of view.

As we see, not all feedback is positive. A feedback signal such as *Huh?* or a raising of the eyebrows does not confirm whatever it is the speaker is saying or assure him that he can proceed. Instead, it queries something about the utterance, though the speaker may be quite unsure exactly what. At one level it could be equivalent to a question about the actual words spoken: *Did I hear you properly?* If you interpret the *Huh?* this way, you can simply repeat your original remark and continue with the topic. You presume that what was sought was some repair in communication necessitated by your listener's momentary inattention, your own poor articulation, a bit of background noise, or some other deficiency in the context of speaking. But at another level the *Huh?* could indicate a comprehension problem, and be equivalent to *Do you really mean that?* or *Did I hear you correctly?* If you interpret the *Huh?* this way, then repetition is not enough; you are being asked to provide a further explanation or justification, which you must do. Your difficulty arises from being forced to choose which of these interpretations you should give to the original query. Merely to repeat when clarification was sought is likely to make you appear to be at least evasive and probably somewhat uncooperative, but to clarify when only repetition was called for will make you appear to be pedantic and excessively concerned with a very simple matter, perhaps over-concerned to the point of defensiveness.

Monitoring behaviour may also involve you in a certain amount of correction, of yourself and of others. Self-correction is relatively easy, if only because you have the floor. If you notice you have made a mistake or observe some confusion in your listeners about what you are saying, you can rephrase your words: *What I meant [intended] to say was . . .* or *What I really [actually] said was. . . .* If your listener has misunderstood you, you can even interrupt him with a *Hold on! I didn't say that, That's not what I said*, or *That's not right, surely!* Then a correction is in order, and you have the floor to make the correction on the understanding that the person corrected will be given the opportunity to continue once you are finished. Of course, many such interchanges never resume but get bogged down in claims and counter-claims about who said what and what particular things mean. The original speaker, may never get back to where his topic was at the point of interruption.

When we monitor ourselves or others, we are not acting uncritically. The feedback we provide allows speaking to continue by indicating that attention is being paid to what is being said. But it can also cause the speaker to focus on specific items or a specific way of speaking. As we have seen, not all feedback is neutral in the sense of meaning no more than *Please continue*. Expressions like *Great!*, *Beautiful!* or *Crazy!* are very obviously not neutral, expressing as they clearly do approval or criticism. Likewise, a *Really?* or *Look here!* is apparently a deliberate attempt to try to stop the flow of words in order to make a change or to get the speaker to somehow modify what he or she is saying. These expressions can provide a combination of monitoring function – 'Yes, I hear you' – and evaluative function – 'I find that surprising' or 'I don't quite understand.'

Almost at the opposite extreme is the kind of behaviour we exhibit when we are less than enthralled by a topic of conversation. Trapped in a conversation which bores us, we are in a quandary. Decency requires that we do not directly inform the other that we are thoroughly bored, but self-preservation requires us to indicate something about our feelings. To pretend to give full attention is to act insincerely, indicating, as it does, an interest we do not have. The usual result is that we have recourse to a prescribed set of small gestures, such as fidgeting, engaging in some secondary activity, or allowing the gaze to wander. Such gestures tell the speaker that what attention we are giving comes from politeness rather than interest, and warns him that it would be wise to move to recapture that interest. In other words, the feedback signals we provide indicate that we seek the speaker's cooperation but in this case to discontinue what should now be seen as boring behaviour. That behaviour is being imposed on us, and we are indicating that we object, but gently; so we ask the speaker to please desist. Once again we see how important it is to recognize that cooperation is behind much of what happens when two or more people converse. We monitor ourselves and others to keep the cooperative enterprise going.

Further Reading

Schegloff's 'Sequencing in Conversational Openings' deals with the general problem of conversational openings; Godard's 'Same Setting, Different Norms: Phone Call Beginnings' and Schegloff's 'Identification and Recognition in Telephone Conversation Openings' deal with the special openings required in using the telephone. Williams' 'Presenting Oneself in Talk: The Disclosure of Occupation' describes how occupations are revealed in conversation. Adler's *Naming and Addressing: A Sociolinguistic Study* is a general discussion of systems of naming and addressing others.

Various kinds of hesitation phenomena, interjecting, and correcting behaviour are dealt with in Blankenship and Kay's 'Hesitation Phenomena in English Speech', James' 'The Use of *Oh*, *Ah*, *Say* and *Well* in Relation to a Number of Grammatical Phenomena', Jefferson's 'Error Correction as an Interactional Resource', Maclay and Osgood's 'Hesitation Phenomena in Spontaneous English Speech', and Schegloff, Jefferson, and Sacks' 'The Preference for Self-Correction in the Organization of Repair in Conversation'.

Cohesion between utterances is the topic of Halliday and Hasan's *Cohesion in English* and Keller and Warner's *Gambits, 1–3: Conversational Tools*.

7
Topics, Turns, and Terminations

A conversation usually covers a number of topics and involves shifts from one topic to another, and sometimes also a mix of topics. However, it is almost impossible to provide a narrow, technical definition for the term 'topic'. A topic is something talked about, but it is very unusual in conversation ever to talk on a well defined topic in a highly systematic way; even well practised lecturers can experience that difficulty. Usually, the kinds of topics we discuss in conversations are by no means well defined; in fact, the participants generally have to figure out what it is everyone is willing to talk about, and that very act of talking about what they perceive to be the topic helps to define it. In addition, whatever you say as a participant must be 'topical' – unless you seek to change the direction of talk completely – so it must relate in some way to the consensus about what matters are appropriate to the topic as it emerges and as it, in a sense, defines itself.

If the topic of a conversation is not explicitly stated – and it usually is not – how do the participants know what it is? The answer appears to be that they must infer it from what is being said, and each participant must do the inferring for himself or herself. The comments the participants make will cluster, and the focus of that cluster is a topic, whether it be the weather, movies in general, a particular movie, a current news story, a round of joke-telling, and so on. Each participant must quickly perceive how any remark made relates – or does not relate – to previous remarks and, in doing so, reshape and redefine for himself or herself the central topic. A considerable amount of ability and knowledge may be called for if the topic is abstruse or veiled. You may not find it possible to fall back on your general knowledge concerning how commonplace topics are dealt with. You may lack the resources you need to make an effective contribution and find yourself forced to choose between being left out and attempting to change the topic.

If topics in conversation are generally not well defined, so that you will hardly ever be able to say that a certain group of people is now going to talk precisely about topic X within such and such parameters for this or that purpose, it must be apparent how difficult it is to try to introduce a new topic into an ongoing conversation. How do you control what you want to talk about and allow others to contribute? If a topic is clear really only retrospectively, how can you try to control it prospectively, that is, before the event? Given all the possibilities that exist for a topic to reshape itself in the course of development, we should not be at all surprised to find that many topics we try to introduce somehow quickly slip out of our control and take on a life of their own. A conversational topic is a consensual outcome, not a private programme or agenda. The latter is more typically realized as a monologue, harangue, or lecture.

Possible topics vary with the nature of the group. Some groups may have no reservations either about topic or manner of discussion. Others may have considerable limitations on both, either formal or informal. For example, debates proceed within prescribed limitations, such as official 'rules of order', with certain kinds of procedures and language prohibited. Other groups may have taboos about particular subjects – sex, politics, religion, participants' private lives, and so on – and about the kinds of language that can be used: nothing 'offensive'. But no matter what the topic and how it is discussed, there is no absolute requirement that you must participate in every part of the discussion. Many things can be ignored or not taken up, and you will be regarded as rude and unsociable if you insist that everything be made explicit. *What do you think, John?* is a question not appropriate to every kind of interaction with John, in that it presupposes the existence of some special relationship between the speaker and John in which John can be asked, or even forced, to express an opinion. We prefer to volunteer opinions, not to have them forced out of us. John may have nothing to say on the topic.

A potential topic can be dropped for any one of a variety of reasons. It may be taboo: *We don't talk about such things.* Or it may quickly be seen to exclude too many participants in the group in which it arises: technical and 'shop' talk are common examples. It may be regarded as too likely to lead to one person holding the floor. Or it may be too sensitive in the particular circumstances in which it is raised: you want neither to embarrass yourself nor to be the cause of another's embarrassment. But a potential topic may also be dismissed because it does not seem to offer the participants much chance to do anything with it – it is exhausted almost as soon as it is mentioned.

Since topics are not well defined, it is possible to drift from topic to topic and to restructure a topic at any point. Speakers can suddenly turn serious or become light-hearted, drop the subject, or give some signal, for instance, silence, that a change of topic is called for. But a new topic may not readily appear, even in circumstances which demand one, for example, at a small dinner party when there is a pause in conversation. Two or more topics may actually compete for a while, but in the normal course of events a single topic will provide a focus for the participants and work itself out in the course of conversation. As we have mentioned, it may not be possible to say what the topic actually was at a particular time until after it has been dropped in favour of some other topic. It may even be difficult to define it precisely in retrospect, for each participant may have quite a different view from any other concerning what was actually talked about.

Once a topic is successfully launched and you want to make a contribution, you must find an opportunity to speak. Sometimes that opportunity may occur just a little earlier than you expected. In such circumstances getting started on what you see as your contribution may require you to seek a moment or two to gather your thoughts. It becomes necessary for you to buy time and, as we would expect, there are numerous expressions you can fall back on to provide you with the time you need: *Well, Well, where should I begin?, Well, it's like this, Let's see now, How shall I put it?, That's a good question [observation, point, etc.], I'll have to think about that.* These expressions tell your listeners that you intend to say something relative to the point at hand, but that you need a few moments to gather your thoughts: you also intend to take some care in phrasing the remarks that you will make.

Once you have acquired the right to speak, your next problem may be that of keeping the floor. You do not want to be interrupted. There are numerous linking devices available to help you mark out what you might want to say into sequences that will discourage others from breaking in. Giving an appropriate example is a one way of keeping your listener's attention and reinforcing a point: a simple *For example* or *For instance* can suffice, as can *One example is . . .* or *To give you an example [idea].* Some more discussion may follow the use of *Take X, for example* since this is likely to produce one or more illustrations of a point, each of which might lead to others' wanting to say something. You can also chain statements together: simple links like *Also, Besides, Concerning [Regarding] X, You can [I might] add, What's more, In that respect* are very helpful, as are more complicated ones such as *When it comes to X, In a case like that,* and *Seeing that.* If the continuation requires a questioning of what has gone before, this may be signalled in expressions like *But then again, But the real point [issue, question, problem] is . . .* and *That raises an issue [problem].*

A word of caution is called for. You must not attempt to dominate a conversation by never letting anyone else get a word in. You should not over-use linking devices so that you slide too easily from point to point, avoid interruption, and deny others natural opportunities for response. Constantly to do so will eventually lead you to violate the cooperative principle that conversations exist for the benefit of *all* participants. Once you cease entertaining others you will become a bore. They may even regard you less as a conversationalist than as an entertaining fool. A witty monologue is not a piece of conversation – it is a piece of theatre.

If a topic has taken the form of a story or some kind of account, you may try to end it clearly so that others can either add to it or change the direction of the conversation. There are several clichéd ways of providing suitable endings: *So it goes, That's life, I suppose, Win some, lose some, We'll wait and see, Something will turn up.* Some of these are available to both the listener and the speaker, particularly *I suppose it's all for the best* and *It makes you think,* and an expression like *What a shame!* from the listener can have the same end-marking function. One characteristic all of these have is their 'sympathy marking', a good indication of either a plea for, or the actual expression of, the cooperativeness of empathy.

Changing topics in a conversation is no easy matter. There may be a period, generally at or near the beginning of a conversation, when various topics get broached with the purpose of developing one that seems to meet everyone's requirements. Once that topic gets established any further topic must compete with it. Of course, on occasion that competition may not be too severe, for everyone may recognize that the current topic is close to being exhausted, since talk has become desultory and a shift appears necessary. At such a time, a remark like *By the way, That reminds me of, Speaking about,* or *Incidentally* may easily lead to a complete change of topic. This kind of remark will be much less successful in bringing about a change if everyone is still actively engaged with the current topic. In such circumstances it will appear to be an interruption and get little or no encouraging response; it will be perceived as an attempt to abrogate the group's rights to continue with its current business, and therefore as a form of uncooperative behaviour.

Sometimes it happens that when one topic is exhausted, several potential topics will compete until one of them prevails. In the hunt for a new topic, you might try to revert to a previous one (*As I was saying earlier*) or use some aspect of a current topic to side-step into a new one (*Speaking of X*). It may also be somewhat easier for the person who introduced the current dying topic to switch to a new one than for someone else to do so. A too early proposal by you to switch away from Sally's topic to a brand-new one of your choice may offend not just Sally. The other participants might think that she is being short-changed – and they themselves, too, if they have not had a 'fair' opportunity to contribute. Of course, coming from Sally herself, a proposal to change topic might be quite acceptable, unless, of course, some participants still feel that there is more to say on the original topic and that Sally should not deny them the opportunity to make a contribution. Sally might be regarded as trying to control not just the topic of conversation but the conversationalists too. In certain circumstances she will get away with this kind of behaviour – if she is a 'queen' and the others are her 'courtiers' – but in others she may find herself gradually ostracized, being perceived as selfish or self-centred.

What can you do if you find yourself in a conversation in which the topic is of little interest to you? You may have nothing to say on the subject or you find it boring, trivial, nasty, and so on. You can always try to change it. But you must exercise great care in doing so. You can meet considerable resistance if you proceed too boldly – for example, if you try to introduce a new topic before the old one is exhausted. A new topic has to survive; there has to be some measure of agreement that it should be allowed to develop; so it should not be prematurely born. Of course, if you have some special position in the group, you may get your way regardless of how the others actually feel about abandoning a 'good' topic to take up the one you have introduced. Your topic may still have a tough time surviving and, should you be forced to leave the group, its members may heave a collective sigh of relief and pick up the old topic again. Of course, if you have little or no status within the group, it is unlikely that your attempt to capture the group's interest in your proposed topic will be successful so long as the old topic is still nowhere near being exhausted. Your behaviour may even appear to be rude, as you are perceived to be trying to force your will – and what right have you to do so? – on others.

A brute-force attempt to change topic can often safely be ignored. Deliberately not acknowledging something in the environment is a common social practice. Not everything is public; certain activities are private, not to be noticed officially. It is much the same in conversation. We can treat an attempt to break into a conversation or to change a topic as a private intrusion into a public activity; we can pretend it never occurred. We disregard certain other linguistic behaviours in the same way: someone's losing himself or herself in the middle of a sentence; certain kinds of small interruptions; mutterings we care not to hear; insulting behaviour or language we prefer not to confront. So long as these are not acknowledged, they can be treated as though they had not occurred. We can try to do the same with a brute-force attempt to change topic against the wishes of the majority of the participants: we can just ignore the attempt, hoping it will go away.

If, for some reason, a topic does get changed without being exhausted – that is, some participants feel there is still much that should be said – an attempt may be made to revive it after a digression, interruption, or change. Either the inter-rupter or some other participant may try to get the convers-ation back on track. Possible ways of doing this include the use of expressions such as *Anyway, Where was I?/were we?*, *To get [going] back to X*, and *As I [X] was saying*. In some instances, even though the old topic was not exhausted, the new topic may have completely superseded it and the attempt to revert will fail. Or it will lead to no more than a brief agreement to make a few more remarks on the original topic before everyone comes back to what is now recognized as a more interesting topic, the new one.

As previously indicated, one way of providing a topic change without appearing to force it is by pretending that the new topic is somehow related to the old: *Oh! that reminds me of X* or *Speaking of X*. Such expressions act as bridges to possible new topics. One of these may become established if most parties to the conversation are happy to abandon the old topic in its favour. Often topics brought up in this manner are completely unrelated to the old one, but the device serves the speaker's pretence that conversation is an orderly, cooperative endeavour. When a proposed new topic is not taken up, we can assume either that the members of the group are not yet ready to abandon the old topic or that they find the new topic somehow uncongenial to their interests.

A topic change may affect the composition of the group. For example, at parties and similar gatherings a topic change can lead to group restructuring: if you do not care for the new topic, you can often remove yourself with a quiet *Excuse me!* The group can be left to get on with the topic without you. A similar move after the topic is well launched requires a more considerable leave-taking. You must avoid appearing to abandon the group in the middle of the collective activity of discussing a certain topic. Consequently, topic-changing and leave-taking can be mutually reinforcing activities.

Some speakers have the ability – not necessarily one that others care for – of being able to deal with almost any topic in such a way that they bring it back to some pet topic of their own. In effect, what they have is a single topic which they try to insist on making everyone else address in some way. Their favourite topic may be sex, politics, economics, religion – it really does not matter. What does matter is that it provides them with a framework for participating in any conversation, no matter what the topic: *Well, it all comes back to X, If you look at it from the point of view of X*, and so on. Such monomania is not unusual, but it quickly stops effective communication. Communication occurs when someone says something that is unpredictable; when you know exactly what he or she is going to say, you are no wiser after the event than before.

One other method of topic selection involves pre-planning. Groups of people meeting for specific purposes usually have their topics pre-assigned through the setting of agendas. But individuals too often have private agendas which lead them to attempt to see that certain topics come up in a conversation. Although a meeting called for a specific purpose is likely to have a pre-arranged agenda of some kind, many of the participants will probably have their own ideas that they want to present. Less formal conversations may also have their agendas. The difference is that on such occasions the agendas are not clearly fixed in advance and the purposes that motivate the participants may be less specific. Possibly the agenda will not reveal itself until after the conversation is finished and the participants have had time to consider what actually happened. What happened, of course, will, in large part, have been determined by what the participants brought with them to their encounter. We might question the use of the word 'agenda' in such circumstances. If an agenda is an explicit programme of activities worked out in advance, then the choice of the term is not defensible. If, on the other hand, we can legitimately use 'agenda' to refer to any kind of process that is unavoidable then its use becomes quite appropriate.

Group talk is difficult to manage unless there is a pattern to which everyone is willing to subscribe in advance. A formal meeting will have a chairperson, an agenda, and rules of procedure. A ceremonial ritual will have its rigid prescriptions concerning who can say what and when. A seminar will have its own structure. And many informal groups will have acknowledged leaders and recognized topics. Even that well known phenomenon the cocktail party will have its ritualistic sub-groupings, its 'safe' topics, and its system for ensuring a proper beginning, middle, and end. But a random group of people brought together by accident may have a real problem in getting any kind of conversation going. At best, individuals may talk to one another, but general talk directed to a common end will be unlikely. We can appreciate how that can happen if we remember the converse: how easily and quickly a poorly organized meeting can break down into a set of conversations between pairs, with the resulting constant calls for 'order'.

Most conversations are orderly affairs and not very exciting at all. But there is something remarkable about that orderliness. How is it achieved? For example, speakers must know and subscribe to a set of principles which governs turn-taking in conversation. Who gets to speak and when? Some events proscribe speaking except by certain individuals, and often they must speak in fixed formulaic utterances: royal weddings and other important public occasions are good examples. Others have an officially appointed dispenser of opportunities to speak: meetings presided over by a chairperson, or by a Speaker in some parliamentary systems. Most events, less formally organized than these, use subtle signals either to allow someone to speak or to make it difficult to do so. A look of encouragement may contrast strongly with the pointed ignoring of one or more individuals. Not everyone in a group has the same rights to speak as everyone else, but just how these rights are recognized and exercised may not always be very clear either to a trained observer or to the participants themselves.

The most general principle governing turn-taking in a conversation is that one and only one person speaks at a time. There may be overlaps and brief interruptions, to be sure, but it is generally quite clear which speaker has the floor at any particular moment. Moreover, that speaker usually gives up the floor voluntarily, that is, he or she willingly hands over the turn to someone else. And just as only one person speaks at a time, so someone speaks at all times. Conversationalists abhor silence; consequently, pauses are usually kept very short and speaker follows speaker in rapid succession. Long pauses are treated almost as embarrassments: they are regarded as indicators of failure, and all participants experience that failure. When we encounter cultural groups which do not require their members to make conversation the way we make it and actually seem to encourage silence, we may find it awkward to be with them. And they, for their part, must wonder why it is we have to talk so much and so inconsequentially.

Having taken a turn in conversation, you can signal that you are coming to the end of what you want to say by using any one of a variety of devices. You can draw out the last syllable or two of what you are saying by pronouncing them extra-slowly and exaggerating the final associated pitch change. Such a signal indicates completion, and someone else can take up the topic. Or you can deliberately pause after you have said something, but without providing any additional change in tempo or pitch. Pauses in conversation tend to get filled. You can attempt to fill the pause yourself – by a *Well!* or some such expression – but others too can use the opportunity that the pause creates either to pick up the topic or to attempt to change it. Some kind of gesture or body movement, for instance, a noticeable relaxation, may also accompany the pause you have created and indicate that you are willing to let another talk. Somewhat more unusually, you can phrase what you are saying grammatically and rhetorically so that it says 'I'm finished': however, that kind of technique is a rather formal one and its use is usually restricted to very narrow sets of circumstances.

You can also indicate your desire to take a turn at speaking in a number of ways. Someone who is about to take a turn in conversation tends to increase bodily tension and make certain body movements which draw the attention of others. A noticeable intake of breath is also a clear signal not only that speaking is about to begin but that it is likely to continue for some time. When the speaking actually does begin, it is likely to be a little louder than normal, as an attention-holding device. And as we saw earlier, in order to make interruption less likely, a person taking up a turn will very possibly avert his or her gaze from the other participants for a few moments. In this way the new speaker can resist possible challenges to his or her right to speak by simply not seeing them.

Sometimes a change of turn is deliberately synchronized by the two parties. One party gives up the turn as he or she begins some other activity, for example eating, drinking, or smoking. The second party is then free to begin. In some circumstances the turn point may not suit the one who is to begin, but some signal is required that the turn has indeed changed. A *Just a moment* or *Let me finish* will hold the turn if some other activity has to be terminated (reading, eating, doing some chore) before the turn can be taken up. Very rarely will the silence that is created at the change point be left unfilled – even a tiny gesture can serve to acknowledge that the turn will be taken up.

Once you have acquired the turn to speak you have a strong right to continue speaking until you voluntarily give up the turn. You can give it up either by indicating who you are passing it to or by ending what you are saying and allowing the next speaker to select himself or herself. Once you have been given a turn there are many ways of keeping it. You can organize what you want to say to prevent inter-ruption. For example, you can indicate that you are making a series of remarks: *First of all* or *To begin with*, followed by *Then, After that, Next, Second*, and so on. Expressions such as *Another thing* and connectors like *So, Because, Moreover, Con-sequently*, and *However* promote continuity. And, of course, in the same way it is possible to signal a deliberate coming to an end: *Finally, This shows [means, suggests], All in all, When you think about what I've said*, and so on. In other words, you can do much to keep the floor if you are able to control those logical, chronological, and grammatical devices which make a series of utterances a cohesive and coherent account rather than a jumble of thoughts and impressions. But you must always remember that you are participating in a group activ-ity. You cannot have the floor for ever, as it were. Conse-quently, there are severe limits to your use of such devices, and you must be conscious at all times as to how your audience is reacting. Does the feedback they are providing you with show that they are bored and inattentive? If it does, possibly you should hand over the turn very quickly and not seek to get it back too soon. Once again we can see how cooperation is the essential ingredient in any successful con-versation.

However, not all conversations proceed smoothly, effort-lessly, and cooperatively. Sometimes it is necessary to inter-rupt what someone is saying and be uncooperative. Any kind of interruption is a violation of another's territory or rights.

One very obvious kind is knocking on someone's door, even when you have been invited to do so. You still need techniques and resources to get you safely across the threshold and into the house. Asking for help or directions of strangers is also to interrupt their activity. In such circumstances you must reassure the other person immediately that your interruption is to be brief by stating its limited purpose. Breaking someone's routine is also an interruption. In this case, too, you must recognize that you have a 'repair' to make; consequently, the janitor or cleaning person you interrupt as you pass merits an acknowledgement. Occasionally, certain interruptions, real or potential, must be completely ignored; this is particularly true of ritualistic and ceremonial events which must either go on, refusing, as it were, to be interrupted or, if interrupted, begin again at the point of interruption as though nothing untoward had happened. We can also distinguish between interruptions designed to break up conversations and interruptions designed to break into conversations.

One kind of interruption for which you need not feel apologetic is that designed to seek clarification concerning something that is being said. Such behaviour is, after all, cooperative: you are trying to help the speaker communicate what he or she wants to get across to you to the extent that you are willing to point out where the attempt is failing. In listening to someone tell you something, particularly if it is rather complicated, you may find yourself confused or lost. If you are not really interested, it may not matter and you may even prefer to daydream and let your attention wander. But then again you may sincerely want to understand what the other is saying: to have an obscure point clarified or an apparent (or real) inconsistency resolved, or to have repeated a remark masked by some extraneous circumstance (a noise, for example, or a moment's inattention). So you must be prepared to break in and request a repetition or a clarification. An *Excuse me!*, *Pardon me!*, or *I beg your pardon!* will allow you to interrupt the speaker, but, once having stopped him or her in this way, you must explain why you did so. *Did I hear you say X?, Do you mind repeating X?, What did you say?, Would you say that again?, Would you repeat what you've just said?, Sorry, I missed that [what you just said], You've lost me!, I didn't catch that, I think you've lost me*, and expressions of this kind will indicate that your motive is one of clarification. The speaker can then simply clear up the confusion and proceed. You have made no attempt to take over the turn or sabotage the account. Of course, if you repeatedly use the same tactic, the speaker may well suspect your motive to be other than that of simply seeking clarification.

Interrupting for the sake of correcting – as opposed to seeking clarification – is a much more delicate matter. Self-correction is always permissible, but too much is likely to reduce your credibility with your listeners. Correcting others, however, is risky in another way: it directly questions an underlying assumption of conversation – that everybody is telling the truth or at least presenting his or her best version of it. The person interrupted with a correction may therefore regard it as a kind of challenge, and, if the correction is a lengthy one, as when one person breaks into another's account to present a very different version of some incident, that challenge is doubly threatening, seeming to question both the speaker's veracity and his or her very right to speak.

Some interruptions *are* challenges. You hear something with which you sharply disagree or you consider that the speaker is badly misinformed. One option you have is to hear the speaker out and, at some later point, attempt to rebut or to clarify the misconception. But that may be asking too much of yourself, particularly if you also want the floor. So you interrupt: *[Just] wait a minute!, Hold on!, That's not right, I don't agree*, or *You've got that wrong [mixed up, confused]*. You deny or reject some point that the speaker made. Such remarks will be regarded as challenges, for you are calling into question the veracity or sincerity of the speaker or the quality of his information. You have also chosen not to wait to see if the speaker will later in some way qualify or other-wise justify the remarks to which you take exception. The likely consequence of this kind of interruption is that the speaker will be silenced. However, he will be rather unhappy about being cut short and/or corrected, and it is not unlikely that some kind of dispute will occur over the point or points at issue. Of course, you may yourself be rebuffed–ignored, drowned out, or squelched – because your move can be rejected by a speaker who insists on holding the floor. The momentum is his if he is prepared to use it to overcome what he may regard not as an interruption but as a potential interruption. He can say *Let me finish* and go on. You must be rather rude if you insist that the speaker cannot be allowed to finish if he wants to.

If you are the one who appears to be in danger of being interrupted, the most effective signal that you do not wish to be interrupted is almost always a gesture of the hand. Your raising of the hand to either a potential interrupter or an actual interrupter clearly signals that you do not recognize the interruption and that you want to continue speaking. You can also use your hand – or both hands if necessary – to support remarks intended to override problems or objections. Used too often, however, hand gestures of this kind are likely to lead to the impression that you are a bore, unfeeling, dogmatic, or even dictatorial, for what they do is turn conversations into declamations. You will suppress the contributions from others that are necessary if there is to be genuine communication.

You can also reduce the probability of being interrupted by attempting to structure what you say in such a way that you allocate a certain amount of time or a certain progression to the remarks you intend to make: *I just have a few comments, There are three points I want to make, I have a couple of observations about that*, and so on. Remarks such as these indicate the extent of the material that you want to communicate and warn others that they will not be cooperating with you if they try to cut you short. You can also attempt to keep the floor by chaining your utterances, using words such as *and, but, however*, and *consequently* in an attempt to add further remarks to ones already made. This device, however, is available to others. They may attempt to use these same words to complete what you are saying and effectively inter-rupt you by continuing to speak after the 'completion'.

Interruptions can always be resisted. Raising the voice to drown out another is often effective. It is really quite difficult to stop someone who insists on talking, particularly if that person can manage to string clauses together in an apparently seamless process or if he or she is facile enough to avoid hesitations of any kind. Even the type of sentence used can help: a speaker can deliberately compound clauses and choose periodic rather than loose sentences – sentences in which the so-called main idea clause is led up to gradually rather than introduced first and then embroidered with subordinate mat-ters. Once having gained your turn to speak, you really can exercise a lot of control over the direction that a conversation will take, and you do not have to give up your turn until you are ready to do so.

As we have indicated, one way of interrupting and taking over a turn which is less offensive than attempting to drown out the speaker is by trying to complete something he is saying. For example, you can finish the sentence he is saying and try to use that opportunity to lead straight into a sentence of your own, thus achieving a certain continuity of topic but a discontinuity of speakers. If you cannot actually complete the sentence, you can use the opportunity the end of the sentence provides to add a further comment on the same topic or just simply to rephrase what the speaker said. The tactic in both these cases is to soften your interruption by just, as it were, changing voices, substituting yours for the other's. Employed too often, of course, this tactic can lead a user into trouble: the others will soon come to resent your taking over their turns and you will therefore kill genuine conversation when they withdraw their cooperation.

If someone does succeed in interrupting you, this does not mean that you must completely abandon your turn. You may, of course, just defer completely to the interrupter and make no attempt to insist that you be given an opportunity to complete your turn. But if you are unwilling to give up you will be seen to have certain rights to continue, and such rights are likely to be recognized if you insist on exercising them. Refusing you your rights will be regarded as rude behaviour: you have been cut off in the middle of speaking, and a refusal to recognize this is a strong violation of that basic cooperative principle that appears to govern behaviour in conversation.

It is possible, therefore, to distinguish between an interruption that completely changes a topic and one that merely puts it on hold for a brief period. The latter variety results in some kind of secondary conversation, sometimes referred to as a 'side sequence'. The expectation is that the original topic will be resumed at some time and that the original speaker will have the floor returned to him. Often we signal this kind of interruption with a remark such as *By the·way*, or by a brief request to the speaker for clarification of a point, or through the interjection of a comment or observation on what was said. What is important is that all parties understand the expression for what it is: a momentary move away from the topic, to be followed by a resumption of the original flow of conversation once the particular point at issue has been dealt with. If the original topic is abandoned, then we no longer have a side sequence but a complete interruption and, therefore, a qualitatively different kind of conversational event.

A typical side sequence is the following one in which B's response to A's opening question is made to depend on an item which B wants clarified:

A. Are you going to walk Rufus?
B. Did the bloke come about the TV yet?
A. No.
B. He'll have to wait then.

The *he* in B's second utterance refers back to the dog in A's first utterance; the BA sequence is the side sequence. Another variant of this total sequence occurred in a shop:

A. Can I have a mirror like that one?
B. Let me see if we have any in stock.
A. OK.

. . . . . .

B. Yes, I do have one.
A. Good.

You can also 'frame' a genuine side sequence in any one of a variety of ways. You can change your voice characteristics to make an aside. You can use an expression like *Excuse me, please!* if you must answer the telephone while conversing. The original topic can then be taken up after the interruption by a shift to your original voice or by the use of such an expression as *Now where were we?* Framing acknowledges that a break has occurred but that the original topic is not thereby abandoned: it is just momentarily set aside as some issue – either a minor one related to the topic or an extraneous one – is dealt with. Then you can go back to where you were almost as though nothing had happened in the meantime.

The grossest kind of interruption to a conversation is, of course, ending it. Bringing it to an end is just as much an art as initiating speech with another person or interrupting successfully. People do not end conversations arbitrarily. They do not just stop talking and turn away from one another abruptly and without explanation. If they are ever forced to do so – for example, because of an interruption – when the conversation is resumed, one will usually apologize to the other or others for the disruption. A telephone call interrupted through an accidental disconnection will resume either with an outright apology (*Sorry, I cut us off by mistake*) or some other explanation (*Somebody cut us off*). When we seek to close a conversation, we must serve notice that we are rapidly approaching the ultimate cut-off which silence brings, but we often pretend that we are reluctant to cease. We want to leave the other with the impression that there is nothing we would rather do than continue what we are doing; however, some exterior condition or event stands in the way: *Well, back to work, I must be going, Sorry!* [*Please excuse me!*] *but, I'd better let you go,* or *I've got to go/run/do X.* Alternatively, we may offer some kind of compliment which acts as a comment on the whole conversation and at the same time marks it as a completed unit: *It's been nice [good] talking to you*. Such a comment indicates that the speaker regards it as time to move on to some new activity because the current one has apparently fulfilled whatever purpose it had – and quite successfully.

You can signal that you intend to bring a conversation to a close in any number of different ways. Diminished eye contact with the speaker can be used to show that you would really prefer to be doing something else. Likewise, a dramatic shift in your posture can signal a new, and different, interest. A glance at a clock or watch is also an effective signal: it indicates that you believe it is time to move on to something else. You can deliberately return to earlier topics that were mentioned and summarize them with words which indicate not only that you are summarizing but also that you are concluding whatever it is you and your listener were doing. Still more deliberate movements and gestures are possible. You can change your position quite drastically – for instance, stand up. You can determinedly put papers away, or you may even use certain dismissal formulas, either dismissing yourself (*I'm sorry but I have to go*, *My next appointment is waiting*) or the other (*You should get back to work*, *Come back this afternoon and we will talk again*). What is important is that all parties recognize the closing behaviour for what it is and agree to it so that, after perhaps a ritualistic exchange of *Goodbyes*, they find that they have negotiated themselves successfully back to silence.

Closing a conversation is a cooperative activity. If one party wants to close and insists on doing so when the other does not, the second party may feel he or she was either shut up or shut out, since the closing was imposed and not negotiated. On certain occasions it may be appropriate to behave this way: a superior may dismiss or abruptly abandon a subordinate. However, in normal conversation both parties are required to manoeuvre jointly toward a closing. They must agree that they have said all there was to say, that no further topics remain, and that they are willing to discontinue. Expressions such as *Well*, *OK*, and *So*, hesitations, references to some other activity, or certain movements and gestures can indicate that the parties are about to break off. Once a sub-routine of this kind is begun, any attempt to bring up an additional topic must be quite clearly signalled: *Oh, I forgot something*. But usually there is no such attempt and the conversation is brought to a conclusion with some form of ritual leave-taking.

Many kinds of expressions are used in pre-closing rituals just before the final *Goodbye*. *I'm sorry I have to go now*, *I mustn't keep you*, *Take care*, *It was nice meeting you*, *See you*, and *Give my regards to Fred* are just a few randomly chosen examples. If something occurs to you after another person has said one of these to you, you must clearly indicate that you are interrupting the closing routine: *Wait, I've just remembered something*, *Wow! it's just occurred to me*. A strong expression is called for to acknowledge the break in the parting routine and to indicate that you are aware that you have caused the interruption and that whatever you are going to introduce as new material is important. But, if you have nothing new to introduce, you can be content with an *OK*, *All right*, a nod of the head, a repositioning of your body, some fixed expression (*Well, I'll be off*), an excuse (*I must go* or *I have to do X*), and so on. These confirm that you agree to the ending. All that is necessary now is for each party to use a *Goodbye* (or some equivalent), and the conversation will be brought to a mutually satisfying end.

You can actually start preparing for a closing quite a long way in advance of the actual moment. You can, for example, near the very beginning of a conversation introduce certain conditions which will govern when you will close. You can warn the other person that you are busy, or that you have only a moment to spare, or that you must leave shortly, or of some other limitation. You can then, at a convenient point, use this kind of information to bring the conversation to an end. It is particularly necessary to relay such information early in any encounter in which the other party has no reason to believe that there will be a premature leave-taking. For example, dinner guests who must leave earlier than normally might be expected will usually warn their host that they must leave early – and provide a reason – very soon after their arrival. A premature parting without such an early warning will almost certainly embarrass the host, and any excuse profferred at the time of leaving will be treated, privately at least, with some degree of scepticism.

One kind of conversation you may find difficult to close is one that you have chosen to get into but, after entering, find quite uninteresting. You may be bored, out of your depth, or insulted, or you may just want to leave and join another group of people, for example, at a party. How do you remove yourself from the conversation? An abrupt leave-taking may work if the group is large, but the smaller the group the more difficult that is, and, if there is only one other, such a remedy is, of course, impossible. Having entered a conversation, you have to stay some minimal time in it. Otherwise, you will appear to be rude and inconsiderate. What is sometimes amusing is to see two people engaged in a conversation because neither feels comfortable in breaking it off, but each is obviously looking for an excuse to do so. The desultory language, the postures, the eyes wandering around the room, all indicate that only the observation of a politeness convention – keep the conversation going some minimal time – holds the two together. A conversation can be so fragile!

It can be extremely difficult for you to close a conversation if the other party is unwilling, or unable, to do so. In the absence of mutual agreement you may feel rude and ill-mannered if you must force a closing, even when you are apparently left with no other choice. It is difficult to stop someone who refuses to adopt any kind of pre-closing routine or who insists on bringing up new topics (*Oh, by the way*). Your only recourse is to an excuse (*I have to run, I think I hear the phone*, and so on) or to some other abrupt behaviour which unambiguously signals your desire or need to bring the conversation to an end. Sometimes only physical removal from the presence of the other succeeds; sharing an office with a constant chatterer can be a most disturbing experience if you need peace and quiet to get on with your work.

If the person with whom you are in conversation refuses to close and ignores all of your pre-closing manoeuvres, you have a problem. Such behaviour almost requires you to be rude, for, if all your signals that you wish to close are ignored, you are really left with very few choices. One is to tell the other person that the conversation is at an end; you can then try to ignore what is said and hope that he will desist. Another is to put some distance between the two of you, physically removing yourself or the other. We realize how difficult this breaking off can be when we recognize how dramatic a gesture is hanging up on someone on the telephone. The same effect is much more difficult to achieve in a face-to-face encounter. And when it is not one person but a large group who refuse to end a 'conversation', for example, a stormy protest meeting, a demonstration, or a sit-in, there is likely to be a strong physical (over-)reaction to what is happening. You are likely to feel disturbed and frustrated if you cannot close, and no less disturbed if you must force a closing. It is a no-win situation for most of us, unless you are the kind who enjoys being nasty to others. It is so unsatisfactory because it signals a clear failure in cooperation.

Further Reading

There has been an extensive discussion of turn-taking in conversation; see particularly Duncan's 'Some Signals and Rules for Taking Speaking Turns in Conversation', 'Toward a Grammar for Dyadic Conversation', and 'On the Structure of Speaker-Auditor Interaction during Speaking Turns', Edelsky's 'Who's Got the Floor?', McHoul's 'The Organization of Turns at Formal Talk in the Classroom', and Sacks, Schegloff, and Jefferson's 'A Simplest Systematics for the Organization of Turn-taking in Conversation'.

Jefferson's 'Side Sequences' is the basic paper on that topic

and Schegloff and Sacks' 'Opening up Closings' is an attempt
to describe how conversations are brought to an end. See also
Clark and French's 'Telephone *Goodbyes*'.

8

Requesting, Informing, Advising, Agreeing, Apologizing, Promising

As we have seen, conversation involves much more than just talking about this and that. It involves us in doing things, in getting others to do things, in eliciting information, in refusals, apologies, promises, and threats, and in a whole list of other activities. Conversation is not just talking; it is also doing. But to appreciate that doing we must be tuned in to the intent of others; we must learn to respond not just to the content of the words. Language offers us a wide range of options: we must learn to use them.

If we examine the apparently simple matter of making requests of others, we rather quickly discover that it is not so simple after all. A request can take any one of a wide variety of linguistic forms, in addition to the standard imperative form: *Stand up!* All the following are requests to do X: *Have you done X?*, *When do you plan to do X?*, *Are you planning to do X?*, *Can you do X?*, *Would you mind doing X?*, and *Shouldn't you do X?* Each is syntactically a question, but if we assume that X has not been done and should be done, that the speaker has some right to see that X is done, and the listener has some duty to do X, then we have a situation in which the question must be interpreted as a request to do X. A statement can perform the same function: *You haven't done X yet, I suppose you are going to do X, X hasn't been done, I shouldn't have to remind you to do X.* Bald request forms (*Do X!*) are generally avoided, particularly between near equals, but even some of the above forms may be too 'strong' for most relationships. One of the first principles you must observe in making a request is that, if you want somebody to do something, you have to be careful about how you go about specifying to that person that it can be done.

We can make requests, that is, we can get others to do things or not to do them, in a variety of ways so far as grammatical devices are concerned. Imperatives, full or abbreviated, are one way: *Give me a pencil!*, *Coffee, please!* We can dress up a request in question form: *Would you hand me that book?*, *Could you get me a doughnut?*, *Do you have the time?*, and *Aren't you going to tell me?* We can even make ourselves the subject of the question: *Can I have the light on?*, or *May I borrow this book?* We can state a simple need: *I need a pen*, *I want an answer*, and *I'll have a coke*. We can ask certain questions in special circumstances: (on the telephone) *Is John there?*; (as a teacher) *Do I hear talking?* Or we can simply make a comment: *My glass is empty*, *You are standing in my way*, *I'm tired*, *My bag is in the car*, *I don't see the salt*, *I wish you'd stop*, or *I don't think you should tell him*. If your intent is clear, that is, the right combination of circumstances prevails, each of the above will be taken by your listener as a request to do (or not to do) something. What is particularly important, of course, in understanding what is said as a request is recognizing the 'right combination of circumstances'. If your listener recognizes what is said as a request, he is obliged to respond appropriately. It is not enough for him to answer the question *Yes* or *No* or to acknowledge the statement. These may be necessary responses, but they are not sufficient ones; a sufficient response requires either the listener's compliance with, or rejection of, the request that you have made.

We can appreciate the tremendous range of possibilities open to us in making requests if we concern ourselves with one simple request situation: asking the time. Among the many possibilities that exist are the following:

Do you have the time?
Do you know what time it is?
Can/Could/you tell me the time?
I wonder what time it is!

You don't have the time, do you?
What time is it [please]?
Do you have/Got/any idea what time it is?
I wonder how we are doing for time.
Anybody have the time?
It must be getting late!
Do you have a watch?
Is it two o'clock yet?
It must be time to go.

What we see here are grammatical devices of various kinds and a range of strategies designed to indicate to the listener that the speaker would like to know the time. Each example conveys something different; each will get the desired response – an indication of the time if the listener has that information – and leave behind a certain impression about how the speaker goes about making requests.

Only a very few bald requests or commands are quite acceptable. Warnings like *Watch out!* and invitations like *Come in!* are good examples, as are expressions such as *Have a good time*, *Write*, *Take care*, and *Do send us a postcard*. But these are somewhat limited in use, concern very few topics, and demonstrate a strong interest in the hearer's welfare. They are quite clearly 'marked' by the circumstances in which they are used, and they impose little or no obligation on either party. In general, though, direct requests (*Stand up*, *Close the door*) are even more restricted in their use than plain questions (*Are you ready?*, *Are you going or not?*, *Why did you say that?*). They are quite 'naked'; therefore they are quite useful in emergencies (*Don't move!*) or when there is an unambiguous power relationship (*Turn to page nine*). However, life itself is inherently ambiguous and power is usually concealed to a considerable extent. So, much more common are indirect requests (*I wonder if you could write to him*) and indirect questions (*Could you tell me what you would like?*). Even statements may find themselves modified in this way (*You know, I was just thinking that it's about time that . . .*).

Making a bald request is generally too direct a way for you

to achieve what you want. Such a request allows for only two possibilities: compliance or refusal. It takes away from your listener a certain room to manoeuvre and does not allow him or her to indicate either that the request is inappropriate or that it cannot be responded to so simply. Consequently, most requests are likely to be more delicately phrased and to allow in their phrasing for the possibility that an answer might not be so readily forthcoming. They may also allow for some other answer than a simple *Yes* or *No* or for a precise item of information. Hence, requests are given such introductions as *Could you tell me?*, *Do you happen to know?*, *Would you know?*, *You don't happen to know?*, and *Do you have any idea?* Suitable answers to such requests can take any one of a multiplicity of forms because of the way the requests are hedged. They do not put the listener directly on the spot; he can, if he chooses, comply with or refuse the request, but he can also deal with any one of the other possibilities that the form of the request opens up to him. If someone says to you *Are you by any chance going to be in your office this afternoon?*, you will undoubtedly hear this as the lead-up to some kind of request, say, to meet you or call you. If you say *Yes*, then you can be sure details will be forthcoming. You can also hardly say *No* by itself if you are not going to be there or wish to discourage the other person, but must add some explanation if you are to appear to be as polite as the other. Note that *No* and even *Sorry* are also entirely inappropriate responses to the following request: *Excuse me, could you possibly move your car forward a couple of feet so I can get mine out of here?* whereas one or the other response might be appropriate to *Going up?* said on the arrival of a lift, or *Got a pencil?*

Whereas a simple request making little or no demand of the listener can be baldly put, a request that makes large demands requires considerably more elaboration. You must do a greater amount of preparatory work and allow for possible refusal. If your request is one that well might be refused or that would impose substantial obligations on the listener, you must make it more delicately. It certainly should allow for refusal and it must recognize that each party – the one making the request *and* the one of whom the request is made – will need to retain face after a refusal. Requests of this kind are sometimes so delicate that third parties may not even be aware that they have been made.

The preparatory work might involve your commenting on some aspect of the listener's appearance, health, or dress, or of the relationship that exists between you. You may even phrase the actual request so as to make it appear to be a very minor concern: *What a nice dress you are wearing today, By the way, could you. . . ?* or *Excuse the interruption, but. . . .* Of course, this kind of lead-in behaviour can become quite long-winded as mitigating and qualifying statements pile up on one another. The listener may want the speaker to get on with it, to stop beating about the bush. While doing extensive preparatory work may be a tactic designed to save the face of both parties, it can sometimes also appear to be extremely manipulative. The lead-in is meant to make refusal that much easier, but excessive lead-in pressure may make it more difficult to refuse, particularly if categorical refusal is impossible and you are reluctant to indulge in a countervailing long-winded procedure of refusal.

You must be prepared to do the right quantity of preparatory work – and not only for requests. Invitations, offers, and other kinds of solicitations require similar work. The right amount of preparation will allow for non-compliance, if that is to be the response. Face will be saved by both parties. A request which is delicately put, politely refused, and gently acknowledged as being refused does no serious harm to a relationship. But a blunt order and an unequivocal refusal are likely to have very different consequences for the parties involved.

We can see how this mitigating lead-in behaviour works in other circumstances, too, in providing some kind of framework for a more direct utterance. For example, an invitation is likely to follow *What are you doing this weekend?* A question like *Have you heard the news?* leads into a story or account of some kind, and *I've got to get back to my books* can indicate a desire to close a conversation, or *I see it's seven* can mark the beginning or the end of a lecture. This kind of utterance serves notice that something is about to happen, and fairly clearly indicates what that something is in that it makes use of a convention that is known to both parties. It therefore becomes part of the later request, story, sequence, or whatever it may be, while at the same time both softening up the change that is required and allowing the other party to voice possible disapproval of or a reluctance to comply with whatever is apparently to occur.

A few requests do not seem to open up the possibility of refusal in most circumstances: *Will you pass the salt?* said at a dinner party is an example. Others like *Do you have the time?*, *Do you have a light?*, *Do you have change for a pound?*, or *Can you tell me how to get to Piccadilly Circus?* can hardly be refused, either, particularly if asked with a prefatory *Excuse me!* and a certain polite deference. You can refuse only if you do not know the time, you do not have a light, you are not carrying any change, and you are a stranger to London yourself. A refusal must also in such a case be accompanied by a brief explanation. A simple *No* would be quite inappropriate: it would be too brusque and impolite. So you have to say something like *Sorry, I don't wear a watch, I don't smoke*, and so on. And, of course, if you answer *Yes* it must be accompanied by the appropriate action. *Do you have the time?* followed by *Yes* with no offer to tell the time or indicate it in some overt manner would be a peculiar response, to say the least.

One way of avoiding the possibility that your request might be refused is by, as it were, seeking permission to make it in the first place. Then, if permission is denied, you do not have to make the actual request. When you ask for permission to make a request, the listener is required to address himself or herself to the issue of permission alone: *Can you do something for me?* or *Excuse me, do you have a moment?* What such a preamble does is attract the attention of the listener and at the same time elicit some signal of agreement that the request which is to follow can indeed be made. You attempt to set up a cooperative situation. Your opening remark can hardly be ignored, and the response is almost certain to be *Yes* or some affirmative gesture. At that point you can make your request in what now appears to be a somewhat cooperative environment. If, alternatively, your opening remark is rejected, then you need not make the request. Indeed, if you were to insist on doing so, you yourself would appear to be uncooperative: you asked for a signal but proceeded to ignore it. If you are granted permission to make the request, but the request is refused, you may want to question the actual refusal. You may· feel denied in some way: why were you allowed to make the request in the first place? You may have felt that the battle was already half won with the granting of permission to detail the request, so that the refusal may appear unjustified. And the refusal will also have to be lengthier than usual, because of the expectations that were probably aroused in the person making the request.

Requests that are mitigated and dressed up in such a way that they attempt to achieve their objectives without being offensively direct are more usual than the bald kind. Few of us are in a position to be able to order others around, and, if we ever did succeed to such a position, we would still find that to be a most unpopular tactic. *Do you have anything to add?*, *What can you say about X?*, *Can somebody tell me X?*, and *Who knows X?*, for example, are requests. Their grammatical form is that of a question, but the intent of each is quite clear: you are soliciting help or a response of some kind. The mitigation the question form provides is particularly useful when the one making the request is superordinate to the person or persons of whom the request is being made, for example, a teacher or a chairperson to a student or a very junior colleague. Power is best exercised subtly rather than overtly; you can then appear to offer others an element of choice. A more naked, but still somewhat mitigated, request is, of course, the teacher's *John, would you like to begin X?*

The two simplest mitigating expressions are the words *Please* and *Let's*. They are both indications of requests and serve to sweeten them. *Please* may go either at the beginning, the end, or somewhere in the middle of an utterance, but all three positions are not possible in all sentences. It can be found with statement, question, and request forms: *Please, I don't want you to do that, Please, can you get me some water?*, and *Please send me his address.* It may also sometimes be used to distinguish a simple statement from a request, for example, to distinguish *I'm ready* from *Please, I'm ready*, the latter appearing to be a request to someone to get on with something. We should note that *I'm ready, please* does not seem to mean anything at all; you cannot just sprinkle *please*s around in sentences. Requests beginning with *Let's* also have to be interpreted in context to find out whether their intent is to include the speaker in the proposed activity. *OK, let's go* probably does, but a nurse's *Let's take our medicine, Mr Jones* or a teacher's *Let's stop our talking and work for a while* undoubtedly are requests only for others to do or not to do something. Hence the ambiguity of an expression like *Let's not rush*: the person uttering the remark may have no desire to move at all or he or she may be willing to move – but only slowly.

We should note that in one way all questions are actually requests: they require responses. That response can be a simple *Yes* or *No* or an item of information. Sometimes it is a reason: questions prefaced with *Why* generally seek a reason. But *Why* questions may not simply be requests for a reason: they may also have a critical import. The listener may interpret *Why are you doing X?* not just as a question seeking a reason for X being done but as a statement that the speaker does not think the other party should be doing X. It is tantamount to a request to stop doing X. *Why not do X?* may be more, therefore, than a question seeking a reason for not doing X; it may be an actual request or suggestion that you do X. Some *Why* questions may also have a rhetorical import: *Why should I give it back to her?* or *Why do people behave like that?* With one couple, this type of question was used quite frequently, but she tagged the other's name to it: *Why do people behave like that, John?* She meant such questions rhetorically; he understood them as genuine requests for information and occasionally was irritated at being asked 'impossible' questions, particularly when she did not (naturally) listen to the replies he tried to offer. Once she learned to drop the *John* – she was not a native speaker of English, though a very good one – the confusion ended.

Once a statement is made to you or a request is made of you, you must react to it somehow. Certain difficulties lie in your way. It may not be easy to refuse a request, or even to signal attention rather than agreement when a statement is made for which the speaker is obviously seeking your approval. Sometimes the speaker, and onlookers too, may actually misjudge what is happening: the speaker may mistake a signal that you are conscientiously listening – nodding, interjected *Uh-huh*s – as an indication that you also fully approve what you are listening to. Lack of agreement, on the other hand – but not, of course, overt disagreement – you can signal by employing such expressions as *Maybe*, *Possibly*, and *Perhaps* to punctuate what you are listening to. They indicate that you are listening, but that you do have reservations. Responses such as *I'll have to think about that* or *We'll [Let's] wait and see* show a much more deliberate withholding of judgement and/or approval, but without indicating disagreement or refusal. Quite often you can use them to signal that you have rejected a request: the convenient fiction is that your response is to be delayed. A request responded to in this way is really a request refused, but refused in such a way that the person making it is able to preserve 'face'.

Turning down requests is a delicate matter. It is often difficult to utter a categorical *No*. Fortunately, quite often a request which is likely to meet with a refusal will be phrased in such a way that you can make the expected refusal gracefully. *You don't have £10 I can borrow, do you?* leads easily to *Sorry, I've got to go to the bank myself.* Occasionally a request is quite pointed and the speaker's expectation seems to be that you will comply; but if you do not intend to comply, you can find yourself in a very difficult situation. Saying *No* may be almost impossible, so you may find yourself either committed to doing something you do not want to do or leaving the other person with the impression that you have agreed. If you do refuse and actually say *No*, you will almost certainly feel obliged to provide a reason for your refusal. Categorical refusals without explanations are rare. In child–adult interaction they prompt children to ask *Why?* and adults to counter with *Because I said so*, which is really a most unsatisfactory state of affairs, being no more than the adults' assertion of power. Among adults a *No* is a clear sign of uncooperative behaviour, and adding reason to your refusal mitigates its uncooperativeness and alleviates to some extent any hurt that refusal might cause to the relationship: it serves as a kind of remedy or repair to the tear in the social fabric caused by the refusal.

As we have observed, questions are a form of request, a form that should be fairly easy to answer. One basic kind of question can be answered simply with *Yes* or *No* (*Are you ready?*), and another with a simple informational response (*Where are you going? Out*). If you are asked a question in a conversation, you can answer it and then the person who did the asking should be able to continue the conversation. But, in practice, matters are not so straightforward. Whereas a *Yes* to the first kind of question generally provides a perfectly adequate answer, a negative response seems to oblige you to provide some further clarification. Conversation is a cooperative undertaking, and your unadorned negative reply to a question asked of you is hardly cooperative. Generally, you must supplement your *No* with some kind of information to justify it. Alternatively, you can omit the negative and offer the explanation directly. On occasion you may want to respond to the second kind of question, the information question, with a question, if the assumptions that lie behind it seem unwarranted. You can do this with the first kind too. Questions are useful devices for eliciting information, but they assume, once again, that speakers and listeners are cooperating. In any case, it may be quite difficult to refuse to answer, to stonewall, or to lie in answering – at least consistently. There seems to be a general principle that those questioned have a strong obligation to provide answers that are full and truthful and to clear up any misconceptions the questioner might have. Law enforcement officers and various types of officials work this principle to their advantage.

Questions must be answered, or not answered, according to how they appear to be related to the immediate context of their asking. When it appears that the answers to questions you are being asked are not being put to immediate use, you are likely to object, or, if not object, to wonder what the purpose of the questioning might be. You may quickly become uncooperative because your understanding of cooperative behaviour leads you to believe that the questions (and their answers) should be relevant to some issue both parties can recognize easily. If you cannot determine a purpose in the questioning, you may justly feel that you are being either interrogated – interrogation is a special kind of conversation – or 'set up' in a trap, that is, the questioner is deliberately holding back something from you and the questioning is designed to test your truthfulness, accuracy, honesty, and so on. This kind of questioning can sometimes serve as a kind of barometer in a personal relationship. When one party starts to question the other about little things, the party questioned is likely to become defensive. A series of questions such as the following to a spouse returning late at night is not likely to be well received: *Where've you been?*, *Who were you with?*, *What were you doing until this time?* Such questions will hardly be interpreted as 'innocent' in their intent.

You can answer a *Yes–No* question with a response that omits the *Yes* or *No*. A question such as *Are you ready?* may well bring the response *In a minute*. In a pair such as the following the answer is obviously affirmative; the second party, B, interprets A's question as a request for shoe polish, not simply as a question concerning what kinds of items B keeps in stock:

A. Do you keep shoe polish?
B. What colour do you want?

With answers of this kind you can always deduce the appropriate affirmative or negative. The initial *Yes* or *No* of the answer need not be expressed if the answerer provides some additional explanation or justification, as in *Are you going to the meeting?* answered by *I've got to mark these papers.* In this case the response is clearly negative. But, even in this last case, it is very likely that if any actual negative does precede *I've got to mark these papers*, it will be something like *I don't think so* rather than *No*. This kind of attenuated refusal is less brusque than a categorical one would be.

When you receive a question response to a question that you have asked, the message seems to be that the answer to the second question has some bearing on the possible answer to your initial question:

A. What are you doing on Sunday?
B. Why?

Once you answer the second question you may expect your initial question to be answered:

A. We are having some friends over.
B. I don't have anything planned.

If A had answered *Forget it*, B would have considered him to be disrupting a perfectly legitimate routine. However, if after A's reply, B does not answer A's original question but brings up some unrelated topic, A will consider B to have dropped the original topic and may feel snubbed for certainly B has not played by the rules. Finally, if this ABAB sequence as outlined above were not followed by A inviting B to join in the Sunday activity, B would be left wondering what A's intent could possibly have been in opening up such an exchange in the first place.

How you choose to frame a question can also indicate to the listener the kind of answer you appear to expect. For example, negative questions function differently from positive questions, which seem to be quite neutral, allowing for either a *Yes* or a *No* answer. You are genuinely seeking either one answer or the other and have no expectation as to which it will be. But a negative question seems to seek a positive response: *Shouldn't we ask them?*, *Isn't it beautiful?*, or *Don't you want to get up?* In the same way a *Why not?* or *Why don't?*

beginning to a question makes a suggestion of some kind of positive activity: *Why not go to the movies?*, *Why don't we stay at home?*, or *Why can't you tell him?* We can compare this kind of pseudo-question with the simple *Why?* type: *Why do it?*, *Why are we going?*, or *Why should I?* The latter suggest some kind of objection, challenge, or refusal to comply. They are in that respect only questions in form, not in intent. If the listener has recourse to a *because*-type answer, that may well lead the speaker and listener into an argument or confrontation.

Still another kind of question has very special uses. The questions that teachers ask in classrooms are peculiar in a number of ways. Most are not genuine questions, if by 'genuine' we mean that a question should be seeking an answer which the questioner does not know. Not only do teachers usually already know the answers to the questions they ask, but those of whom the questions are asked know that the teacher knows the answers. Very few such questions, then, are of the type one person asks another in most other circumstances, unless that 'conversation' itself is a highly specialized one, for example, a lawyer eliciting information from his own witness in a courtroom. Then, too, in the classroom a kind of bidding system prevails for providing answers to the teacher's questions; the teacher selects who is to give the answer from among those who bid in some way for this position. Conversationalists are not usually quite so manipulative about who gets to answer questions, although they can limit the possibilities, or the circumstances in which their questions are asked can limit the possibilities. A waiter may find that he wants to answer a question asked by diner A of diner B, particularly if he knows the answer when B does not, but he may have second thoughts about the propriety of the act, depending on the nature and urgency of the initial request.

Teachers' questions also involve a fairly circumscribed set of concerns. They can seek information, either a precise fact (the date of the Battle of Waterloo) or an illustrative fact (the name of the king). Some may require students to explain a process, reason through an argument, or just make a choice. However, another important set of concerns involves neither requests for information nor the relating of information to some emerging intellectual pattern. These questions involve a kind of social control, and are actually veiled requests for students to perform certain specified actions: *Will you turn to page nine?* and *Could we have some quiet at the back?* Classrooms are typically full of questions; but they tend to be the teacher's, not the students'; they tend toward the factual rather than the thought-provoking; and they contain plentiful instances of veiled social control, that is, the questions are really not questions at all so far as their actual intent is concerned.

The question-answering behaviour that occurs in classrooms actually bears less resemblance to that which goes on in everyday conversation than to what happens in courtrooms, doctors' surgeries, and other settings in which unequal relationships exist. The questions are often challenges or are investigatory, and either cannot easily be evaded or require responses of a predetermined kind. Moreover, in classrooms, as in courtrooms, both questions and answers are regarded as entities to be judged by third parties and may be analysed closely, disregarded, or treated in still some other fashion. They are also highly regulated according to the external demands of the situation: proceeding through a curriculum, eliciting evidence, and so on. The relationship is unequal in another respect, too. Only one party can terminate a sequence, intrude on the other, comment on what the other has said – sometimes to a third party – or require the other to speak or be silent. So question-answering is often not a neutral activity, one shared in equally by both parties.

There is another sense in which questions are not neutral. A question can tell you a lot about the person asking it: beliefs, attitudes, world view, and so on. In recent years, an early question asked in a conversation between strangers is often *What are you?* The answer sought is not something like *A teacher* or *A police officer* but *A Taurus* or some other sign of the Zodiac. If the first kind of answer is rejected as unimportant and the second kind insisted on as being somehow relevant to the other's being able to 'understand' you, it may indicate quite quickly the possibilities – or impossibilities – for further communication. If your being a Taurus is somehow significant to the questioner, then it may well raise in you considerations about the whole system of beliefs of your questioner. You may not care to explore them in any detail – or you may have discovered a kindred spirit. Questions, just like many other components of a conversation, can provide a great deal of information about the person from whom they originate.

In some circumstances questions are deliberately asked to find out things about others for purposes of classifying or in some way evaluating those being questioned. Teachers' questions often fall into this pattern. So do the questions asked by doctors and psychiatrists. In interviews, too, the questions asked of candidates are evaluated by those asking them: does the candidate know this or that, or does he or she even know what an appropriate response to the question is? When questions are used for this purpose and the interviewee has no sense of what an appropriate response is (for example, to a question like *What particularly interests you in working here?* to a candidate for a position), then he or she may have real difficulty in being considered seriously. Knowing how to answer such questions is a sophisticated bit of learned behaviour, and not everyone may have equal opportunities to learn such behaviour.

If we were to ask ourselves how many questions, that is, genuine grammatical questions signalled quite clearly by interrogative syntax or intonation, are immediately answered by an appropriate grammatical or behavioural response, the answer might seem simple: the vast majority. But there is considerable evidence to suggest that in many conversations less than half of the questions get such immediate responses. Instead, we find that questions are sometimes countered with other questions, or the questioner answers his or her own question, or the respondent answers a question other than the one that was asked or provides an elliptical answer, or the questioner adds a further question to the original question before it can be answered. Questioning does not necessarily lead to answering. Indeed, it may not be intended to, as when you ask a purely rhetorical question, one designed to make a point rather than to elicit a genuine response. If a question is also a device for handing over a turn in the conversation to some other party than the questioner (to be returned when the reply is given), it is not a particularly successful device in that respect either, since many questions go quite un-answered and no change of speaker results. Questions and requests can be properly understood only in relation to their contexts; it is not enough to try to understand them from their grammatical forms alone.

Requesting and questioning comprise only a small – though not insignificant – part of conversational activity. A lot of conversation is almost ritualistic, as the parties go over mat-ters familiar to one another. In addition, some conversation may be devoted not just to checking information known to both (or all) but to passing on information that is new, in a kind of updating process: X wants Y to know something that X knows and Y does not.

One of the main purposes of conversation, therefore, is to pass on information to others. However, as we have indic-ated, not all information passed on is new information. Often we just want to be sure that everyone has access to the same information that we have, so we check up on what infor-mation is available rather than pass on anything that is par-ticularly novel. For that reason much conversation is quite banal, and when we must pass on brand-new information, we have to be careful: it is not always easy for others to grasp a novel idea or even a new fact.

Presenting brand-new information is not easy in any set-ting, but in a very casual setting it may be next to impossible. Brand-new information of any complexity, particularly of the kind that requires listeners to adopt a different way of looking at phenomena, requires a very slow and careful introduction. You will undoubtedly have to repeat large chunks of it in order to allow the recipients time to reorganize their old knowledge in such a way that the new can fit in. At best, you may expect to do little more than plant an idea in a conversation, to open a new door to someone. To expect to accomplish much more would be to attempt to turn the conversation into a sermon or a lecture, or to turn oneself into a teacher or a salesman. Most of us have had the experience of conversations changing in this way: a casual, equal relationship shifts into an unequal one when the roles of the participants change as a consequence of one setting out to change the ideas of the other, or others. It is not surprising that most societies have developed very formal means for allowing individuals or groups to converse so that new information and new ideas can be presented to other individuals or groups: schools, training establishments, and meetings of various kinds designed specifically for such purposes. Those who work in such settings will usually be the first to admit how difficult it is in fact to get brand-new information across, even in optimal conditions. Most people seem incapable of accepting much new information on a single occasion. A casual conversation, therefore, is not the place to attempt to do much beyond occasionally planting the seed of a new idea.

Information that we pass on to others can also have qualitative characteristics: we are more certain of some things than of others. Indeed, you may have good reason to believe that some of the information you wish to pass on to others is 'tainted' in some respect. You may not be entirely sure of it because of its source, or it may not ring true because of other things you know, or you yourself may be doctoring it for a special purpose. However, you may not want to lie, that is, present the information as though you were absolutely sure about what you are saying. You may not want to appear to be actually warranting what you are saying. There is good reason for your caution: you would not want later to be caught out in a lie. Therefore you may have recourse to one of a variety of ways of feeding information to others without warranting it completely. You can represent yourself, as it were, as the agent of others: *People [They] say [are saying], I've heard [read], Rumour [The grapevine] has it, The story is going around that, It seems,* or *Did you hear [see] that. . .* ? This kind of introductory statement allows you to feed information to others without making you responsible for the complete accuracy of that information. Of course, this device is also readily available to gossips and rumour-mongers, so information dispensed in this way is often heavily discounted by those who receive it.

In much the same way you can avoid the expression of direct opinions by offering them indirectly. Instead of saying *I believe* or *I know* you can preface an opinion with *I'm told, I've heard, It may be that,* or some equivalent framing expression. This kind of introduction allows you to make the same kind of statement but succeeds in distancing you from it. If it is accepted, then you can take some credit for it; if it is rejected, you need not feel slighted in the way that you might were the statement warranted by a prefatory *I know*. Of course, you may be criticized for offering the report, but it is easier to meet that kind of criticism than to meet a denial of the content of the report itself. After all, you did not warrant the content, as your choice of the 'hearsay' introduction indicates.

You may also want to transmit information in conversation confidentially. But it is unusual to swear someone to secrecy and, even if you do that, few such oaths have any legal sanction anyway. Indeed, you must expect most information given in such a manner to be leaked. You may even count on that happening in some cases! Consequently, while it is possible for you to relay information to others with such qualifying remarks as *Confidentially, Unofficially, This is just [sort of] between [the two of] us, This should go no further* – and, that favourite of leaders of all descriptions, *Off the record* – you should not be dismayed to find how quickly your 'secret' becomes general information, but not always the information that you communicated originally. Information is not a 'pure' thing: it gets changed in the retelling, confidential information no less than any other kind.

It sometimes seems necessary to give a kind of personal 'marking' to words or sentiments that you are expressing, so that those who are listening to you can be left in little or no doubt as to what you believe or feel about what you are saying. This is clearly 'warranting' behaviour, and a whole variety of warranting expressions exists: *Between us, Frankly, Personally, In my opinion, As far as I can tell, To be honest [frank, blunt], Actually, Realistically,* and *In fact, I'll be perfectly [absolutely, quite] frank.* Such expressions allow you to show the degree of commitment you have to what you are saying, but, of course, like all such expressions they can also be used to deceive, since not all remarks prefaced by *To be honest* are offered honestly.

There is an affective, emotive side to conversation as well as a purely informational one. But that too is a kind of information. Conversations are often used to indicate our feelings, rather than some rational or intellectual concern, about issues and other people. They do not serve merely to exchange information about factual matters; it is quite possible that the exchange of information may often be little more than a minor function of conversation and that the major function is an empathetic one. In seeking conversational partners, you usually search out those with similar ideas, backgrounds, and feelings to your own rather than strangers or those you know or suspect to be deliberately antagonistic to you. Most of your conversational exchanges, therefore, are likely to be with people you feel you can get along with, and much of what happens in them will focus on keeping this 'getting-along-with' purpose alive. Consequently, you are probably inclined to be somewhat sympathetic to the other person, you are likely to punctuate his or her accounts of grief or injustice with expressions like *I'm sorry to hear that!, Wow!, How dreadful [awful, sad, excruciating!], What a pity [shame, nuisance!],* and *That's awful [too bad, dreadful!].* In similar circumstances but with someone with whom you do not have the same close bond or whose feelings you cannot share, you may comment in quite different words: *It's your own fault, What else would you expect?, You asked for it, Serves you right, You've got no one to blame but yourself,* or *That will teach you a lesson.* Such remarks will be perceived not only as unsympathetic (which they obviously are) but as somewhat antagonistic. The speaker is probably looking for sympathy from you, but what he or she gets is the rubbing of salt into a wound which he or she would obviously prefer to have your help in closing. Your words do not cooperate in that intent, so all you can expect is perhaps an increase in tension between the two of you.

In general, opinions are not likely to be stated unequivocally and bluntly: we are usually not so 'opinionated'. Instead, we hedge or modify what we say. *It's kind of interesting, That may be true but, In one way, It's fine but, It usually happens that,* and *That's not very nice* are less strong than *It's interesting, That's true, It's fine, It's always the case that,* and *That's bad.* The latter do not leave your listener much room to manoeuvre or too much opportunity to save face if things turn out to be different from what you expected or predicted. You will have to make a later denial, and you would normally want to avoid that situation. It is much easier to make a statement that equivocates somewhat and be 'called' on it, rather than to make a definitive one and later be shown to be quite wrong. Complex and important matters are much more likely to be discussed with hedges and modifying statements than without, and opinions on them offered with caution. Unhedged language on important topics is a sure sign of dogmatically held beliefs: *X is right* [*wrong, good, bad*], and so on.

But some people deliberately do seek to speak with authority. They may do this not by reason of any position they hold but by the manner in which they choose to express themselves. They boldly assert their beliefs so as to appear to be decisive: *The truth is, I'm* [*absolutely, pretty*] *sure* [*certain, positive*], *There's no doubt* [*in my mind*], *Undoubtedly, As far as I can tell, The fact of the matter is, As a matter of fact,* or *You must admit.* Such expressions leave little or no doubt as to where the speaker stands on the point under discussion. But people who insist on constantly using this kind of framing device for statements are likely to be seen as hard and inflexible; they leave little room for cooperation with others who might not share their opinions.

The kinds of words you use to frame or qualify your utterances can also indicate a lot to others about how you view the world. As we have just indicated, some speakers are unequivocal; for them most issues are black and white – things *never* are or *always* are. But others live in a more-or-less world in which things happen *usually, generally, normally, by and large, on the whole*, and *as a rule*. If things are unusual they are indicated to be so, occurring, as they do, *rarely, occasionally, from time to time*, or *sometimes*. If they are peculiar, abnormal, or unexpected, they are so marked: *funnily [strangely, peculiarly] enough*. Our words therefore reflect the view we have of the universe in one respect, at least: some of us are much more equivocal and uncertain about where we fit into that world than others!

The more uncertain among us resist making bold statements and prefer to hedge what we say. We *believe, think,* or *suppose* things rather than come right out and assert them. We prefer to qualify statements with *seem* and *appear* rather than warrant their complete veracity with *certain, positive, definite, absolute*, and so on. We qualify with *perhaps, maybe, sort of,* and *kind of*. We approximate with *roughly* and *about*, and prefer an introductory statement like *I recall* rather than the more categorical *I definitely remember*. We gloss over claims with a word like *anyway*. Direct, frank, unambiguous utterances have a place in what we say, but they do not comprise the majority of our statements. People who insist on making them the preponderant majority may often have difficulty in finding others on whom to practise their conversational art a second time.

Normal behaviour requires the avoidance of extremes. It tends to be ambiguous and non-committal. It allows doors to remain open to others. There is a definite reluctance to close oneself off from others, and this reluctance shows itself in various ways. For example, most people hesitate to commit themselves on many issues, except perhaps with very intimate friends. They may readily acknowledge their limitations in knowledge, and refuse to make categorical statements which could prove to be impossible to defend and leave little room for negotiation, striking as they would at the heart of cooperation should others have different views of the topic under discussion. Their words show this reluctance and hesitation: *I guess* [*wonder, suppose, think, suspect, assume*], *It looks like, It may, It could be, Maybe, Perhaps, Possibly, My guess is, It seems to me*, or *I'm afraid*. There is no appearance of finality in such remarks: they leave the door open to other opinions and tend to promote discussion of any differences that appear to exist rather than to provoke challenges or denials from others.

However, you cannot equivocate for ever unless you are quite happy to be regarded as a wishy-washy person who has no opinions on any topic and who is never certain about anything in life. You can certainly try never to either accede to or refuse a request outright, always to dodge hard questions, always to treat every statement you hear with considerable reserve, and never to express a firm opinion on anything. Such behaviour is not at all unusual, but you will require a lot of skill if you are not eventually to offend others. Carried to extremes, equivocation must prove unsatisfactory, because it is not ultimately cooperative behaviour. A perpetual equivocator really has nothing to offer others in a conversation. Since cooperation involves giving as well as taking, if you refuse to give you become a burden to others, who will find that talking to someone who has nothing of substance to say is a complete waste of time.

So sometimes you need to be definite. The secret is knowing when to be definite, and how often. Indeed, there are actually occasions for exaggeration and overstatement, occasions when words like *marvellous* and *fantastic* are required. It is quite usual for people to *have a great time*, weather is sometimes *absolutely awful*, and certain events turn out to be *disasters*. In this way you actually heighten certain feelings and incidents for the listener in an attempt to engage his or her attention, though within prescribed limits. However, not everything can be described in superlatives, for employed repeatedly they lose any effect that their occasional use can have on the listener. You must not be *too* cooperative!

As well as using conversations to request, question, and inform others, we also use them to do a variety of other things. Living requires us to give others advice, to make promises and agreements, and even on occasion perhaps to threaten. What we must have, therefore, are everyday ways of doing these things, or of recognizing them when others advise, promise, or threaten us in some way. We must even learn to negotiate such a simple matter as agreeing on something.

What conditions must prevail if you are genuinely to offer advice to another person in a conversation? First of all, you must assume that he is likely to do (or not to do) something if you refrain from offering advice, and you must regard a different course of action as more appropriate for him and in his best interests. In offering advice, you want the other person to know this, to know what you think, and also to understand that you believe that the course of action you are setting forth is quite within his capabilities. Moreover, you assume that the other person wants to know all this. If these are the necessary preconditions for advising another person, it is easy to appreciate how the process can go wrong. Your perception of what someone else proposes to do or not do may be incorrect; your opinion about what he might find an acceptable alternative may be without foundation; or your role as a possible adviser may be called into question. Not everyone can offer advice: a certain amount of familiarity between the parties is necessary, or at the very least some shared concern around which the advice can be structured, for instance, a fireman's *I would advise you to leave the building immediately*, or his brusque *You'd better leave quickly* in more critical circumstances.

Advising another person or making a suggestion requires you to have a sense of identity with him or her. As well as indicating a course of behaviour that you think will benefit the other person, your advice must be something that he or she finds possible to do in the circumstances. Neither *I suggest you cut your throat* nor *I suggest you jump ten feet in the air* is likely to be treated as a serious suggestion. In everyday life, the *I suggest* formula is quite often avoided and less direct means used, but the effect is the same. You suggest a course of action which you consider to be beneficial to the listener: *Why don't you?*, *If I were you, I'd*, *Why not?*, *How about?*, *You can [could] always*, *One thing you can [could] do would be*, *You might try*, *Perhaps you can [could]*, *Might it not be?*, and *Can [Can't, Could, Couldn't] you?* Such expressions suggest a possibility of one kind or another, and some indicate directly that this is what you yourself would opt for if you found yourself in identical circumstances. The listener is forced to assume that this is a very strong suggestion as to a course of action, for you are openly stating your opinion and lending your authority to what is proposed. We must observe, however, that it is the listener, not you, who will be at risk. It is just possible that you have some ulterior motive and are counselling the listener to do something detrimental to his or her interests and favourable to yours.

You may not find it easy to respond to an utterance like *Why don't you do X?* It is not just a simple question, but a suggestion that you actually do X. If you are not anxious or willing to do X, you will probably have to provide some kind of reason for not doing it. But something more is involved: the speaker has suggested a course of action to you, and, in a sense, has put himself into a superior position – particularly if you proceed to act on the suggestion – for he has proposed a solution you apparently did not see or were reluctant to adopt without the proffered advice. We can observe that if you consider the suggestion to be a poor one, you can, in refusing it, exhibit a certain superiority of your own. Quite often, though, a *Why don't you?* type suggestion seems to be the natural outcome of previous discussion – the listener seems to draw it out of the speaker, as though the speaker had been 'set up' to make it. This is a particularly effective manoeuvre when instead of a *Why don't you?* the conclusion is a *Why don't we?*, and you gain the maximum amount of cooperation possible from the other.

Even when the parties are at odds, cooperation is the hallmark of successful conversation. There may be signs of considerable disagreement as suggestions are ignored, advice not taken, and statements questioned, but strong disagreement is not a characteristic of normal conversation. It is, rather, a characteristic of heated argument, of the *Yes, it is – No, it isn't* variety. Much more usual is very mild disagreement expressed in the *Yes, but* form, or through statements like *I don't know that I agree* or *I wouldn't say that exactly*, and so on. Modifying or altering a response in some way, or rephrasing, or half-agreeing (and therefore half-not agreeing) are the usual strategies preferred to outright denial or confrontation. Even when you perceive someone to have made quite contradictory statements to you, you are more likely to reserve them for future resolution or to probe carefully to see whether there is a genuine contradiction than to say something like *But look you said just the opposite a few minutes ago.* Such a remark is likely to heat up a conversation significantly, even between close friends. It is appropriate only in very few circumstances: a cross-examination, a seminar, an interrogation, a demanding interview (it is also one of the defining characteristics of such a situation).

Asked your opinion of something, you can express your agreement or disagreement or some uncertainty you have. There is a considerable variety of linguistic devices to draw on. You can agree by using words such as *Okay, Right, Quite [so], Yes, That's it, Of course, Good, Agreed, That's right [true], Correct, Exactly, I'll say, For sure*, and even such expressions as *I knew it, No, of course not, I'm afraid so, I don't think so*, and *You can say that again.* For disagreement you can choose from an even broader range, depending on how strongly you want to disagree: *No, Ridiculous, Nonsense, Not true, Not really, I'm afraid not, No way, Not quite [exactly], I doubt it, I disagree, but, Yes, but*, and *I couldn't agree less.* Your uncertainty or indecision can be communicated by words and expressions such as *Maybe, Perhaps, I'm not sure, I can't [really] say*, and *I don't know*. The decision you face in each case involves not just the fact that you agree, disagree, or have no strong opinion, but also how firm you want to appear to be in showing what it is you think. There is a strong likelihood that in a great many circumstances you may wish to equivocate or be somewhat circumspect in what you say. Then, on those occasions when you actually do want your opinion to count, you can be forthright in stating it.

Sometimes a statement or suggestion may be made to you that you find quite unacceptable. However, you may not wish to reject it out of hand. A denial or a *No* or *Absolutely not* would be rude, just as would be a refusal prefaced by such words as *I refuse to*, *I'm not going to*, *I can't stand*, *I don't accept*, or *I don't want to*, not to mention the categorical rejection *That's none of your business*. You may prefer to turn aside a statement or suggestion that you do not agree with by resorting to some device that diverts the other person's attention. For example, you can raise an associated issue that you are apparently prepared to discuss in place of the suggestion or statement that was actually made. If successful, you shelve the original remark and leave it shelved with the agreement of the person who made it. You can then proceed to discuss some more palatable topic, one that might lead to some measure of agreement.

You may be content initially to warn the other person that you are reluctant to agree with something that has been said to you. You do not want categorically to refuse or reject, but you do want to indicate your reservations. Expressions such as *I don't think it would be a very good idea to. . .* , *Do you really think we. . .?*, *I'm not really very keen on. . .* , and *I don't quite see how . . .* can indicate your lack of enthusiasm or reluctance. You have not entirely closed the door to agreement but you have indicated how difficult it might be to achieve it.

Agreement, of course, often comes very slowly indeed. We sometimes have to be persuaded or to persuade others, and the process can be a lengthy one. Sometimes reluctance to agree may be shown in the manner in which the agreement is expressed: *Well*, *OK then*, *[Well] in that case*, *On second* thoughts, *Now that I've thought about it*, *Well, possibly*, or *Put that way*. What these remarks say, in effect, is something like 'I agree with you but be aware that this agreement did not come readily.' A person who gets this kind of response would be wise to assess what is happening. A series of such admissions is likely to indicate that there is considerable disagreement between the parties and that one is forcing the other to agree (superficially at least) with him. The party doing the coercing may find the consequences of such a conversation rather different from those which he expected.

If you are coerced and feel quite strongly about the situation in which you find yourself, you will almost certainly indicate your objection in some way. You can also indicate the amount of pressure you feel yourself to be under. *That [it] doesn't seem to leave me much choice*, *If I must [have to]*, *There seems to be no alternative*, and *I haven't much choice* show great reluctance to comply, but compliance nevertheless. In contrast, *It seems I* and *I guess I* do not indicate such extreme negative feeling, but they do not show any enthusiasm either. It is also quite possible to indicate agreement while attaching a mild protest to that agreement: *I mean it's not that I don't*. What we observe in each case is someone forcing his or her will on you, but you are prepared to voice a protest while apparently going along with the course of action that the other has suggested.

Another kind of conversational behaviour that people have to be able to handle is that of apologizing. 'Never apologize' is bad advice for the vast majority of people, since few of us are in a position not to need occasional forgiveness for some error or omission. Never to apologize would make you appear to be unfeeling and uncaring. But, of course, the opposite kind of behaviour, apparently endless apologizing, is also difficult to deal with. A person who constantly requests your forgiveness for this and that – almost to the extent of forgiveness for his or her very existence – is likely to prove an extremely burdensome companion indeed! Nor is 'Never apologize' particularly good advice to follow if you are apt to make mistakes and use power and position to cover them. Unfeelingness and arrogance are the least of the accusations such behaviour is likely to provoke.

Only occasionally are apologies perhaps best not given at all. A formal ceremony that somehow gets off its set course is sometimes best put back on course without resort to apology. Indeed, a profuse apology may make a farce of the whole performance. Speeches, announcements, and most formal addresses are best not interrupted by apologies when they come to grief over some trivial matter. At most, some kind of distancing is called for: when it goes wrong the speaker should handle the performance from the outside, as it were, and then quickly step back into it once a repair is made. To try to incorporate either your own mistakes or the interruption into the performance may lead to it getting out of control: its sincerity or effect can be quickly called into question or the performance may be transformed into some other kind of theatre, as when a political speaker tries to get the better of a heckler and is himself bested.

Apologizing is an open acknowledgement that the speaker did something that he should not have done, or did not do something that he should have done. The apologizer also expects the offended party to indicate forgiveness. And if he makes a suitable expression of regret, the apologizer also expects the offended party to indicate forgiveness. But the apologizer must be sincere in his regret. An apology can be a simple *Sorry!*, *Excuse me!*, *Pardon me!*, or *Oops, my mistake [fault]!* It can also be more extensive: *I'm dreadfully sorry*, *Please accept my apologies for X*, or *I must apologize for X*. You can even add a promise to it that the offence will not be repeated: *I promise I won't do it again [that it won't happen again]*. The act of apologizing is not completed until the offended party has accepted or acknowledged the apology: *That's OK*, *Don't let it happen again*, and so on. Alternatively, a refusal to accept the apology may be indicated by an unwillingness to listen to it or a comment such as *It's too late*, or, if the apology is felt to be insincere, *I don't think you mean it*.

To be truly effective, an apology must be accepted. Only then is the breach that has occurred properly repaired. If an apology is rejected, then the injury is still deemed to exist. If an apology is ignored, the party offering it may be at a loss to know where he or she stands, because without a definite sign of acceptance the apologizer may well consider it to have been refused. Finally, if an apology is accepted, the party who offered it may feel somewhat angry if the offended party continues to press for further apologies or in some other way keeps the issue alive. It is even less acceptable to continue to demand apologies for an injury than to keep offering them, particularly if the very first apology was accepted.

In that they must be accepted to be valid, apologies are much like compliments. A compliment calls for some indication of appreciation. How you express that appreciation is important; on the whole it is better to do so playing down the compliment a little rather than exaggerating its import or fishing for further compliments. The person offering the compliment has to have a valid reason for complimenting – just as he or she must have a valid reason for apologizing. To compliment the wrong person for an act may be to embarrass that person. Similarly with inappropriate compliments, for it is not just anyone who can compliment any other – who can compliment the Queen on her newest outfit?

Compliments may often be required by social convention; their absence can be quite noticeable. They often take the form of saying how *good, pretty, great,* or *beautiful* something is, or using an expression of admiration, as in *I enjoyed your talk, I like your shoes, He did a fine job, That was quite a performance,* or *Nice try!* Compliments usually require an acknowledgement such as *Thank you, I thought you might like it, It's not bad, is it?, No bother, really!,* each of which serves a different function in the way it suggests how the complimenter should view what occasioned the compliment: acceptance, agreement, playing down, and so on.

Promising is another activity deserving of comment. According to the philosopher John Searle, certain conditions must obtain if an utterance you make is to be interpreted as a genuine promise. It must be made in the first person, that is, it should contain an explicit *I* or *We,* and it must have a future

orientation. Whereas *I promise* or *We will do it* may be promises, *You are to do it* is some kind of request and *I promised* is a
report. Second, you must believe that the person (or persons)
to whom the promise is made really wants something done
(or not done); if he does not, then you are not promising –
you are threatening. Consequently, *I promise I'll beat you up*
(unless said to a masochist) is a threat. Third, you must
believe that whatever is promised would not otherwise be
done (or be left undone) unless promised; hence the strangeness of a sentence like *I promise you that the sun will rise
tomorrow.* You must also seem to be sincere in making a
promise: you should support it by appropriate looks and
gestures. It also helps to have a reputation for veracity.
Finally, you must find some suitable verbal expression, frequently a sentence beginning *I promise* or *I will.*

A threat is different from a promise, since it proposes a
course of action which is in some way inimical or harmful to
the person to whom it is made. Whereas you expect to
benefit from a promise made to you, you expect to be diminished in some way if a threat is carried out. So what can you
do when faced with a threatening remark such as *Do you want
a punch on the nose?* You can even meet it with a physical
response, if it appears the threat is to have drastic and/or
unacceptable consequences. But there are numerous other
alternatives. You can attempt to pass off the threat as a kind
of joke, laughing it off or ridiculing it in some way: *You can't
be serious!* Or you can attempt to ignore it, by pretending it
was never uttered, or by acting as though you had not heard
it, or by responding with silence. A variation on this technique is to attempt to divert attention to some other topic. If
you wish to treat the threat somewhat more seriously, you
can attempt to deal with it in a vague, abstract, almost
theoretical way and try to defuse it thereby. An alternative,
related technique is to involve a third party, not necessarily as
a mediator or arbitrator but again in an attempt to broaden
involvement and reduce tension. Or you can take up the issue
that occasioned the threat and try to talk about it seriously,
by arguing a point of view or defending a course of action. In

this way you are attempting to answer the threat directly. Finally, of course, you can simply back off and apologize, if this seems necessary in the circumstances or if no other course of action seems possible. For, after all, you may on occasion deserve to be the victim of threatening behaviour, if you have violated some other person's territory or space or in some other way offended grossly. Sometimes it might even be the wisest kind of cooperative behaviour.

Further Reading

Ervin-Tripp's 'Is Sybil There? The Structure of Some American English Directives' discusses certain aspects of requests; Garvey's 'Requests and Responses in Children's Speech' is limited to an analysis of how children use requests. Goffman's 'Response Cries' deals with replies and other kinds of responses. Churchill's *Questioning Strategies in Sociolinguistics*, Goody's *Questions and Politeness: Strategies in Social Interaction*', Merritt's 'On Questions Following Questions in Service Encounters', and Robinson and Rackstraw's *A Question of Answers* discuss various aspects of questioning and answering behaviour.

Language interaction in the classroom is the topic of Bellack, Kliebard, Hyman, and Smith's *The Language of the Classroom*, Cazden, John, and Hymes' *Functions of Language in the Classroom*, Edwards and Furlong's *The Language of Teaching*, Flanders' *Analyzing Teaching Behavior*, Johnson's *Discussion Dynamics: An Analysis of Classroom Teaching*, McHoul's 'The Organization of Turns at Formal Talk in the Classroom', Pride's 'Analysing Classroom Procedures', and Sinclair and Coulthard's *Towards an Analysis of Discourse: The English used by Teachers and Pupils*.

Fraser's 'Hedged Performatives' describes various kinds of hedging behaviour, and politeness is the concern of Brown and Levinson's 'Universals in Language Use: Politeness Phenomena'.

9

Samples of Conversation

We are now in a position to look at a few sample conversations to see how the various bits and pieces discussed so far fit together in practice. The conversations that follow are not unusual, because our subject is the structure of an ordinary activity. Indeed, all except the last were collected somewhat casually within the space of a few days; each conversation was recorded as accurately as possible immediately after it occurred but without the benefit of taping. In contrast, the last conversation is from a corpus of conversation deliberately recorded for research purposes, so, although there is nothing really remarkable about it either, it does have some special characteristics that we will refer to later. What we can discover from these fragments of ordinary living is how structured they all are when you examine them closely.

The first conversation is a simple home-coming routine. Speaker B is in the house as Speaker A enters and takes off his coat.

A. [Loudly] Hi, Sue!
B. [Loudly] Hi, John!
A. [Quietly] Hi, Charlie! Had your dinner?
B. [Quite loudly] I've fed the animals already.
A. [Walks to kitchen] Been home long?
B. Just a few minutes. I was out in a school all afternoon.
A. Ah! We eating at home?
B. Could, I suppose.
A. No. Let's go out. I've got to look for a book.
B. OK. Give me a few minutes to get changed. By the way. . . .
A. Yes?
B. Oh, nothing. Chinese food?

A. Yeah. If you want. I'll take the dog out for a walk while you get ready. [Loudly] Rufus!

The first pair of utterances is a routine exchange of greetings. With this couple the one who enters the house usually greets the one who is already home from work with a fairly-loud *Hi!* type utterance. Thus, the arrival of the second one home is quite clearly signalled. The next greeting does not involve an exchange: Charlie is a cat; she – Charlie is also female and is never *it* – usually comes to the door when either of the two adults who live in the house enters. The question that follows (*Had your dinner?*) while addressed to the cat is paired not with a reply from the cat (which would be quite a surprise!) but with one from Speaker B, the one to whom it is indirectly addressed. It really means something like 'Have you fed the animals?' This meaning is apparent from the response *I've fed the animals already.* The animals are two cats and a dog, which customarily are fed by the first person who gets home in the evening. This is a routine understood by both A and B – and by the three animals.

The exchange involving the feeding of the animals acts as a second check that normal conditions exist this day on home-coming. The opening greeting exchange was the first such check. Now comes a third: *Been home long?* Speaker A already 'knows' the answer to this question: it should be some kind of negative if normal conditions prevail. And so it is. Not only has B just got home, but she adds that she has been in one of the two places she almost certainly had to have been that afternoon – in a school. (The other would have been her office. Any other response would have been quite unusual, given the nature of her employment, as would also the response that she had been home a long time.) Once again the home-coming situation has been checked out by A as normal. And, of course, by B too.

At this point a little bit of negotiation occurs, but negotiation well within the bounds of what this couple consider to be normal behaviour. They eat out a considerable amount of the time, but rarely on a planned basis: that is, whether they eat out or at home is often a decision made at 5.30 to 6.00 p.m. each evening when they return from work. So, after acknowledging B's response as to when she got home (*Ah!*), Speaker A brings up the question of dinner, directly questioning B on the matter: *We eating at home?* Speaker B's reply is interesting: *Could, I suppose* is clearly a response showing some reluctance and one that A reacts to immediately with a firm *No. Let's go out.* Speaker A appears to have used the inquiry concerning eating merely to see if B had already begun to prepare food for dinner or had definite plans to stay at home and eat. The *Could, I suppose* response seems to have been the one he expected, for it allows him to propose going out to eat, a proposal which he reinforces with a reason. However, both A and B know this is not a full-blown reason: A is always looking for books, either specific ones or just any that might be interesting to acquire. (We should note that *a book* is ambiguous in this respect – it could mean a particular book or any book.)

Speaker B readily accedes, asking for no more than a few minutes to get changed. But then something just a little out of the ordinary occurs. She says *By the way*, which prompts A to answer *Yes?*, only for B to drop the subject. This little side sequence is not pursued. However, an item has been put on the agenda for later discussion. Speaker B has left A wondering what the *By the way* was all about; however, A is willing to accept that, whatever it is, it is not a matter of any great importance but one that he can expect B to bring up in the fairly near future. What he does not do is insist that the topic be fully presented at this time. He is perfectly aware that this exchange is *not* about anything of substance: it *is* about re-establishing contact between two people at the end of a busy day, looking after pets, and having the evening meal together. So B's *Oh, nothing* is quite acceptable to A as a response.

Chinese food? shows that the conversation is back again on track as a piece of routine behaviour. A knows that B prefers Chinese food to any other, so this question signals B's request to eat what she prefers most. B readily accepts (*Yeah*) and his *If you want* further acknowledges his willingness to go along with A's choice of cuisine. He then offers to walk the dog while she gets ready. Rufus is, of course, the dog.

This conversation is about coming home and re-establishing a normal routine. It has little or no substance to it, being almost entirely 'phatic' in Malinowski's scheme of things. The ordinary business of life is its concern, but we can see that even that business requires careful negotiation through the use of fixed routines and fixed topics. So there is a large amount of ritualistic activity in the exchange. Only the brief side sequence introduced by *By the way* hints at something just a little out of the ordinary, but this is not the moment evidently to pursue a new topic. Two people have cooperated in beginning an evening together and expressed their willingness to make their time together fit into the normal pattern of their everyday existence. To a third party many of the remarks must appear peculiar – the routines of others often are – but to the participants they are quite transparent because what is unsaid is just as much part of the exchange as what is said. Expressions like *Had your dinner?*, *the animals*, *We eating at home?*, and so on make sense only in the lives of these two people at this particular point in time enjoying the special relationship they have with each other.

The second conversation is quite different. The setting is a neighbourhood shop and the time 11 p.m. Speaker A is a woman in one of the two queues at the cash registers. These queues are quite closely packed because there is not much space in the area in front of the registers. Speaker B, a man, is directly behind A in the same queue. He is looking around at shelves and at other people in the shop but is paying no particular attention to the woman in front of him – she is just one of those 'other people'.

A. [Looks directly at B] Would you like to get in front of me?
B. [Surprised] No!
A. You know I can feel your tension.
B. [Edges back] I'm sorry but I'm not aware of it. [Turns

away, raises his eyebrows, and shrugs his shoulders,
directing these last two actions toward the next one in
line, C, who has overheard the brief exchange]
C. [Similar shrugging behaviour]

The opening remark in this exchange surprises B, because
he understands the words to be a genuine question, that is, he
reacts to the syntax of the utterance. He has no desire to get
in front of A. Indeed, while he answers A, he looks at the
two or three things she is carrying and, as he answers,
wonders why she is making such an offer: getting in front of
A would get him out of the shop only marginally more
quickly than retaining his place in the queue.

However, A's next remark changes completely B's interpretation of the original question. A tells B she can feel his
tension. Her *You know* partly mitigates that observation but
mainly serves to introduce a reason. B suddenly realizes that
A perceives him to have encroached on her space – certainly
her psychological space and possibly too her physical space.
His normal behaviour in a queue is to dissociate himself from
the boredom of waiting by doing things: picking up magazines if they are available, reading labels, looking around, and
so on. A obviously finds this behaviour intrusive in the small
space in which those in the queue are confined. She reacts by
drawing B's attention to his behaviour. She cannot really say
Stop fidgeting! or *You are making me nervous.* Instead, she offers
to give up her space to get rid of what she perceives to be this
intrusive person next in line. But to do so she must confront
a complete stranger. B is genuinely unaware of what has
caused A to challenge him for he now reinterprets A's opening remark as a challenge and not an offer. He declares his
lack of awareness and prefaces it with an apology. However,
it is obvious from his actions that the apology is not genuine
and that his words are uttered mainly to placate A. He directs
the gestures that follow his words toward a third party, who
is thus directly brought into the conversation. Up to this
point C has been only a witness; now he is forced to make a
response. He does so by mirroring some of B's behaviour. At

the time B's interpretation of that mirroring was that C agreed with B's view of the incident. However, in retrospect, he decided that C's behaviour could only be interpreted as ambiguous. C obviously does not want to get involved, for after all everyone is a stranger to everyone else. C is both an unwitting and an unwilling witness, but B confronts him by directly turning to him. He can choose to ignore what B does or comment in some way. His comment is perhaps the minimal one he can make in the circumstances: some kind of action which indicates mild agreement but no words. C's real lack of involvement is apparent: he just wants to get out of the shop.

Undoubtedly A and B both interpreted this incident quite differently. A must have felt violated in some way; B certainly felt challenged. A saw B as an intruder; B perceived A to be somewhat paranoid. What seems quite clear is that the queuing behaviour of these two people is quite different. Whereas B would never challenge A, not being aware of A's concerns, A was prepared to challenge B. B could only ask himself whether A went through life in this way and what really caused her to issue such challenges. People do not usually go around confronting others in our society, even in this mild way.

Just how unusual such confrontations are and sometimes how fleeting can be seen in a third brief example. In this case B is a man walking his dog at dusk on a dreary wet autumn evening. His dog, which is on a leash, has just stopped at a building site to relieve himself. B stands waiting, his hands in his pockets. A woman, A, walks by briskly, head under an umbrella. Her pace never falters.

A. Don't you clean up after your dog, Mister?
B. [Silence]

Just how unusual such a confrontation is can be judged by the simple fact that this comment is the only instance of its kind in ten years of B's dogwalking.

The exchange is, of course, a confrontation. First of all, A and B are strangers passing each other in the street. In this city strangers do not need to exchange pleasantries to indicate that they mean no harm to each other – the city is a 'safe' one, making such exchanges unnecessary. Usually people just pass by each other without comment, although dog-walkers sometimes find that strangers will comment on the dog, invariably favourably, particularly adults with accompanying children, and particularly when the dogs are well behaved ones on leashes. A does not choose this approach. She knows that B does not clean up after his dog, since he is obviously not in possession of any of the necessary equipment. Her question is rhetorical. But is is, after all, a question. It is not *You should clean up after your dog*, *Why don't you clean up after your dog?*, nor *Do you clean up after your dog?*, which would be even more challenging and inviting of response. She also adds *mister*, which B interprets to be a kind of politeness-marker. *Sir* would seem to be unavailable in the circumstances, so *mister* is the next best thing.

B is temporarily lost for an answer, which the comment (or question) uttered by A seems to require. He cannot say *no* since that would be stating the obvious and might sound defiant. He cannot lie and say *yes* since such a lie would be too transparent and, anyway, lying does not come easily even in such circumstances. He can say *Mind your own business* but does not, since, being fully aware of her concerns, he recognizes that it is genuinely part of her business what his dog does – they live in the same city – but he prefers that such business stay private and not be made public. Above all, he does not want to argue with a stranger, and it is also quite obvious, from her unbroken pace, that the stranger does not want to argue with him. So B says nothing: his silence or refusal to say something is his response. It expresses his ambivalence and possibly at the same time reassures A in her views: she does, after all, express her opinion on this matter and hears no kind of rebuttal. Even though only one person speaks in this exchange, it has been a cooperative endeavour because the one who remains silent does not seek to contradict or deny in any way the criticism of the one who speaks. Indeed, he tacitly acknowledges its validity.

The next conversation also involves complete strangers, but is an encounter of a very different kind. The setting is a park adjacent to a university, one frequented by students and also by the general public. It is small, tree-filled, and pleasant. The time is a fine autumn afternoon and the park is well populated. Speaker B is sitting on a park bench. She is dressed in the style favoured by students. There is an open book on her lap and some books on the bench beside her. Speaker A approaches her. He is a young man dressed in jeans and a black leather jacket, not a style of dress favoured by students. As A approaches B, he speaks.

A. You look a little lonely.
B. Not at all.
A. You smoke hash?
B. I don't want to buy any, and I don't have any to sell.
A. How about coke?
B. Look! I'm not bothering anyone and I *was* quite content until . . .
A. Two's company.
B. *You're* a crowd.
A. Don't get fresh with me.
B. [Stands up, picks up books, leaves]

Speaker A is a stranger to B. He approaches her and enters space which she has quite firmly established for herself, sitting as she is on a park bench surrounded by books. She is also clearly signalling that she is a student; she has been looking at the book in her lap. And this is not a known pick-up area. Moreover, Speaker A would not appear to be the kind of person B would be interested in. His opening remark is directed toward establishing some kind of pairing: *You look a little lonely.* B immediately denies that she is lonely. The opening exchange is completed. Speaker A changes his approach and asks a question which B replies to with two negative assertions. But these are directly related to the question asked. She has the option of telling A to get lost – she would be quite safe doing so in the circumstances – but instead gets involved with the substance of the question. She is actually cooperating with A by treating his approach seriously. So A gets bolder and asks a further question.

At this point B decides the conversation has gone far enough. A has intruded on her space and activities. She had rejected his initial approach but then proceeded to undo that rejection by treating his question about hash seriously. Now it is time to stop matters from going any further: she is a student and he is interested in drugs, and, though she appears to know something about the subject, she does not want to get involved with this particular young man. Her *look* acts as a strong attention-getting signal which prefaces her declaration that she wants to be left alone. However, she cannot make even this declaration clearly and unambiguously. Instead, she says *I'm not bothering anyone and I was quite content until*, a declaration which A interrupts with the trite *Two's company*, which refers back to his opening remark. At last B's sharpness shows in her quick rejoinder *YOU'RE a crowd*. This is the first time she addresses A directly, and she does so by deliberately twisting the saying he has chosen and throwing it back at him in a way that clearly indicates her displeasure. Speaker A's next remark shows that this rebuff has had the intended effect. He is clearly outwitted verbally so he resorts to a 'tough-guy' type response, accusing B of 'getting fresh' with him, ignoring the fact that he was the original violator of the 'Don't speak to strangers' injunction. Of course, in the circumstances such a response is somewhat threatening to B even in a 'safe' public park. She does not attempt to reply, but picks up her possessions and leaves.

This encounter shows how difficult it is for the young woman to ignore the verbal advances of the young man. She goes along with him, pairing her responses to his various remarks until finally he gets frustrated. But that frustration does not occur until B directly addresses A and puts him down, an affront to his self-image. It is a verbal defeat that threatens him and causes him to change his approach, an approach which B this time resolves to ignore by a physical act – removal of herself from the space which she has occupied. Speaker A can follow, but he chooses not to. That would be too aggressive a move to make in such a public place. He also has his self-image to preserve: being defeated publicly is no part of that self-image.

In a sense this is a piece of theatre. The two characters act out their roles for each other: student and macho intruder. Dress, mannerisms, and language are all in character. So is the student's verbal politeness and the intruder's verbal agressiveness. Even the choices of topic and approach are appropriate: 'pick-up' language, drugs, triteness, and threat opposed to polite refusal rather than complete rejection, a reasoned statement of present intent, a verbal rejoinder to put down the other, and then a final flight if not to safety at least to a less distracting environment. The characters stay in role throughout even as they create their roles: they know what to do and they do it.

The last conversation is rather different. It is from Svartvik and Quirk's *A Corpus of English Conversation* (pages 408–11), a large collection of recordings that has been made available for research purposes in book and computer-tape form. The text reproduced here follows the original, except that Speaker a in the original is relabelled Speaker B and the supplementary markings for various voice characteristics have been removed. Left in, though, are the symbols used to show overlapping talk (★ and + in various combinations), unclear utterances (⟨⟨ ⟩⟩), and pauses (−·). A capitalized word is one that carried the stressed tone. All utterances are numbered for identification. The two speakers are male academics aged about fifty.

B. [1]I don't know whether you have talked with Hilary about the diary situation

A. [2]WELL [3]she has been EXPLAINING to me [4]rather in rather more general TERMS [5][ə:m] · what ★ you are sort of DOING and ★

B. [6]★⟨⟨5 to 6 sylls⟩⟩ what it was all ★ about · yes ·

A. [7]I gather you've been at it for nine YEARS −

B. [8][ə:m] by golly that's true yes yes it's not a long time of course in the [ə] in this sort of ★ work ⟨⟨you know⟩⟩★

A. ⁹☆ well NO ☆ ¹⁰but it's quite a long time ⟨⟨syll⟩⟩ by ⟨⟨[m]⟩⟩ ANY standards –

B. ¹¹yes suppose so ⟨⟨1 syll⟩⟩ –

A. ¹²she TOLD me what YOU DID - - ¹³and we decided we were [ə] both a bit out of DATE ¹⁴compared with present-day · STUDENTS and –

B. ¹⁵well I suppose that that's true - - - [əm] – you

A. ¹⁶but I don't really KNOW that I'm ¹⁷going to be a vast amount of HELP to you · ¹⁸I was INTERESTED in your ADVERTISEMENT ¹⁹and and [əm] - - · [?ə] but [ə] I gather you're AFTER ²⁰ ⟨⟨an⟩⟩ enormous amount of INFOR-MATION ²¹and I don't REALLY know that I've got - YOU know ²²whether WHAT I've got ²³is [?] of any HELP ²⁴I mean it's really for you to DECIDE ²⁵REALLY - - -

B. ²⁶the private correspondence that you mentioned [əm] we can probably match you know we've got some private correspondence

A. ²⁷YES

B. ²⁸[əm] what we have been desperately short of is [əm] the most intimate kind of writing and speaking

A. ²⁹[mhm]

B. ³⁰now [əm] you know [ə] the way one speaks as no doubt Hilary has been telling you [əm] when your hair is let down.

A. ³¹ ☆ YES ☆

B. ³² ☆ the ☆ kind of things that the one can allow oneself to say I don't mean merely the subject matter because the subject matter is of no particular concern˙☆ to us ☆

A. ³³ ☆ [m] ☆

B. ³⁴[əm] but as you well know the way in which you will write a letter to your son or your wife or your mother or something ☆☆ is very ☆☆ different from the way you write to almost anyone else [ə] because the threshold of criticism becomes very different and the possibilities of criticism your reaction to criticism becomes so ☆ very different ☆

A. ³⁵ ☆☆YES☆☆ - - - ³⁶ ☆ [m] ☆

B. ³⁷well if you if you admit that if you admit that the

private letter the private conversation with with one's
wife will be very different [əm ə] will be much less
selective about structures and so on that one uses then
you will admit the further points that the talking to
oneself that one does on paper in one's private diary
☆-☆ is probably the most genuine expression of oneself
that [ə] is ever permitted one one talks to oneself [ə]
either + subvocally

A. [38]☆ [m] ☆ [39] + (laughs - -) +

B. [37]or in the case of + of [ə] some unfortunates actually
vocally [əm ə] but the obviously this is not a possible
subject of study since the people ☆☆ who talk to themselves aloud ☆☆ are crazy

A. [40]☆☆ ⟨⟨3 to 4 sylls⟩⟩ ☆☆

B. [37]and the people who talk to themselves ☆⟨⟨10 to 12
sylls⟩⟩☆

A. [41]☆ ⟨⟨but⟩⟩ I've always ⟨⟨been told⟩⟩ that DIARISTS☆
are crazy [42]as WELL [43]☆☆ (laughs - -)☆☆

B. [44][əm] ☆☆well there may be of course something in this
but there's ☆☆ an awful lot of them in that [in] in that
case cos diarists you see are of two kinds apparently the
the the sort of Harold Macmillan the the [əm] Harold
Nicolson type who write their diary because they are
aware of having their pulse on the on the goings on of
the time ·

A. [45]☆YES ☆

B. [44]☆ and ☆ think well this is history ·

A. [46]☆☆ [mhm] ☆☆

B. [44] ☆☆ and ☆☆ posterity ⟨⟨6 sylls⟩⟩ and so they're not
really writing a private diary at all they're writing a
rough draft of a history book [hm] - ☆ you see ☆

A. [47] ☆ YES ☆·

B. [44]and they're aware all the time ·

A. [48] [mhm]

B. [44]that this is going to be converted and [ə] and I made a
slight study of Harold Nicolson [ə] Harold Nicolson's
diary from this point of view and the diary from the ☆·
from the☆

A. ⁴⁹✫ from his✫ BOOK you mean ·

B. ⁵⁰yes from ✫✫from the book from the book surely surely✫✫

A. ⁵¹ ✫✫ [m] · ⁵² [m] · ⁵³ [m] ✫✫

B. ⁵⁴[əm] and the kind of [əm] revelation that he puts in his diary is much more guarded than that which he puts in letters to Vity

A. ⁵⁵yes well we've ✫SEEN this ✫

B. ⁵⁶✫ you see ✫

A. ⁵⁷YES ⁵⁸YES

B. ⁵⁹ [ə] well this shows that the private diary is not in fact a genuine diary at all it's preliminary memoirs ✫[hm]✫

A. ⁶⁰✫ YES ✫ ⁶¹YES

B. ⁶²but the private diary that you write or that I write and which we hope will always remain under lock and key and which we will the last act on earth that we do ⟨⟨will be the⟩⟩ destruction thereof [ə] this is a diary which is genuinely talking to ourselves [ə] on paper and as I say a lot of people go in for it we may be crazy but there are other manifestations of craze of ✫ some kinds ✫

A. ⁶³ (laughs ✫-✫ -)

B. ⁶⁴do sit down -

A. ⁶⁵WELL ⁶⁶ [əm] · I thought

B. ⁶⁷so really what I'm leading up to is saying if you can let us have ⟨⟨your⟩⟩ private letters [əm] we should be very grateful

A. ⁶⁸YES

B. ⁶⁷but we should be even more grateful if you can let us have this diary and you point out in your last letter [ə] and I am quoting very much from memory but [əm] you've got some misgivings about the [ə] use of the diary if the thing was going to be open to the public

A. ⁶⁹oh YES

B. ⁶⁷or was going to be ✫⟨⟨4 to 5 sylls⟩⟩✫

A. ⁷⁰ ✫any any [s]✫ FORM ⁷¹ of of of RECOGNITION ⁷²I should be very very RELUCTANT

B. ⁷³right well I mean [əm] this this would be entirely

taken care of I don't know whether Hilary mentioned but we have [əm] recordings made under similar conditions you know of intense privacy

A.　[74] [m]

B.　[73]which we use [əm] and and we dissect with coolly and calmly despite the fact that what is what is being talked about is extremely private and in the transcription that we make we replace all the proper names including place names ·

A.　[75] ☆YES ☆ [76] + [mhm] +

B.　[77] ☆ by ☆ fictitious ones + - + [ə] so that anybody coming across the only record that is public namely the one that's in the in the filing cabinet ⟨⟨2 sylls⟩⟩ that's not public but ☆☆semi-public☆☆

A.　[78]☆☆YES☆☆

B.　[77]I mean the all all the the gang get at it

A.　[79][m]

B.　[77][əm] would never be able to [əm ə m] understand what was going on so far as living persons are concerned

A.　[80]☆YES☆

B.　[81]☆ it is☆ it is + ⟨⟨10 sylls⟩⟩+

A.　[82] + ⟨⟨well I don't know ⟩⟩ [83] I mean I have KEPT a diary + [84] for some YEARS - [85] [əm ·ə ? æ] and I mean I've never showed it to ANYBODY - [86][əːm əm] · I tend to [ɔːf] always wonder what on EARTH is going to HAPPEN to it - [87][əːm] · and I have GOT [88]as I EXPECT [89] a CERTAIN number of letters [90]because I [m?in] never[s] never seem to throw anything AWAY you KNOW - [91][əːm]

B.　[81]that's another form of madness

A.　[92]another form of MADNESS YES [93][m] · but they turn OUT in · [94]few GENERATIONS [95]to be extremely INTEREST-ING [96] ⟨⟨2 sylls⟩⟩ one is very GRATEFUL. [97]that one's ANCESTORS ☆ didn't throw things away ☆

B.　[98] ☆ [m - m]☆ quite

A.　[99]☆☆do you☆☆ SEE

B.　[100] ☆☆yes☆☆ yes ☆ yes☆

There are many interesting features in this conversation. The first has to do with the unclarity of the actual text in many places, an unclarity which we can attribute not just to the failure of the tape recorder to catch everything that was said but also to a characteristic of many conversations: we do not hear everything that others say. We do not hear everything because not everything said is spoken clearly enough to be fully heard, and some of what is said is drowned out by what someone else says because there is a certain amount of overlapping in actual speaking and listening. Although at any one time only one speaker in this conversation clearly has the floor, the other can be seen to be interjecting remarks of various kinds which produce overlap, and there is also some additional overlap as speakers change turns. The resulting unclarity in the text does not in fact stop or confuse either speaker in the conversation itself because, as we can readily observe, there is a considerable amount of redundancy in the text, particularly in the repetitions that the speakers seem compelled to make of even the simplest points.

The conversation itself involves a piece of negotiation. Speaker B is trying to persuade Speaker A to let him have a very personal diary for research purposes. Speaker A is not reluctant to allow the diary to be used by B for this purpose, but needs to be persuaded. B knows this and understands that protocol demands that he go through a persuasive ritual to gain access to the material he seeks. One direct reflection of these two different approaches to the conversation – agendas, if you will – is that whereas Speaker A is hesitant, speaks less, and shows a much greater range in the kinds of tone groups he uses – note the words in upper-case letters – Speaker B's speech is less uneven and more fluent, and, moreover, dominates that of A. Whereas A has taken the initiative to visit B in his territory – B's *do sit down* (64) to A assures us of that – it is B who must persuade A and who must therefore take the initiative in speaking and sustaining the topic.

One dimension we can look at, then, is the relative smoothness of the utterances of A and B. It is quite easy to contrast B's 34, 37, 44, 62, 67 and 73 with A's 16–25, 82–91, and 92–7. B knows what he is about: his task is to persuade A. A knows his role too: he has to let B convince him (though he may be quite prepared to be convinced) and so has to appear hesitant and uncertain. The language of the two is in that respect a direct reflection of the roles each is playing at the moment. In some other circumstance we would not expect this same distribution of smoothness and hesitation for, after all, the two seem to be quite well acquainted, as the reference to Hilary at the very beginning shows.

Since this is a piece of persuasion, Speaker B must be prepared to state and restate his case. This he does by repeating himself from time to time, as in 34 and 37, for example. Sometimes the repetition is of a single word: *the the the the sort* in 44 or of more than one word: *on the on the goings on*, again in 44. Sometimes the restatement involves fairly minor changes: *because the threshold of criticism becomes very different and the possibilities of criticism your reaction to criticism becomes so very different* in 34. We can contrast this kind of repetition with the kind favoured by A, the more hesitant speaker: his repeated *really* in 21 to 25 and the *I've got* of 21 and 22. The two also repeat each other: for example, A repeats in 92 B's *another form of madness* in 81. Each is also prepared to complete in some way a statement begun by the other: B adds in 6 *what it was all about* to A's *what you are sort of doing and* in 5, and A completes B's *and the diary from the* in 48 with *from his book you mean* in 49, even as B repeats *from the* and then acknowledges A's completion: *from the book from the book surely surely* in 50.

Since each party must explain something to the other, there is also a lot of hedging and mitigation. There are plentiful examples of *well, you know, you see, I mean, sort of*, and so on. A particularly interesting example occurs in 73: Speaker B begins *right well I mean [əm] this this would be entirely taken care of* . . . The *right* shows B's acknowledgement of A's feeling of reluctance, the *well* seems to be a kind of filler, the *I mean* indicates that B is searching for the right words needed for the occasion, the *[əm]* shows these words do not come easily to him, and the repetition of *this* shows that when the words finally do come B makes a false start. Speaker A is just as capable of doing this kind of thing, as 82–91 quite clearly shows with its *well I don't know* (82), its *I mean* (83) repeated in 85, its repeated *never* in 90, its final *you know* (90), and the various forms of *[əm]* interspersed throughout.

Both speakers use variations of this last [əm], recorded here as [əːm], [ə], [ə?], [hm], [əm], [m], [?ə], and [?]. B seems to use it much less frequently than A, with much bigger chunks of language occurring between instances. And when B is in full flight of explanation, as in 34, 37, and 44, he has little resort to this kind of filler. A, on the other hand, uses it very frequently when he tries to string together several utterances. The [əm]s serve to create (and fill) the gaps he needs to express his hesitation and reluctance. So the [əm]s tend to function differently in the two cases: in B they signal some kind of switch to a new argument or reason, whereas in A they show that B must be prepared to work harder if he is to convince A.

However, A is quite willing to cooperate with B in his attempt to win over A. The feedback that A provides to B is considerable: the use of *yes*, [mhm], [m], and so on as well as the three outbursts of laughter in 38, 42, and 63, the last of which prompts B to ask A to sit down, a move which immediately precedes B's direct request in 67 to have access to A's private letters and diary. A's *yes* in 68 is of particular interest because, whereas it is possible to interpret some *yes* responses as expressions of agreement with a proposition made by another (for example, 50 with 49), the *yes* of 68 seems to be in a different category – in the class of 'I'm listening' rather than 'I'm agreeing.' We can see how this is so if we look at what happens after 68: B feels obliged to explore the matter of confidentiality so that A's mind can be set at rest. This next prolonged exchange would hardly have been necessary if the *yes* of 68 were A's unqualified agreement. A provides B with far more feedback than B provides A – for example, see 51 to 53, 74, 75, 78, 79 and 80 – but, after all, it is A who must carry the burden of talk in this situation. A's feedback works, as we can see if we look at how many of B's utterances begin with continuity markers like *and, but, which, or, so,* and so on. A encourages B to get on with the job of persuading him; he willingly cooperates in the agenda B has set for himself.

This kind of cooperation is actually apparent throughout. The speakers express agreement with each other (11 with 10, 15 with 14, and so on) or help each other out (particularly at the beginning, as in 5 to 9). In this last case even the denial in 9 (*well no*) is done gently, and then mitigated immediately with a further clause introduced by *but.* And the conclusion (97 to 100) shows how A looks for B's agreement even in the circumstances when overall it is B's task to win A over to his point of view. In numerous other ways too we cannot but note that without cooperation such a conversation could not proceed very far: whether that cooperation involves accepting the other's position for what he represents it to be, finding topics to reach consensus on (Harold Nicolson's diaries), picking up topics and circling around them for a while (the length of the research projet, the issue of confidentiality), or avoiding any kind of unpleasantness (through the requisite amount of indirection and politeness in making a request). The result is a civilized bit of negotiation which maintains face, satisfies both parties, and allows them to meet again on another occasion with a feeling of mutual accomplishment. We feel that business will be done – B will get access to the material he seeks from A – but we know too that the conversation is a lot more than just a business transaction: it is a piece of social interaction that requires a considerable set of skills. And it is just such conversations that help keep people living and functioning together in society.

Further Reading

The last conversation is from Svartvik and Quirk's *A Corpus of English Conversation*, a large collection of conversations made available in various forms to researchers.

10

Consequences

In the last decade or so, conversational analysis has formed an increasingly important part of language study. Philosophers, psychologists, sociologists, educators, and linguists have examined conversation from a variety of perspectives. What is surprising is the amount of agreement they have achieved, because so often when academics from various disciplines approach a problem they look at it so differently that they cannot even begin to talk to one another about it. Not so with conversation. Indeed, we have made almost no attempt to identify a particular point of view with a particular discipline, since that might tend to give a misleading impression of differences where few or none exist.

What is slowly emerging in conversational analysis is a view of conversation as a many-faceted, structured activity. To some linguists, none the less, it has appeared much too 'messy' to be of any interest to them in their concern to identify certain properties and rules which give human languages the characteristics they have and make them learnable by human beings. But if we recognize that languages are not just formal systems of properties and rules, that they are indeed complex and multi-faceted systems used by real people to go about the business of real living, we soon become much more tolerant of their apparent disorder, which we seek to sort out with fewer *a priori* assumptions about what we must find.

Once we recognize that more than just formal properties and rules are used in communication, we can acknowledge those functional aspects of language and human behaviour that come into play in conversation. That is when matters such as cooperative behaviour, mutual trust, individual speech styles, and cultural expectations begin to play an important part in determining who says what and how on a particular occasion, and how that saying relates to what others say or do not say. And that must be of concern to anyone who is seriously interested in why languages have the characteristics they do have.

It is of serious concern because, while it is a completely legitimate interest to study the formal properties of human language, it must also be of interest to study how humans use language in conducting their affairs. This surely must be a topic of abiding interest, and one that cannot wait until the first has been exhausted. Conversation provides an excellent – and ready – source of materials with which to study language in use, to form and test hypotheses, and to develop the kinds of theories in which scientists are often interested. What we have seen in recent years is an attempt to develop such a theoretical understanding.

There is also a practical side to the analysis of conversation. We spend a considerable part of our waking lives listening and talking. Conversation, after all, is a commonplace activity, one to which we do not usually give very much thought, except perhaps when a particular exchange goes badly for us. But most of us would like to do a little better some of the time, at least. Consequently, analysis can help us to know just what makes conversations tick: to be aware of the various subtleties; to understand something of the general dynamics; to know how our words and those of others relate to gestures, movement, and so on; and to be able to express our intent clearly and to recognize the intent of others. Knowing a language is more than knowing a large number of words in that language, or how to construct an endless variety of sentences, or even how to construct some basic dialogues. Knowing a language is knowing how to converse and interact like a native: knowing English in this sense is knowing how to behave like a speaker of English. You know English only when you can communicate competently in English. So the analysis of conversation helps us to understand just what is involved in such competence, and it may also encourage those of us who wish to do so to try to improve our competence. The previous chapters contain numerous insights which may be of some use in that respect. They may also be helpful to those of us who perhaps too readily put our trust in others – to be forewarned, as they say, is to be forearmed.

In recent years theoreticians and practitioners have used this developing knowledge of conversation and of what it means to use a language to communicate with native-speaker-like competence in order to conduct research and develop materials for a variety of purposes. Our understanding of the acquisition of language by children is no longer confined to deciding which sounds, words, and structures are learned in what sequences. What children use this learning for is also of concern, as is the issue of how the two types of learning are related. A child may be a 'language acquisition device', that is, he or she may somehow be programmed from birth to acquire a human language, but without access to a specific human language used meaningfully for communication, it is doubtful that any language-learning could occur. So the development of conversational competence in children is a serious issue in research into language acquisition.

There is an increasing awareness, too, that language is used to educate and mould children in certain ways, both by parents and teachers. Children are taught *about* language and *through* language, and that teaching has very definite characteristics and consequences. Classroom talk, as we have seen, is conversation of a very special kind: it does not follow the rules which generally prevail when I speak to you informally. Its structure is different and its purpose is different. That we should be alert to the consequences of these differences seems obvious once they are drawn to our attention; that we should also undertake to see that those in charge of educating the young know of them may also be a worthy task to set ourselves.

When we teach a language like English to speakers who already know another language, we must be aware that we have to teach more than new sounds, words, and grammatical structures. Learning to speak English with a skill something like that of a native must involve learning to use the various subtle devices that the natives use. Conversational analysis can throw light on such devices. It helps us to pick out those things which give words and expressions the conviction that enables the learner who uses them to be understood rather than misunderstood. Hence the concern in recent years with teaching a new language as a system of communication – without denying that the various structures are also important. Attempts to do this have been numerous, but as yet there appears to be no clear consensus on just what exactly is involved in restructuring a curriculum to teach a language such as English to speakers of other languages on a thoroughly communicative principle.

Any activity that involves conversation is likely to be further illuminated by any understanding we can achieve of the dynamics of conversation. Many such activities are highly specialized, as, for example, radio communication between airline pilots and air traffic controllers. Some may be routine on most occasions but critical on others, as between doctors and patients. And many may be routine on just about all occasions but cumulatively have profound consequences, as between parents and children and husbands and wives. A large amount of resources in modern societies is devoted to 'conversational repair', that is, to activities designed to mitigate and patch up the consequences of failure to communicate. This misunderstanding is unfortunately a fact of life, but fortunately one located within a much larger context of understanding and cooperation – the very cement of society.

Human beings are uniquely language-using creatures. They are not uniquely social creatures. Language is important to human beings in creating the kinds of societies in which they have come to live. Human social structure is in large part created and maintained through language use. Ordinary everyday conversation comprises a significant part of that language use, and it is for this reason, if for no other, that it forms such an important area of study in modern approaches to language and linguistics.

Further Reading

Keenan's 'Conversational Competence in Children' is an attempt to show how such competence develops. Further suggested reading on the topic of the use of language in the classroom is indicated at the end of chapter 8. For discussions of teaching a language 'communicatively' to speakers of another language see Brumfit and Johnson's *The Communicative Approach to Language Teaching* and Widdowson's *Teaching Language as Communication*. For matters to do with changes in syllabus design necessitated by such an approach see Munby's *Communicative Syllabus Design* and Wilkins' *National Syllabuses: A Taxonomy and its Relevance to Foreign Language Curriculum Development*. Larsen-Freeman's *Discourse Analysis in Second Language Research* discusses a variety of related research issues. For further discussion of language used in doctor–patient relationships see the sources suggested at the end of chapter 4.

Bibliography

Adler, M. K., *Naming and Addressing*: *A Sociolinguistic Study*, Hamburg: Helmut Buske, 1978.

Argyle, M., 'Non-Verbal Symbolic Actions: Gaze', in R. Harré (ed.), *Life Sentences*: *Aspects of the Social Role of Language*, London: John Wiley and Sons, 1976.

Argyle, M., and M. Cook, *Gaze and Mutual Gaze*, Cambridge: Cambridge University Press, 1976.

Argyle, M., A. Furnham, and J. A. Graham, *Social Situations*, Cambridge: Cambridge University Press, 1981.

Austin, J. L., *How To Do Things With Words*, Oxford: Clarendon Press, 1962.

Austin, J. L., *Philosophical Papers*, 2nd edn, London: Oxford University Press, 1970.

Basso, K. H., 'To Give up on Words: Silence in Western Apache Culture', *Southwestern Journal of Anthropology*, 26 (1970) 213–30.

Bateson, G., D. D. Jackson, J. Haley, and J. Weakland, 'Toward a Theory of Schizophrenia', *Behavioral Science*, 1 (1956) 251–64.

Bauman, R., and J. Sherzer (eds), *Explorations in the Ethnography of Speaking*, Cambridge: Cambridge University Press, 1974.

Bellack, A. A., H. M. Kliebard, R. T. Hyman, and F. L. Smith, *The Language of the Classroom*, New York: Teachers College Press, 1966.

Birdwhistell, R. L., *Introduction to Kinesics*, Louisville, Ky: University of Louisville Press, 1952.

Birdwhistell, R. L., 'Paralanguage: 25 Years after Sapir', in H. W. Brosin (ed.), *Lectures on Experimental Psychiatry*, Pittsburgh: University of Pittsburgh Press, 1961.

Birdwhistell, R. L., *Kinesics and Context*: *Essays on Body Mo-*

tion Communication, Philadelphia: University of Pennsylvania Press, 1970.

Blankenship, J., and C. Kay. 'Hesitation Phenomena in English Speech', *Word*, 20 (1964) 360–72.

Brown, G., and G. Yule, *Discourse Analysis*, Cambridge: Cambridge University Press, 1983.

Brown, P., and S. Levinson, 'Universals in Language Use: Politeness Phenomena', in E. N. Goody (ed.), *Questions and Politeness: Strategies in Social Interaction*, Cambridge: Cambridge University Press, 1978.

Brumfit, C. J., and K. Johnson (eds), *The Communicative Approach to Language Teaching*, Oxford: Oxford University Press, 1979.

Cazden, C. B., V. P. John, and D. Hymes (eds), *Functions of Language in the Classroom*, New York: Teachers College Press, 1972.

Churchill, L., *Questioning Strategies in Sociolinguistics*, Rowley, Mass.: Newbury House Publishers, 1978.

Cicourel, A. V., 'Basic and Normative Rules in the Negotiation of Status and Role', in D. Sudnow, (ed.), *Studies in Social Interaction*, New York: The Free Press, 1972.

Cicourel, A. V., *Cognitive Sociology: Language and Meaning in Social Interaction*, Harmondsworth, England: Penguin Books, 1973.

Cicourel, A. V., 'Language and Medicine', in C. A. Ferguson and S. B. Heath (eds), *Language in the USA*, Cambridge: Cambridge University Press, 1981.

Clark, H. H., and J. W. French, 'Telephone *Goodbyes*', *Language in Society*, 10 (1981) 1–19.

Cohen, L. J., 'Speech Acts', in T. A. Sebeok (ed.), *Current Trends in Linguistics*, Vol. 12, The Hague: Mouton Publishers, 1974.

Cole, P., and J. L. Morgan (eds), *Syntax and Semantics, Volume 3, Speech Acts*, New York: Academic Press, 1975.

Coulmas, F. (ed.), *Conversational Routine*, The Hague: Mouton Publishers, 1981.

Coulthard, M., *An Introduction to Discourse Analysis*, London: Longman, 1977.

Coulthard, M., and M. Montgomery (eds), *Studies in Discourse Analysis*, London: Routledge and Kegan Paul, 1981.

Coulthard, R. M., and M. C. Ashby, 'A Linguistic Description of Doctor–Patient Interviews', in M. Wadsworth and D. Robinson (eds), *Studies in Everyday Medical Life*, London: Martin Robertson, 1976.

Crystal, D., 'Paralinguistics', in T. A. Sebeok (ed.), *Current Trends in Linguistics*, Vol. 12, The Hague: Mouton Publishers, 1974.

Crystal, D., *The English Tone of Voice: Essays on Intonation, Prosody and Paralanguage*, London: Edward Arnold, 1975.

Crystal, D., and R. Quirk, *Systems of Prosodic and Paralinguistic Features in English*, The Hague: Mouton Publishers, 1964.

Duncan, S., 'Some Signals and Rules for Taking Speaking Turns in Conversation', *Journal of Personality and Social Psychology*, 23 (1972) 283–92.

Duncan, S., 'Toward a Grammar for Dyadic Conversation', *Semiotics*, 9 (1973) 29–46.

Duncan, S., 'On the Structure of Speaker–Auditor Interaction during Speaking Turns', *Language in Society*, 2 (1974) 161–80.

Duncan, S. D., 'Nonverbal Communication', *Psychological Bulletin*, 72 (1969) 118–37.

Dundes, A., J. W. Leach, and B. Özkök, 'The Strategy of Turkish Boys' Verbal Dueling Rhymes', in J. J. Gumperz and D. Hymes (eds), *Directions in Sociolinguistics: The Ethnography of Communication*, New York: Holt, Rinehart and Winston, 1972.

Edelman, M., *Political Language: Words that Succeed and Policies that Fail*, New York: Academic Press, 1977.

Edelsky, C., 'Who's Got the Floor?', *Language in Society*, 10 (1981) 383–421.

Edmondson, W., *Spoken Discourse: A Model for Analysis*, London: Longman, 1981.

Edwards, A. D., and V. J., Furlong, *The Language of Teaching*, London: Heinemann, 1978.

Ervin-Tripp, S., 'On Sociolinguistic Rules: Alternation and

Co-occurrence', in J. J. Gumperz and D. Hymes (eds), *Directions in Sociolinguistics: The Ethnography of Communication*, New York: Holt, Rinehart and Winston, 1972.

Ervin-Tripp, S., 'Is Sybil There? The Structure of Some American English Directives', *Language in Society*, 5 (1976) 25–66.

Flanders, N. A., *Analyzing Teaching Behavior*, Reading, Mass.: Addison-Wesley, 1970.

Frake, C. O., 'Struck by Speech: The Yakan Concept of Litigation', in L. Nader (ed.), *Law in Culture and Society*, Chicago: Aldine, 1969.

Fraser, B., 'Hedged Performatives', in P. Cole and J. L. Morgan (eds), *Syntax and Semantics*, Volume 3, *Speech Acts*, New York: Academic Press, 1975.

Garfinkel, H., 'Studies of the Routine Grounds of Everyday Activities', *Social Problems*, 11 (1964) 220–50.

Garfinkel, H., *Studies in Ethnomethodology*, Englewood Cliffs, N. J.: Prentice-Hall, 1967.

Garfinkel, H., and H. Sacks, 'On Formal Structures of Practical Actions', in J. C. McKinney and E. Teryakian (eds), *Theoretical Sociology*, New York: Appleton-Century-Crofts, 1969.

Garvey, C., 'Requests and Responses in Children's Speech', *Journal of Child Language*, 2 (1975) 41–63.

Giglioli, P. P. (ed.), *Language and Social Context: Selected Readings*, Harmondsworth, England: Penguin Books, 1972.

Giles, H., and P. F. Powesland, *Speech Style and Social Evaluation*, London: Academic Press, 1978.

Godard, D., 'Same Setting, Different Norms: Phone Call Beginnings in France and the United States', *Language in Society*, 6 (1977) 209–19.

Goffman, E., 'On Face-work: An Analysis of Ritual Elements in Social Interaction', *Psychiatry*, 18 (1955) 213–31.

Goffman, E., *The Presentation of Self in Everyday Life*, New York: Anchor Books, 1959.

Goffman, E., *Interaction Ritual*, New York: Anchor Books, 1967.

Goffman, E., *Relations in Public: Microstudies of the Public Order*, New York: Harper and Row, 1971.

Goffman, E., *Frame Analysis: An Essay on the Organization of Experience*, New York: Harper and Row, 1974.

Goffman, E., 'Replies and Responses', *Language in Society*, 5 (1976) 257–313.

Goffman, E., 'Response Cries', *Language*, 54 (1978) 787–815.

Goffman, E., *Forms of Talk*, Philadelphia: University of Pennsylvania Press/Oxford: Basil Blackwell, 1981.

Goodwin, C., *Conversational Organization: Interaction between Speakers and Hearers*, New York: Academic Press, 1981.

Goody, E. N., (ed.), *Questions and Politeness: Strategies in Social Interaction*, Cambridge: Cambridge University Press, 1978.

Gordon, D., and G. Lakoff, 'Conversational Postulates', in P. Cole and J. L. Morgan (eds), *Syntax and Semantics, Volume 3, Speech Acts*, New York: Academic Press, 1975.

Gosling, J., 'Kinesics in Discourse', in M. Coulthard and M. Montgomery (eds), *Studies in Discourse Analysis*, London: Routledge and Kegan Paul, 1981.

Green, J. R., *A Gesture Inventory for the Teaching of Spanish*, Philadelphia: Chilton Books, 1968.

Grice, H. P., 'Logic and Conversation', in P. Cole and J. L. Morgan (eds), *Syntax and Semantics, Volume 3, Speech Acts*, New York: Academic Press, 1975.

Gumperz, J. J., *Discourse Strategies*, Cambridge: Cambridge University Press, 1982.

Gumperz, J. J. (ed.), *Language and Social Identity*, Cambridge: Cambridge University Press, 1982.

Gumperz, J. J., and D. Hymes (eds), *Directions in Sociolinguistics: The Ethnography of Communication*, New York: Holt, Rinehart and Winston, 1972.

Hall, E. T., *The Silent Language*, New York: Doubleday, 1959.

Hall, E. T., *The Hidden Dimension*, New York: Doubleday, 1966.

Halliday, M. A. K., *Language as Social Semiotic: The Social Interpretation of Language and Meaning*, London: Edward Arnold, 1978.

Halliday, M. A. K., and R. Hasan, *Cohesion in English*, London: Longman, 1976.

Hacher, M., 'The Classfication of Cooperative Illocutionary Acts', *Language in Society*, 8 (1979) 1–14.

Hinde, R. A. (ed.), *Non-Verbal Communication*, Cambridge: Cambridge University Press, 1972.

Hudson, R. A., *Sociolinguistics*, Cambridge: Cambridge University Press, 1980.

Hymes, D., 'Models of the Interaction of Language and Social Life', in J. J. Gumperz and D. Hymes (eds), *Directions in Sociolinguistics: The Ethnography of Communication*, New York: Holt, Rinehart and Winston, 1972.

James, D., 'The Use of *Oh, Ah, Say* and *Well* in Relation to a Number of Grammatical Phenomena', *Papers in Linguistics*, 11 (1978) 517–35.

Jefferson, G., 'Side Sequences', in D. Sudnow (ed.), *Studies in Social Interaction*, New York: The Free Press, 1972.

Jefferson, G., 'Error Correction as an Interactional Resource', *Language in Society*, 2 (1974) 181–99.

Johnson, M. C., *Discussion Dynamics: An Analysis of Classroom Teaching*, Rowley, Mass.: Newbury House Publishers, 1979.

Keenan, E. O., 'Conversational Competence in Children', *Journal of Child Language*, 1 (1975) 163–83.

Keenan, E. O., 'The Universality of Conversational Postulates', *Language in Society*, 5 (1976) 67–80.

Keenan, E. O. 'The Universality of Conversational Implicatures', in R. W. Fasold and R. W. Shuy (eds), *Studies in Language Variation*, Washington, D.C.: Georgetown University Press, 1977.

Keller, E., and S. T. Warner, *Gambits, 1–3: Conversational Tools*, Ottawa: Minister of Supply and Services, Canada, 1976–9.

Kendon, A., 'Some Functions of Gaze Direction in Social Interaction', *Acta Psychologica*, 26 (1967) 1–47.

Kendon, A., 'Movement Coordination in Social Interaction', *Acta Psychologica*, 32 (1970) 1–25.

Kendon, A., 'Some Relationships between Body Motion and

Speech', in A. W. Siegman and B. Pope (eds), *Studies in Dyadic Communication*, Elmsford, N. Y.: Pergamon, 1972.

Kendon, A. (ed.), *Nonverbal Communication, Interaction, and Gesture*, The Hague: Mouton Publishers, 1981.

Key, M. R., *Paralinguistics and Kinesics: Nonverbal Communication*, Metuchen, N. J.: Scarecrow Press, 1975.

Knapp, M. L., *Nonverbal Communication in Human Interaction*, New York: Holt, Rinehart and Winston, 1972.

La Barre, W., 'Paralinguistics, Kinesics and Cultural Anthropology', in T. A. Sebeok, A. S. Hayes, and M. C. Bateson (eds), *Approaches to Semiotics*, The Hague: Mouton Publishers, 1964.

Labov, W., 'Rules for Ritual Insults', in D. Sudnow (ed.), *Studies in Social Interaction*, New York: The Free Press, 1972.

Labov, W., *Sociolinguistic Patterns*, Oxford: Basil Blackwell/ Philadelphia: University of Pennsylvania Press, 1972.

Labov, W., and D. Fanshel, *Therapeutic Discourse: Psychotherapy as Conversation*, New York: Academic Press, 1978.

Lakoff, R., 'Language in Context', *Language*, 48 (1972) 907–27.

Larsen-Freeman, D. (ed.), *Discourse Analysis in Second Language Research*, Rowley, Mass.: Newbury House Publishers, 1980.

Laver, J., and S. Hutcheson (eds), *Communication in Face to Face Interaction*, Harmondsworth, England: Penguin Books, 1972.

Leiter, K., *A Primer on Ethnomethodology*, New York: Oxford University Press, 1980.

Levinson, S. C., *Pragmatics*, Cambridge: Cambridge University Press, 1983.

McHoul, A., 'The Organization of Turns at Formal Talk in the Classroom', *Language in Society*, 7 (1978) 183–213.

Maclay, H., and C. E. Osgood, 'Hesitation Phenomena in Spontaneous English Speech', *Word*, 15 (1959) 19–44.

Malinowski, B., 'The Problem of Meaning in Primitive Languages', in C. K. Ogden and I. A. Richards, *The Meaning of Meaning*, London: Routledge and Kegan Paul, 1923.

Merrit, M., 'On Questions Following Questions in Service Encounters', *Language in Society*, 5 (1976) 315–57.

Mitchell-Kernan, C., 'Signifying and Marking: Two Afro-American Speech Acts', in J. J. Gumperz and D. Hymes (eds), *Directions in Sociolinguistics: The Ethnography of Communication*, New York: Holt, Rinehart and Winston, 1972.

Moerman, M., and H. Sacks, 'On Understanding in the Analysis of Natural Conversation', in M. Kincade (ed.), *Relations of Anthropology and Linguistics*, The Hague: Mouton Publishers, 1978.

Morris, D., *Manwatching: A Field Guide to Human Behaviour*, London: Oxford University Press, 1977.

Morris, D., P. Collett, P. Marsh, and M. O'Shaughnessy, *Gestures: Their Origins and Distribution*, London: Jonathan Cape, 1979.

Munby, J., *Communicative Syllabus Design*, Cambridge: Cambridge University Press, 1978.

Opie, I., and P. Opie, *The Lore and Language of Schoolchildren*, Oxford: Clarendon Press, 1959.

Pittenger, R. E., C. F. Hockett, and J. J. Danehy, *The First Five Minutes: A Sample of Microscopic Interview Analysis*, Ithaca: N. Y.: Paul Martineau, 1960.

Pride, J. B., 'Analysing Classroom Procedures', in H. Fraser and W. R. O'Donnell (eds), *Applied Linguistics and the Teaching of English*, London: Longman, 1969.

Psathas, G. (ed.), *Everyday Language: Studies in Ethnomethodology*, New York: Irvington Publishers, Inc., 1979.

Robinson, W. P., *Language and Social Behaviour*, Harmondsworth, England: Penguin Books, 1972.

Robinson, W. P., and S. J. Rackstraw, *A Question of Answers*, London: Routledge and Kegan Paul, 1972.

Ruesch, J., and W. Kees, *Nonverbal Communication: Notes on the Visual Perception of Human Relations*, Berkeley: University of California Press, 1956.

Sacks, H., 'An Initial Investigation of the Usability of Conversational Data for Doing Sociology', in D. Sudnow (ed.), *Studies in Social Interaction*, New York: The Free Press, 1972.

Sacks, H., 'Notes on Police Assessment of Moral Character', in D. Sudnow (ed.), *Studies in Social Interaction*, New York: The Free Press, 1972.

Sacks, H., 'An Analysis of the Course of a Joke's Telling in Conversation', in R. Bauman and J. Sherzer (eds), *Explorations in the Ethnography of Speaking*, Cambridge: Cambridge University Press, 1974.

Sacks, H., E. A. Schegloff, and G. Jefferson, 'A Simplest Systematics for the Organization of Turn-taking in Conversation', *Language*, 50 (1974) 696–735.

Saville-Troike, M., *The Ethnography of Communication: An Introduction*, Oxford: Basil Blackwell/Baltimore: University Park Press, 1982.

Scheflen, A. E., *Body Language and the Social Order*, Englewood Cliffs, N. J.: Prentice-Hall, 1972.

Scheflen, A. E., *How Behavior Means*, Garden City, N. Y.: Anchor Books, 1974.

Schegloff, E., 'Sequencing in Conversational Openings', *American Anthropologist*, 70 (1968) 1075–95.

Schegloff, E. A., 'Notes on Conversational Practice: Formulating Place', in D. Sudnow (ed.), *Studies in Social Interaction*, New York: The Free Press, 1972.

Schegloff, E. A., 'Identification and Recognition in Telephone Conversation Openings', in G. Psathas (ed.), *Everyday Language: Studies in Ethnomethodology*, New York: Irvington Publishers, Inc., 1979.

Schegloff, E., G. Jefferson, and H. Sacks, 'The Preference for Self-Correction in the Organization of Repair in Conversation', *Language*, 53 (1977) 361–82.

Schegloff, E., and H. Sacks, 'Opening up Closings', *Semiotics*, 8 (1973) 289–327.

Schenkein, J. (ed.), *Studies in the Organization of Conversational Interaction*, New York: Academic Press, 1978.

Searle, J. R., 'What is a Speech Act?', in M. Black (ed.) *Philosophy in America*, London: George Allen and Unwin, 1965.

Searle J. R., *Speech Acts: An Essay in the Philosophy of Language*, Cambridge: Cambridge University Press, 1969.

Searle, J. R., 'Indirect Speech Acts', in P. Cole and J. L.

Morgan (eds), *Syntax and Semantics, Volume 3, Speech Acts*, New York: Academic Press, 1975.

Searle, J. R., 'A Classification of Illocutionary Acts', *Language in Society*, 5 (1976) 1–23.

Searle, J. R., *Expression and Meaning: Studies in the Theory of Speech Acts*, Cambridge: Cambridge University Press, 1979.

Sinclair, J. and R. M. Coulthard, *Towards an Analysis of Discourse: The English used by Teachers and Pupils*, London: Oxford University Press, 1975.

Sommer, R., *Personal Space: The Behavioral Basics of Design*, Englewood Cliffs, N. J.: Prentice-Hall, 1969.

Soskin, W. F., and V. P. John, 'The Study of Spontaneous Talk', in R. G. Barker (ed.), *The Stream of Behaviour*, New York: Appleton-Century-Crofts, 1963.

Speier, M., *How to Observe Face-to-Face Communication: A Sociological Introduction*, Pacific Palisades, California: Goodyear, 1973.

Strawson, P. F., 'Intention and Convention in Speech Acts', *The Philosophical Review*, 73 (1964) 439–60.

Stubbs, M., *Discourse Analysis: The Sociolinguistic Analysis of Natural Language*, Oxford: Basil Blackwell/Chicago: University of Chicago Press, 1983.

Sudnow, D. (ed.), *Studies in Social Interaction*, New York: The Free Press, 1972.

Sudnow, D., 'Temporal Parameters of Interpersonal Observation', in D. Sudnow (ed.), *Studies in Social Interaction*, New York: The Free Press, 1972.

Svartvik, J., and R. Quirk (eds), *A Corpus of English Conversation*, Lund: Gleerup, 1980.

Trager, G. L., 'Paralanguage: A First Approximation', *Studies in Linguistics*, 13 (1958) 1–12.

Trudgill, P., *Sociolinguistics: An Introduction to Language and Society*, rev. ed, Harmondsworth, England: Penguin Books, 1983.

Turner, R., 'Some Formal Properties of Therapy Talk', in D. Sudnow (ed.), *Studies in Social Interaction*, New York: The Free Press, 1972.

Watson, O. M., 'Proxemics', in T. A. Sebeok (ed.), *Current*

Trends in Linguistics, Vol. 12, The Hague: Mouton Publishers, 1974.

Watzlawick, P., J. H. Beavin, and D. D. Jackson, *Pragmatics of Human Communication: A Study of Interactional Patterns, Pathologies, and Paradoxes*, New York: W. W. Norton, 1967.

Widdowson, H. G., *Teaching Language as Communication*, Oxford: Oxford University Press, 1978.

Wilkins, D. A., *National Syllabuses: A Taxonomy and its Relevance to Foreign Language Curriculum Development*, London: Oxford University Press, 1976.

Williams, M., 'Presenting Oneself in Talk: The Disclosure of Occupation', in R. Harré (ed.), *Life Sentences: Aspects of the Social Role of Language*, London: John Wiley and Sons, 1976.

Index